GENERAL MARSHALL
REMEMBERED

GENERAL MARSHALL REMEMBERED

By

Rose Page Wilson

PRENTICE-HALL, INC.

ENGLEWOOD CLIFFS, NEW JERSEY

To my family

ACKNOWLEDGMENTS My friend, Father R. L. Bruckberger, a French Dominican priest, is solely responsible for my undertaking to write this book, although he is in no way responsible for its contents. Father Bruckberger, a staunch admirer of General Marshall, is himself a man of rare qualities. Author and artist, he is also a recipient of the Croix de Guerre and Legion of Honor for his work in the French resistance. Father Bruckberger convinced me that it was my obligation to write what I know about General Marshall and more than once, he urged and encouraged me to finish this book. My gratitude to him is immeasurable.

I thank my husband, John, and our sons, Page and Thomas, for their limitless patience for certain neglects they endured while I was writing the book. I especially thank our daughter, Celeste, who left her own pursuits to lend a helpfully critical ear to certain parts of the manuscript that were troublesome to me. I want to thank my sister, Celeste Morgan, for her stimulating responses after reading sections of the manuscript as I sent them to her. I am deeply indebted to my niece, Virginia Rose Page, for her invaluable professional advice.

My thanks are due to the many friends who demonstrated an abiding interest in this book, particularly the Reverend John W. S. Davis and his wife, Sarah, and Mr. Lambert Davis and his wife, Isabella.

Finally, I should like to express my appreciation to the three young women who were adept at deciphering my rough drafts and who typed sections of the manuscript for me, Olive Sherman, Harriet Gordon, and Bette Craig.

GENERAL MARSHALL
REMEMBERED

❦ CHAPTER I ❦

My sponsor in baptism was not selected by my parents, who had forfeited their prerogative by the simple process of not having me baptised. I came into the world in 1911 but when I finally got around to being "born anew," I was eleven years old and chose my own godfather whom I had picked up in an elevator nearly four years before.

In 1919, Colonel George C. Marshall, aide to the illustrious World War I Commander of the A. E. F., General John J. Pershing, came to Washington, D.C. Colonel Marshall leased an apartment at 2400 Sixteenth Street which was the same apartment house where I was living with my family. A little crony of mine at 2400 had given me intriguing reports about "that wonderful Colonel Marshall" who had moved in, but I did not see him until the day we happened to be the only passengers riding down in the elevator. It had seemed a worthwhile gamble to me to chance incurring the consequences of breaking parental rules of etiquette in order to reap the benefits of striking up an acquaintance with a man reputed to be a whiz with children. This was a providential opportunity.

"Good evening, Colonel Marshall!" I shouted at him before I lost my nerve.

"And good evening to you," he replied amiably. "How did you know my name?"

"Well," I explained breathlessly, "you're new at 2400, you're tall, have on a uniform, and Eleanor Pierce told me she'd had a lot of fun on a walk with a nice, new, tall Army officer named Colonel Marshall, so I guessed you must be Colonel Marshall."

He laughed. "Now that's a fine compliment, or is it a hint to come walking with us next time?"

I was taken aback that he had jumped right to the point so I blushed, hesitated a moment, then decided if I hadn't fooled him I might as well speak up.

"Yes, thank you, I'd love to come if it's all right with you."

Smiling, he reassured me. "It certainly is all right with me, it's a splendid idea. Meet us in the lobby at two thirty next Sunday afternoon."

We got off the elevator, and as he strode down the lobby, I called after him, "My name's Rose Page!"

He waved back at me and disappeared through the front door.

I had just turned eight years old and had acted on a childish impulse. But with that fortuitous quirk of fate, a mutually affectionate relationship began which was to endure for forty years—until General Marshall's death in 1959.

Although our friendship began on that long ago Sunday afternoon walk, my enthusiasm for establishing the friendship was considerably lessened by the necessity for hoodwinking my mother. I knew that she would not only disapprove of my introducing myself to a grownup whom she herself had not yet met, but would also be outraged that I had angled for an invitation. Nevertheless, my curiosity to find out whether Colonel Marshall offered as good a time as my friend claimed he did outweighed any possibilities of future hell and damnation. I deceived Mother with earnest assurances that Eleanor had asked Colonel Marshall if I could join them and that he had agreed. But unexpectedly, my mother's warnings against the consequences of falsehood were more effective than I realized. She had repeatedly cautioned me that each of my transgressions etched a "black mark on my soul" and I was terrified that this whopper might show through.

I set out for the appointment wishing that I had never heard of Colonel Marshall and not caring if he was the incarnation of the Pied Piper; nothing was worth the acute discomfort of telling a lie.

He and my friend Eleanor were waiting for me in the lobby when I got off the elevator, and as I walked slowly toward them, Colonel Marshall called, "Come along, hurry! It's two thirty-five. You're late!"

Some greeting! All my guilt and reservations about the afternoon churned into frustrated rage. Late, late, late—that's all I ever heard, and this time, for a measly five minutes, when I didn't even want to come! Mother's parting admonition clanged in my ears: "Be polite." And in my family, discourtesy was only a trifle less wicked than dishonesty. I wasn't about to add to the day's sins but I was equally determined not to apologize.

"Thank you for waiting," I replied as coldly as the dignity of my eight years and the strain of fighting back angry tears would allow.

Colonel Marshall glanced briefly into my unhappy face. Then, to my astonishment, he saluted me gallantly, made a jaunty little bow, and said gaily without a trace of mockery, "Not at all. It's a pleasure to wait for a charming young lady."

My spirits soared and I warmed to him at once.

"Oh my goodness!" I cried. "You really are nice!"

My anger melted instantly, and quite as suddenly, the blemish on my soul faded to insignificance as we started off happily for our afternoon's outing.

"Where shall we go?" Colonel Marshall asked when we emerged onto Sixteenth Street into a bright fall afternoon.

"Rock Creek Park!" Eleanor and I shouted in unison.

"Rock Creek Park it shall be," he agreed and started briskly up Sixteenth Street.

Colonel Marshall was still in uniform, as were most Army officers in the fall of 1919. As I jogged along, trying to keep up with his long, springy steps, I thought how lithe and tall he looked, and how much younger than my bald, portly father. Indeed, compared to my father, Colonel Marshall seemed positively boyish.

When I joined my father on his "constitutional" strolls, he carried a silver-knobbed cane which he managed with dignified decorum. Colonel Marshall was carrying a riding crop which he swung jauntily back and forth, every now and then slapping it against his leg or holding it out as a bar to prevent Eleanor and me from approaching too close to the street. We covered the couple of miles to Rock Creek Park in record time. Once there, Colonel Marshall said we could run about as freely as we pleased. Eleanor and I ran hither and yon through the woods until we hit upon the idea of jumping from rock to rock down the creek. Colonel Marshall walked alongside the creek, pointing out which rock looked steady enough for our next leap, until, characteristically, I missed my step and filled my shoes with water.

Colonel Marshall calmly instructed me to take them off. He then set about cutting two forked sticks which he stuck into the ground in a sunny spot. Instead of scolding me, he told me to hang my shoes and socks on the sticks, and asked me if my feet were cold. He made a game of the whole procedure and said that he used to dry his own shoes just the same way when he was a young Lieutenant in the Philippines. While we sat down in the sun to wait for my sneakers to dry, he entertained us with tales of his experiences in the Philippines. I remember little of what he said but I remember very well the enchanted mood he created and how he looked that day. The picture of Colonel Marshall lolling in the warm Indian summer sun comes back to me vividly. I did not observe his features closely, only his expression,

4

but I noticed how the sun lit up his thick blond hair, and that his strikingly blue eyes were lively and full of fun. His cap lay on the ground beside him; he had loosened his Sam Browne belt, and leaned comfortably on one elbow with his long legs stretched out before him. His easy relaxed manner dispelled all vestiges of the restraint that I usually felt with other adults, even with those of whom I was fond. Eleanor was right. Colonel Marshall was a "wonderful man"!

I sat enthralled by his stories. As I searched his face for an expression of adult condescension and found none, I thought he was the handsomest man in the world. It took a couple of years before I could admit to myself that he was homely.

I had a glorious time that Sunday, an afternoon of heavenly freedom from the restrictions of apartment house living and the innumerable rules of conduct laid down by my sensible but extremely strict mother.

On our way back home, Colonel Marshall allowed Eleanor and me to sprint ahead of him or lag behind and run to catch up, while he maintained his steady pace. I even dared ask him to let me carry his riding crop. He turned it over without so much as a comment, and I began to imitate him, holding my head high, swinging the crop, and slapping it against my leg. Colonel Marshall laughed and warned me to watch where I was swinging his crop or I'd put Eleanor's eye out. Eleanor begged for her turn so Colonel Marshall instructed me to give her the crop when we reached the end of the next block. We were all in high spirits, and when Eleanor's turn came, she began waving the crop about happily. We were nearly back at 2400 and were about to pass in front of the French Embassy, which was at the head of our block, when Eleanor, intoxicated by her exuberance, miscalculated the extent of Colonel Marshall's leniency. She darted quickly behind him, reached up with the crop, and knocked off his cap. I stood paralyzed with shock as I watched his splendid officer's cap roll crazily down the sidewalk, while out of the corner of my eye I

5

saw the French ambassador, about to get into his car, pause and stare at us in astonishment. Eleanor realized she had gone too far and giggled nervously to conceal her chagrin. Colonel Marshall halted abruptly. He neither raised his voice in angry reproof nor made a move to retrieve his cap. He stood stone still, and perfectly calm. His face froze into marble severity, his friendly blue eyes turned cold, and in a voice icy with disapproval, he commanded, "Get my cap at once."

Even children accustomed to obeying are apt to delay long enough to plead their innocence—"It was only in fun. I didn't mean to do it . . ." But when Colonel Marshall spoke, Eleanor did not hesitate an instant. She streaked down the sidewalk to fetch his cap.

"Brush it off," he told her. "Give it to me. Give me my crop."

The devil himself would not have dared defy that voice of authority, and certainly not little Eleanor, who hastily carried out his orders like an automaton.

Colonel Marshall put on his cap and, tucking his crop under his arm, took hold of our hands as the three of us waited for the ambassador's car to ease out of the Embassy driveway into Sixteenth Street. The ambassador raised his hat and, with a little Gallic shrug, directed a sympathetic grimace at Colonel Marshall. Colonel Marshall released Eleanor's hand, and I looked up at him apprehensively as he saluted the ambassador. To my relief and surprise, he smiled back pleasantly, quite unconcerned that his dignity had been affronted only a moment before. His former cheerful expression had returned as suddenly as it had vanished.

We proceeded down the rest of the block to 2400, my spirits still somewhat dampened while I waited for Eleanor's scolding; but none was forthcoming. Colonel Marshall did not dissipate the chastening effect the demonstration of his authority had clearly made on us. He had shown us that he was indisputably the boss and that there were limits not to be transgressed. The incident was closed.

6

The apartment house at 2400 Sixteenth Street, where I was living at the same time Colonel Marshall and his first wife, Lily, moved there, was a unique establishment. It is difficult to convey its intangible qualities. *Twenty-four hundred*—it had no other name—has an important place in my memory, not only because I spent most of my childhood and youth there, but because it is integrally associated with my earliest memories of the Marshalls.

My family came to Washington in 1918 because my father, Dr. Thomas Walker Page, with considerable reluctance, I suspect, had relinquished his professorship at the University of Virginia to accept an appointment by President Wilson to the United States Tariff Commission. In 1918, Washington was extremely over-crowded with the influx of people who had swarmed to the Capital in wartime. My parents gave up trying to locate a house, and considered themselves fortunate to find a comfortable, if slightly cramped, apartment in 2400 to accommodate their little brood: my elder brother, my sister, and me.

Because 2400 had been built in time to benefit from the housing shortage, its owner-landlords could afford to pick and choose their tenants. But their choice was by no means limited by a tenant's ability to pay high rents. If this had been so, neither the Marshalls nor the Pages could have lived there! Applicants were simply turned away if the owners thought they would not "fit in" with the residents already there. *Twenty-four hundred* operated as an apartment house, although it was in fact more like a private club. Compared to the Old-World grandeur of de luxe European hotels, 2400 was not outstanding, but it did have a certain unpretentious elegance quite unlike the gaudy opulence of today's public palaces. The marble-columned lobby was spacious and there were various separate rooms downstairs for the "members'" use: a gentlemen's smoking room with a large fireplace, a "French room" for ladies' parties, a glassed-in palm court, a dining room (never referred to as "restaurant"), and a ballroom. Except for the rococo gold and white ballroom, the lobby and

7

other rooms were furnished in restrained good taste designed for gracious living.

The clientele was made up of a dozen or more senators, a few congressmen, a goodly number of high Government officials, a sprinkling of diplomats, a handful of native Washingtonians, several professional men, and many Army Colonels and Generals, most of whom were friends of the Marshalls. There were also a fair number of "unemployed" who chose to live in the exciting atmosphere of the Capital, and the usual complement of well-to-do widows who flock to Washington. There were very few young children at 2400 besides the Pierces and the Pages because the majority of couples there either had grown children or none.

The first six years of my life had been spent in a Virginia country house, but the bucolic simplicity of those earliest years changed radically when our family moved to Washington the year before Colonel Marshall and I rode down alone in the elevator. At the age of seven, I was suddenly thrust into a sophisticated milieu overpeopled with adults. At first, I clung to my elder sister, Celeste, who courageously acted as spokesman for us both, but by the time I spoke so boldly to Colonel Marshall, a year's exposure to the peculiarities of adults had sufficiently conditioned me so that I no longer required my sister's intercession.

The clublike atmosphere of 2400 was particularly in evidence at the dinner hour, for most of the tenants dined in the "dining room" where each family had its own special table and waiter. After dinner the ladies drifted into the lobby gathering into groups to wait for their husbands, who disappeared briefly to enjoy their cigars in the smoking room—except for my father. He went directly upstairs to enjoy the solitude of his books and pipe. My brother Tom, who was six years my senior, also went straight upstairs to read, study, or tinker with his homemade radio set.

Sis and I, trailing after Mother, would stay in the lobby an hour or so every evening before she sent us up to wrestle with our homework. Ostensibly, we were kept downstairs to enjoy the "lovely" music and learn to behave like "little ladies." The same three musicians, a cellist, violinist, and pianist, played chamber music in the lobby every evening for nearly ten years. The music was pleasant enough but Celeste and I eavesdropped on the conversations far more than we listened to the music. Sitting quietly side by side, ankles crossed, dresses "neatly pulled to the knees," we kept so quiet that Mother and her friends often forgot the two little pitchers sitting in their midst. Consequently, we frequently not only overheard the latest social and political gossip, but also listened in on many informed discussions of current affairs. We probably missed most of the innuendos and understood little more than half of what was said, yet we could not have helped but absorb a vast store of information.

Thus my first favorable impression of Colonel Marshall was not altogether naïve, for I had become used to a select company of more than ordinarily interesting adults. Furthermore, since there were so few children at 2400, my sister and I came in for a good deal of attention and both of us had made special friends among the grownups.

For example, my next best friend to Colonel Marshall was Senator John B. Kendrick of Wyoming. He was a genial gentleman who used to take me to lunch in the Senate dining room and ride me back and forth on the underground railway that shuttled between the Senate Office Building and the Capitol. Senator Kendrick had played an important role in the history of the West and he told me many fascinating tales about his cowboy days when he drove cattle up the "long trail" from Texas to Wyoming.

Years later, when I reached my teens, the old *Colliers Weekly* magazine featured an article on Senator Kendrick's colorful career. Colonel Marshall gave me a copy and suggested that I write a congratulatory note to the Senator. I read the article with enthusiasm and interest but put off the letter with one excuse after another until Colonel Marshall browbeat me into writing it. He knew that I had long admired Senator Kendrick and repeated ad infinitum that the old gentleman would be pleased to have evidence of my continuing interest in him.

"Oh, nuts!" I cried one day. "Why do you keep saying that? Senator Kendrick wouldn't give a damn if he heard from me or not."

In exasperation, Colonel Marshall replied that I could damn well take the time to write a note in view of the fact that the Senator had taken the time to be nice to me when I was a child. He summarily ordered me to write, mail the letter the next day, and then report to him that it had been done.

In spite of Colonel Marshall's prediction, I was surprised when Senator Kendrick's prompt reply to my note revealed that he was genuinely touched that I had bothered to write to him. I had "bothered" because Colonel Marshall had insisted. But then, few people are as thoughtful as he was and fewer still trouble to act on a kind impulse.

Another of my friends from 2400 was a certain General who used to invite me to go horseback riding with him when Colonel Marshall was out of town. One afternoon, I tactlessly sang Colonel Marshall's praises to such an extent that the General interrupted. "Really, Rose," he said irritably, "don't you think I sit a horse as well as your *Colonel* Marshall? Do you find me so boring compared to your hero?"

The General's outburst sprang from a deeper source than a little girl's admiration for another adult. Lobby talk was soured from time to time by jealous comments about Colonel Marshall's extraordinary ability, though they usually came from ambitious Army wives rather than their husbands. One Colonel's lady made a classic remark: "I know my Sidney has every bit as much personality and just as good brains as George Marshall if he would only show them."

Whenever I tried to repeat lobby gossip to Colonel Marshall, whether about him or anyone else, good or bad, he would cut me off saying such talk wasn't worth listening to. If I persisted, he would skillfully change the subject to divert my interest. One of the few times Colonel Marshall was ever angry with me resulted from gossip I told him, and it was not about him, at that.

It concerned a vivacious, voluptuous young Cuban woman who lived at 2400, a female cyclone known to me only as Ramona, who used to whirl through the lobby trailing a heady scent of exotic perfume. I transmitted the exciting news to Colonel Marshall that people were saying that Ramona was General MacArthur's sweetheart. Not understanding the implications, I asked if it were true. I simpered that people in the lobby made all sorts of jokes about General MacArthur, such as, "Napoleon had the MacArthur strut."

To my dismay, Colonel Marshall exploded. "Don't you ever repeat talk like that again!" Brusquely, he said that he didn't know if the slander about Ramona and General MacArther was true, and neither did anybody else. He reminded me he had told me often enough that he wasn't interested in idle rumor, and said he expected me to abide by his wishes.

Colonel Marshall had frequently corrected me before but never in anger and I was hurt and shaken by his unaccustomed harshness. I began to cry, and apologized miserably, saying I was sorry if I had said something bad. He curbed his anger immediately and replied gently that perhaps he hadn't made it clear to me why he disapproved of gossip. It was wrong, he explained, because careless talk might unfairly and seriously injure a person's reputation.

"All gossip, whether it's flattering or unkind," he pointed out, "has a numerator of personal opinion, a denominator of doubtful facts, and is multiplied by exaggeration. So you see, Rosie, the answer is bound to be wrong."

He purposely chose that figure of speech because he knew that I was just beginning fractions. Colonel Marshall always baited his instructions with some familiar image that would hook my memory. When he was trying to teach me something that he held to be right and useful, he did not talk down to me in the ex cathedra manner used by most adults which I automatically resisted. Colonel Marshall's basic principles may appear prudish by ordinary standards, but in fact they were fundamental rules rooted deeply in his uncomplicated Christian faith and supported by his incorruptible honor. I disagreed with him on occasion but I trusted Colonel Marshall implicitly. He never failed me. Not once.

Colonel Marshall's influence on me and my deep affection for him went far beyond a pleasant relationship between a child and an adult outside the family circle. To be sure, our friendship began because we happened to live in the same building. Colonel Marshall loved children and I was available. It grew for many reasons. In the early years, my constant exposure to sophisticated, knowledgeable adults possibly sharpened my comprehension sufficiently to free him from the boring necessity of expressing himself in *ABC* language. Unquestionably, he responded to my open admiration for him. More significantly, my relationship with my parents and my position in our family increased my dependence on Colonel Marshall and my devotion to him.

Although I loved and admired my father, I thought of him as an old man, whereas Colonel Marshall, who was only thirty-eight years old when we first met, was many years younger and much more active. My father was more like a grandfather to me. I was proud of his erudition and courtly dignity, but his sedentary habits were not alluring to a little girl. But he was a kindly grandfather-father who took infinite pains and interest in directing his children's intellectual development. He left the practical business of raising us entirely up to Mother. I seldom went to him with childish problems and if I did, he usually dismissed them, telling me, "Run along and play, things will work out by themselves." My father was the personification of the serene professor isolated in his ivory tower.

Mother was his exact opposite. She was thirteen years younger, exceedingly pretty, sensitive, pragmatic, high-strung, and quick-tempered. Ambitious for her children, she demanded perfection. We were admonished to "carry the torch" further than she and our father ever would, which was a big order considering our parents' achievements. Both were members of *Phi Beta Kappa.* Mother won her Master's degree in history at Randolph-Macon College in Virginia at a time when few women even attended college. Dad had earned his Doctor's degree in economic history and philosophy *summa cum laude* from the University of Leipzig.

My brilliant elder brother, Tom, an only son, easily fulfilled Mother's stringent requirements for mental prowess. He was, however, a frail boy whom she nursed anxiously and tirelessly through one serious illness after another. Mother was almost pathologically preoccupied with Tom's welfare.

My sister Celeste, the middle child, was born an adult. Dainty, neat, perspicacious, and blessed with an uncanny sense of tact, she was Mother's mainstay—and mine. I turned to Celeste for maternal comfort far oftener than to my mother.

As for plump, robust, careless me, I so rarely lived up to our mother's lofty expectations that she relegated me to the bottom of the heap, although she never gave up prodding me to climb for the top. I was obsessed with a desire to please her, but I usually fell into deeper trouble by attempting to avoid her disapproval with all sorts of ill-considered maneuvers. I revered my mother, but I was afraid of her.

Colonel Marshall was my bulwark of security. I never felt uneasy with him or that I had to strain to win his affection or approval. He expected a lot of me as my mother did, but he never showed disappointment if I failed. As for punishment, he resorted to it only three times throughout my childhood. Somehow, Colonel Marshall always succeeded in making me believe I was more than I was, bigger than myself. Starting from the edge of baby-hood, I was the lucky beneficiary of his sympathetic understanding and genuine concern for a child's happiness. In turn, I substituted for the child he never had. So I fulfilled a need for him. Hence, a strong and unique attachment grew between us which remained unshaken through the widely changing circumstances of future years.

CHAPTER II

WHEN I FIRST RODE DOWN THE ELEVATOR WITH COLONEL MARSHALL, I already knew that he was General Pershing's aide. I had learned it in the lobby but did not mention it to him because at the time, my young friend's information about him was more important to me. Indeed, before I ever saw him, I had gathered various other disjointed "George Marshall" tidbits from the after-dinner talks. I had heard that he was a "brilliant officer," that he did not tell risqué jokes, did not like to be interrupted when he was talking, was an amusing dinner partner, always won an argument, and had a "simply charming" wife named Lily who was a "raving beauty." I also found out that Mrs. Marshall was visiting her mother because her husband was traveling extensively with General Pershing and only returned to Washington for a day or so at a time.

Colonel Marshall was away with General Pershing most of the time during the fall of 1919 and early winter of 1920, but when he showed up in Washington, he always invited me to come out with him. I was a lucky kid. Colonel Marshall invited me because he was lonesome with his own special kind of lonesomeness. His wife was not in Washington and Colonel Marshall was always a man who absolutely had to have someone to come home to, someone disassociated from the formalities and duties of his job. In short, I acted as a pinch hitter for Lily Marshall.

Although our delightful excursions were intermittent, they were quite enough to put us on a familiar basis, for it came easily to Colonel Marshall to make friends with children. As for me, I responded promptly and open-heartedly to his genuineness.

While he was traveling with Pershing, Colonel Marshall kept in touch with me through a stream of postcards he sent from all over the country, most of them picture cards. He chose cards he thought would interest a little girl, and on the backs, he wrote piquant comments about the pictures. One card showed a powerful white horse rearing up grandly against a brilliant blue sky. Colonel Marshall wrote, "Some day I want you to manage a horse like this one." He meant it, too! By the time I was sixteen, he expected me to be sufficiently competent to handle Pegasus in a steeplechase.

Occasionally, he sent a plain card with a notation of the long distances he had traveled, where he'd be when he would send the next card, and a suggestion that I look up his route on the map.

Several times, I was thrilled to get a postcard addressed in Colonel Marshall's handwriting but inscribed with a brief message from his celebrated "boss." "Hello, Rose," General Pershing wrote; or "Hello, Rose, by consent of Colonel Marshall." The General filled the rest of the message space with his huge flourishing signature.

Colonel Marshall once arranged for me to receive a postcard from the Supreme Allied Commander of World War I, Marshall Ferdinand Foch. It was a wonderful treat for me, as Foch and Pershing were touring the United States at the time under the glare of national publicity and acclaim. Marshal Foch's signature was neatly written over a picture of the *Circle Militaire,* and

Colonel Marshall's note said, "Here is a French postcard Marshal Foch autographed for you at breakfast this morning in his private car. We are just leaving St. Louis . . ."

Colonel Marshall traveled with General Pershing for years, but by the spring of 1920, his trips tapered off so that he was able to settle down in Washington long enough for his wife to join him. As far as I knew, Mrs. Marshall had been with her mother in Lexington, Virginia, throughout his absence and I had just as soon she stayed there. I was not at all anxious for the reputedly charming and beauteous Lily to butt in on Colonel Marshall and me. I know he sensed my reluctance about her return because on the day I was to meet her, he gave me a bang-up, red-letter, good time.

We were walking in our favorite Rock Creek Park, but I was so apprehensive at the prospect of coming back to meet Mrs. Marshall that Colonel Marshall was not having much luck in arousing my usually exuberant spirits. After a while, he spotted a long, thick, wild grapevine hanging from a massive oak tree standing at the edge of a deep ravine. Casually, he called my attention to it.

"Oh boy!" I cried, forgetting my doldrums. "Wouldn't it be fun to hang on to that vine and swing out over empty space?"

Smiling, he walked over to it. "Let's test it and see," he replied, "I don't want to carry you back home in small pink chunks."

He grasped the vine, hung on it with his full weight, and, looking up into the tree, tugged at it with quick, strong jerks.

"It's okay," he announced. "Hold on tight and I'll give you a push."

He showed me how to hold the vine, putting my right hand above my left, with the vine twined around my legs so I could get a firm grip with my feet. When I was all set to his satisfaction, he gave me a mighty shove and I sailed out high and free above the shadowy green ravine, swinging back to the bank like a living pendulum. He pushed me again and again while I shouted, "More! More!" until my hands were raw from clinging to the rough wood and Colonel Marshall called a halt.

On the way home, he bought me an ice-cream cone and kept up an animated, though one-sided, conversation, for as we approached nearer and nearer to 2400, my spirits sank lower and lower.

The time had finally come for me to face up to the fact that Mrs. Marshall was in Washington for good, and I had to meet her and pretend that she was nice. I dreaded she would put an end to the friendship between Colonel Marshall and me, and even if she didn't, I thought, I would surely be demoted to second fiddle. Alas, it had been so grand to be Number One for a change. I had heard plenty about Mrs. Marshall to verify my forebodings. Colonel Marshall's conversations had frequently been punctuated with, "Lily and I . . . ," "Lily thinks . . . ," "Lily says . . . ," but his references to his wife had seemed remote, a part of his life somewhere else at some other time. Only the previous evening, an Army wife's remark I overheard in the lobby cut through to reality and had the most disturbing effect on me—"Oh, how George adores her!" Well, if he adored Lily, I adored him! At eight years old, I was jealous and didn't know it.

On the awful moment we entered the Marshalls' apartment, I clutched Colonel Marshall's hand and clung to it, terrified.

Lily laid aside her novel when we came in. As that lovely creature rose to greet us, I was most painfully conscious of my tubby, ungraceful self. Miserable, I felt like Humpty Dumpty waiting to crash into pieces.

"Lily," Colonel Marshall said with a gaiety impossible for me to share, "here's the little Virginian. Here's Rose."

"Come over and let's have a look at you," she bade me pleasantly.

Obediently, I released Colonel Marshall's hand and walked stiffly toward her while she looked me up and down, her big brown eyes dancing with amusement. Before I reached her, she took a few quick steps to meet me halfway and, swooping down, hugged me to her copious fragrant bosom, exclaiming, "So this is our little girl!"

Never have I felt more welcome!

I wish I could tell you about Lily, do justice to her charm, her *joie de vivre,* her great beauty. She was affectionate and gay, spirited, loyal, yielding one minute, stubborn the next, absurdly frivolous and gravely thoughtful. She was vain about herself but charitable toward others, unmistakably well-bred, and bewitchingly alluring. Lily was the mysterious magic essence of femininity.

When I knew her, she stood on the threshold of middle age, and although the delicate loveliness of girlhood was behind her, the contours of her face and neck were firm, and her skin as smooth as cream. Youth still graced her features, while maturity added character and substance to her beauty.

Lily suffered from heart trouble but I never heard her complain about it or witnessed any evidence that she enjoyed any imaginary ailments. Her weak heart prohibited strenuous activity but it is incongruous to think of Lily participating in athletics or roughing it—not that tender exquisite darling! She abhorred the newfangled suntanned look and carefully avoided the sun to protect her delicate, lily-white skin from which her nickname derived.

Lily's one physical flaw was uneven teeth and she knew it. She had a way of smiling without revealing them, curling up her closed lips at the corners in a most captivating smile.

Although she dressed in impeccably good taste, Lily's physique was completely out of fashion. At a time when flat chests and angular boyish figures were high style, she was full-bosomed and round-hipped, all softness and curves. When most of her contemporaries fell willing victims to the "shingle bob," Lily's waist length, heavy, auburn hair was brushed a half hour or longer every night.

The perfection of skin and features and luxuriant auburn hair were hers through a lucky combination of genes, but these gifts of nature were enhanced by Lily's habitually pleasant expression. Petty irritation and sulkiness were foreign to her—not that she didn't flare up from time to time. Although she was seldom roused to anger, on the rare occasions she was, Lily's eyes would flash fire, her full lips compress into a tight line, and a flush would darken the cameo perfection of her neck and face. When that happened, Colonel Marshall had better stop teasing, and Rose had better stop laughing!

Whenever I saw a storm gathering, I would hush at once, but Colonal Marshall wouldn't give up so easily. He tapered off, turning aside her caustic retorts with weaker and weaker gibes until finally he apologized. Lily would accept his apology at once and switch immediately to a new tack so that no sullen wake would linger on to depress us.

Lily's good nature and quick wit contributed to her popularity with her own sex, while her charm and beauty attracted many male admirers. She delighted in the flowers or candy gentlemen sent her and she always made a big show of her loot in front of Colonel Marshall.

"Oh Rose!" she'd say, holding out a five-pound tin of Sherry's chocolates, "have a piece of this delicious candy. My last night's dinner partner sent it to me. Wasn't that sweet of him?"

Sherry's was her favorite candy, and to this day, when I see one of those violet tins I think of Lily and suffer a little pang of nostalgia.

There was never the slightest breath of scandal about Lily. Certainly, she enjoyed being an object of admiration, but her interest in other men stopped there and Colonel Marshall knew it. Sometimes he pretended to be jealous to make her happy, but he was a lousy actor and even I could see it pleased him that his friends idolized his lovely and loving wife.

After I had known Lily a very short while, I laughed at myself for ever worrying about her, for far from destroying my friendship with Colonel Marshall, she encouraged it and became my warm and benevolent friend herself. Colonel Marshall and Lily were recognized in the Page family as "Rose's friends" though both of them got along very well with my parents and with my brother and sister too.

The Marshalls usually came down to dinner fifteen or twenty minutes after we did, and nearly every evening they stopped by our table to exchange a few pleasantries. At first, they would invite me to join them after I had finished my dinner, but before long, it was taken for granted that I would come over to their table to talk with them until they had finished theirs. Colonel Marshall always ordered ice cream for me and if Lily suggested half-heartedly that, in view of my chubby figure, it might be better for me to have fruit instead of a second dessert, Colonel Marshall and I would hoot her down.

I looked forward all day to those dessert sessions, because Colonel Marshall geared the conversation to interest me, without ever letting me suspect that he was patronizing me. On the contrary, he encouraged me to speak up on whatever subject we were discussing, listening as attentively and respectfully to my opinion as if I were his equal.

"Is that so?" he would inquire, "What makes you say that?" If I gave him a careless answer, he would dismiss it, saying that I'd have to do better if I wanted to bring him around. But if I offered substantial facts or creditable ideas, no matter how childish, he would exclaim, "Well, I've learned something!" Since I was usually considered to be the family booby, his recognition that I had said something worthwhile was stimulating, to say the least.

But the most fun was when Colonel Marshall launched into an account of one or another of his various past experiences. He was a capital raconteur and his talents were by no means limited to entertaining a little girl. Within the circle of his close friends, when I was privileged to listen in, I noticed he held the grownups' attention as closely as he held mine.

I have forgotten many of the anecdotes and stories Colonel

Marshall told me in the *2400* dining room almost fifty years ago, but I remember bits and pieces of some of his tales and nearly all of others.

There was a motherly French matron in whose house he lived during World War I who was the heroine of many stories, but I can remember only one incident about her. I suppose I remember that one because Lily thought it was so funny. It seems that Colonel Marshall's French landlady went into a screaming, weeping frenzy when he returned to her house one evening, bleeding profusely from a superficial wound. The following day, to his great embarrassment, she marched resolutely into the bathroom while he was taking a bath.

"The lady barged in on me because the door had no lock," Colonel Marshall said, laughing. "She ignored all my protests, rattling off something about her *cinc fils adultes,* and scolded me for being foolishly modest when I needed help to wash my feet."

Colonel Marshall had another unsought experience with a woman which was not amusing and indeed, came perilously close to ruining his career. It had to do with the attractive wife of one of his superior officers when he was a young Lieutenant in the Philippines.

The lady was a victim of what Colonel Marshall described to me in the *2400* days as "a sudden attack." Her husband was away on an inspection trip, but why the Post doctor was absent I cannot recall. At any rate, the frightened lady sent for the only person she felt she could trust, Lieutenant George Marshall. When he received her summons, Lieutenant Marshall was attending a lively officers' party. He left it immediately to go straight to her house, where he stayed most of the night administering first aid. Unknown to him, another young officer, well in his cups, had followed him at a distance and returned to the party with the hot tip that woman-shy George Marshall was alone in the house with the absent officer's pretty wife. Several other drunks left the

22

party, and, laughing and shouting coarse jokes, they banged on the lady's front door demanding to be let in. The lady entreated Lieutenant Marshall not to let anyone in and not to tell a soul what was the matter with her, so he ignored the ribaldry until, exasperated by the clamor, he summarily ordered his friends to go away.

By mid-morning the following day, the hottest gossip of the year was dispelled by the news that the officer's wife was seriously ill and George Marshall had probably saved her life. Nevertheless, her husband chose to be Marshall's bitter enemy, and instead of offering him gratitude, never forgave him for "trespassing" on his property. He was restrained with difficulty from permanently injuring young Lieutenant Marshall's career, through the combined efforts of fellow officers who were reasonable enough men when sober.

Twenty-odd years after he told me that story, Colonel Marshall had become General Marshall, United States Chief of Staff, and our nation was in the midst of World War II. He and I were out horseback riding one afternoon, when he suddenly asked me, out of the blue, "Do you remember the woman in the Philippines I told you about who got sick and caused me so much trouble?"

"Sure," I replied, "What about her?"

"Well," he said, "she had a female hemorrhage; it was a helluva predicament. Unfortunately," he continued, laughing, "V.M.I. neglected to give me a course in gynecology."

Obviously, he had been thinking about her husband in connection with the war, but when I queried him as to who the fellow was, he refused to tell me.

Of all Colonel Marshall's tales about his experiences, he especially liked to elaborate on his rigorous life as a cadet at the Virginia Military Institute in Lexington, Virginia. Much of it sounded unbearable to me: the incessant drilling, short vacations, strict rules, small allowance, and, worst of all, no heat in his room during winter. He told me that he and his roommate used to

23

draw straws on cold winter mornings to see which one had to break the ice in their washbasin. One morning, he said, obviously enjoying my repugnance, he drew the short straw and was so sleepy he banged his fist down too hard and the ice scraped all the skin off his knuckles.

Once I asked him why he thought V.M.I. was so wonderful and what was the best or most useful thing he'd learned there. He replied that he had liked V.M.I. because he wanted to be a soldier and the most important thing he had learned there was discipline. "Why didn't you go to West Point, then, if you were so crazy about being a soldier?" I asked, "especially since you're a Yankee anyhow." (General Marshall was born and raised in Uniontown, Pennsylvania.)

He laughed and answered that even if he was a "damyankee," his father had been a Democrat in a Republican district and couldn't get him an appointment to West Point. It made no difference to him, he added, since he had received excellent training at V.M.I.

Colonel Marshall touched lightly on his most noteworthy successes at V.M.I., although he did tell me that in his last year there he fulfilled his two greatest ambitions—he was chosen cadet First Captain and he made the varsity football team. Of the two achievements, he talked much more about the football team. He told me he'd been too skinny for his six-foot-plus height, which had somewhat hampered his effectiveness as left tackle but had not diminished one whit his desire to excel. It was his bullheaded desire that helped him "hold that line," but I thought he had paid a high price to play so vehemently for the good old team. In the final game, his most spectacular tackle—which he remembered down to the minutest detail—had resulted in permanent injury to a muscle in the back of his neck.

I regretted his mishap as much as he did because his neck still bothered him from time to time and I was called upon to massage it. He showed me how to work my fingers around and knead

24

with the heel of my hand, which I did willingly enough until they got numb. But invariably, when I'd want to stop, Colonel Marshall would let out a loud remonstrative groan and complain I didn't care how much discomfort he suffered, so I'd be hooked for another five minutes.

Besides being First Captain and making the football team during his last glorious year at V.M.I., Colonel Marshall found Lily.

Lily, baptized Elizabeth Carter, lived with her mother, Mrs. Coles, in a modest little Victorian house described by Colonel Marshall as "all gingerbread and curlicues"; the house was situated scarcely a block from the entrance to the V.M.I. grounds. Mrs. Coles and Lily managed with dignity on a small income which I assumed from experience was the hallmark of "First Families of Virginia," for Lily and her mother, like the Pages, were members of that anachronistic Brahmin tribe known as "F. F. V.'s."

Colonel Marshall's account of his courtship of Lily was, I suspect, liberally sprinkled with his homemade stardust, but it fascinated me. He had admired Lily from afar, he reminisced, but had had the very deuce of a time arranging to meet her. After dismissing several plans as impractical, he decided the best way to attract her attention would be to spend his Saturday leaves strolling up and down the sidewalk in front of her house. He used up several precious Saturday afternoons marching "ten paces forward, about face, and ten paces back" while Lily, who knew perfectly well what he was up to, entertained him by playing her piano but did not condescend to show her face. Finally, one memorable Saturday, his strategy paid off. Lily relented.

Mrs. Coles opened the door to the persistent young cadet and smilingly inquired his name as she ushered him into their charming, slightly overfurnished living room. Cadet Captain Marshall had composed himself to make a debonair entrance, but because his eyes were fixed on radiant Lily standing beside her piano, he stumbled over a delicate heirloom chair as clumsily as any awkward plebe. Apparently, only Mrs. Coles was disturbed about her shattered treasure, for to hear Colonel Marshall tell it, he was a goner from the moment he met Lily. To hear Lily tell it, pinwheels whirled, sparks flew, and bells rang, then all went calm and nothing was left in the world except a tall, slender youth whose intense blue eyes riveted her to his side forever.

The year was 1901, Colonel Marshall was twenty years old, and Lily, they say, was a few years older. Colonel Marshall never volunteered to confirm the rumor and I never asked him about her age because I didn't care.

I did ask him what became of the wonderful discipline that he had learned at V.M.I., when he told me about the rules he'd broken to spend more time with Lily.

"All's fair in love and war," he retorted; so I left off teasing him, because I wanted to hear about the dangers he had overcome to see his lady love. He told me he used to leave a pillow stuffed in his bed and slip past the guard after taps. Then he had to scale a wall very quietly and sneak through the dark to Lily's house. Lily, he said, spent the anxious moments waiting for him by playing sweet music on her piano so that he would hear it and know she was languishing for his company.

Colonel Marshall liked to boast that he had won Lily over large and lively competition. He often bragged about her fabulous popularity with the V.M.I. cadets and students at nearby Washington and Lee University. Lily always reacted to his tributes with little shrieks of coquettish laughter and coy denials that she wasn't ever *that* famous a belle.

One evening at dinner, when he had been regaling me with Lily's talent for catching beaux, Colonel Marshall turned to her and said, "It will always be the greatest moment of my life, dear, that moment when you accepted me."

Lily gave him a loving glance and smiled her captivating smile. I was melting with the romance of it when Colonel

Marshall asked her, with mock solemnity, "And if it was my greatest moment, it was your luckiest, wasn't it?"

They were married February 11, 1902, in the Coles' little gingerbread house, only six weeks after Colonel Marshall's twenty-first birthday. The interval between his graduation and wedding had been a rough time for the bridegroom, who had irrevocably decided on a military career, but lacked an essential prerequisite—his commission. A diploma from V.M.I. certified his military training, but, unlike West Point, did not automatically guarantee a commission. Added to this dilemma, his father and older brother were violently opposed both to his choice of career and his decision to marry. They insisted that the Army offered a poor future and that he was much too young and too poor to consider matrimony.

After Mr. Marshall was thoroughly convinced that nothing would change his son George's mind, he helped him get his commission and resigned himself to his marriage. Colonel Marshall told me his father wrote "chain" letters to all his influential acquaintances and asked them to write, in turn, to their prominent friends. He said that his father had a pretty low opinion of his ability, and had enjoyed an unaccustomed pride in spreading abroad the "swell" recommendation that the V.M.I. Superintendent had written about him. According to the V.M.I. Superintendent, George Marshall was highly qualified to make a superior officer through training, ability, and temperament.

Mr. Marshall's efforts plus a timely Congressional authorization to enlarge the Army finally assured George Marshall a place on the list of candidates selected to take the examinations for a commission. He passed the exams!

He received his commission as Second Lieutenant in January 1902, along with his assignment to an Infantry Division in the Philippines. I was aghast when he told me that Lily could not go to the Philippines with him.

He was not due to leave for his faraway post until the first part of April, but was ordered to report for duty the end of February. Meanwhile, he wanted to get married.

This was a major part of his plans, he told me, and he proceeded to see that it was carried out. When I reminded him that it might have been part of his plans to get married in a hurry but he sure couldn't have carried them out if Lily hadn't agreed, he reminded me that they were in love, and of course she had agreed. Their home wedding was very simple with only members of the family and intimate friends present, which seemed a pity to me. I thought Lily would have made a gorgeous bride, all decked out in white with a long train trailing down the church aisle behind her.

They had a short honeymoon in Washington—only about a week, I believe. It would have been even shorter, Lily said, if some good-hearted officer had not arranged for a few days' extension of Lieutenant Marshall's leave. They stayed at the old Willard Hotel, which was a swanky place for visiting bigwigs, and Colonel Marshall said if the honeymoon had lasted any longer, he would have been broke anyhow.

At the end of the week, Lieutenant Marshall and his bride parted, not to see each other again for two years. Although hasty marriages followed by long separations were common enough in World War II, when I was a little girl I had never heard of anybody getting married and parting immediately for two whole years.

"How could you stand it?" I asked in shocked bewilderment, and the answer was simply, "We were in love."

❧ CHAPTER III ❧

ONE OF MY CLEAREST RECOLLECTIONS OF GENERAL MARSHALL IS THE dynamic force of his attitude and appearance when he spoke to me in deep concentration. He would drain his mind of all irrelevancies on a moment's notice, and focus his attention exclusively on his subject. His words poured out ever more rapidly, as if speech were inadequate to keep pace with his agile brain. His body remained motionless and his face composed, but the expression of his keen blue eyes changed constantly as they reflected the mood and meaning of his thought.

It was thus he spoke to me one evening about the 1919 victory parade in Paris, one of several that had taken place the previous year. Colonel Marshall, as aide to General Pershing, had ridden in all of them, but the Paris victory parade, or rather the people who came to see it, made the most profound impression on him.

He tailored his story to suit my nine-year-old intellect but he did not destroy its significance by softening harsh facts to spare my "tender little psyche." Although his frank exposition shattered my childish fancies of conquering heroes and the glories of war, the power of his concentration was such that I was caught up by it and listened spellbound by everything he said.

He began by revealing the extent of the devastation that the war had brought to France. He described shelled cities, smashed villages, and destroyed farmlands. He spoke of carnage, bravery, fear, sorrow, desperation, and anguish.

After he was sure that I understood the magnitude of the suffering in France, Colonel Marshall proceeded to talk about the crowds who came to the Paris victory parade. They were not appreciably larger or noisier than the throngs at the London and New York victory parades, he said. Nevertheless, there was a marked difference. In London and New York, the air had tingled with exhilaration. In Paris, the atmosphere was charged with pathos. Britons and Americans had shouted and cheered with abandon. The French had exploded in screaming, weeping, laughing relief.

"As long as I live," he said, "I will never forget the faces I saw that day."

As he looked into one distraught face after another, Colonel Marshall told me that he felt no exultation of victory, only great sorrow that millions of humble people had suffered so extensively for reasons beyond their control and which they did not understand.

"You see, Rosie," he concluded, "because France was the actual battlefield, I don't suppose there was a single person there who had not lost someone dear. Can you imagine the feelings of the French people at that parade?"

All these years, I have remembered my first glimpse into the depths of General Marshall's compassion. But at the time, I was unaware of the indelible impression it had made on me, for only a few evenings later, I temporarily forgot all about it.

I was placidly enjoying my usual second dessert with the Marshalls when Lily casually mentioned that tomorrow was the night General Pershing was coming to dine at 2400. I never gave a thought to Colonel Marshall's moving account of the people at the Paris victory parade. Instead, I envisioned the great General, ramrod erect, astride his famous horse Jeff, riding grandly through the Arc de Triomphe. I was sure that he was the most famous man in the world and I wasn't too far wrong. Although General Pershing's star may be obscured today by the constellation of illustrious World War II Generals, in 1920, he was the Number-One national hero. I was thrilled at the prospect of seeing him close up, but in one short second, Colonel Marshall killed my enthusiasm.

General Pershing was coming to a private dinner party upstairs, he told me, and added as an afterthought, "By the way, Rosie, I think it would be nice if you'd introduce yourself to him when he comes through the lobby."

"By *myself!*" I wailed. "Won't you and Lily be here?"

He replied they would be dining out, and reminded me with a grin that I had had no qualms about introducing myself to him, so why should I be afraid to speak to General Pershing?

I looked desperately at Lily who did her level best to help me. It was a very different situation, Lily said, my wanting to know Colonel Marshall and being forced to speak to General Pershing. She didn't blame me one bit, she added indignantly.

Colonel Marshall was adamant, insisting it would be valuable experience for me to handle the introduction myself. Lily countered that it was all well and good to learn self-confidence, but he was unreasonable to ask a nine-year-old to go up cold and introduce herself to the distinguished General of the Armies.

Colonel Marshall interrupted firmly. "I know what I'm doing, Lily; please don't upset Rose any more than she is already."

He turned to me and said he would never ask me to do anything beyond what he believed I could do. It was important, he explained, for me to be able to face up to an unusual situation and to learn something from the experience. Smiling affectionately, he patted my hand, and delivered his punch line: "I have absolute confidence you will carry it off. Otherwise, I wouldn't have suggested you do it."

I had known from the start there was no way out, although I had counted on fighting back. But Colonel Marshall had won before I could say a word. I could have resisted persuasion or balked at an order, but his expression of confidence left me helpless.

"What must I say?" I asked on the verge of tears.

Colonel Marshall urged me to "be yourself." Lily advised me to say the first thing that came into my head, at which both of them laughed as if she'd made a big joke.

I did not dare rely on "the first thing that came into my head," so the next day I painfully composed a patriotic little speech to recite when I came face to face with the General of the Armies. It was one of the worst days of my life.

After dinner that evening, when Mother, Celeste, and I came out into the lobby, I was appalled to see that it was packed with people four deep all the way from the front door to the elevators. I guessed that practically all of the tenants at 2400 had assembled to see the great Pershing, and all of them must have invited guests. One of Colonel Marshall's Army officer friends spotted me cringing beside my sister and urged me to come forward where I could see better. Everybody at 2400 knew about the close friendship between Colonel Marshall and me, so I stumbled through a path made for me by smiling adults, and ended up pressed against one of the marble columns a little more than halfway down the lobby from the front door. I leaned against the column, stiff with fright, repeating my speech over and over to myself, when suddenly, a horrible thought hit me. No one knew Colonel Marshall had "suggested" I speak to General Pershing. What if everybody would think I was a show-off? Colonel Marshall hadn't thought of that! Of all people, he despised show-offs. I would have given up the project right then if the orchestra hadn't struck up the first bars of "The Star Spangled Banner."

All heads turned toward the front door as a tremendous wave

of applause rolled down the lobby. I leaned forward and saw General Pershing, followed by a retinue of officers, advancing at a rapid pace toward the elevators. He looked neither right nor left, his stern, handsome face masked with the impersonal courtesy characteristic of great men of the hour. When he came abreast of my column, everything in my mind went blank except that Colonel Marshall was counting on me. I marched straight out and planted myself squarely in front of the august General, who nearly tripped over me before he could halt. Pershing glared down at me with a chilly, annoyed little smile which sent my memorized speech flying off into the wild blue yonder.

"Yes?" he asked uninvitingly, almost rudely.

"Sir," I faltered, "I'm Colonel Marshall's Rose Page and he suggested I come up and speak to you."

General Pershing's smile broadened and warmed, "Well, well," he said heartily, extending his hand, "So you are Rose. How do you do?"

As we shook hands, an important part of my speech came back to me, "Thank you for winning the war," I said.

"Thank you for the compliment," he replied, "but you mustn't think I won the war. We won the war, hundreds of thousands of us."

"Yes sir," I answered, and catching the finality in his voice, I stepped aside and General Pershing strode on, unhindered, to the waiting elevators.

The first thing I remember after he had gone was Colonel Marshall's same Army officer friend rushing up to me all smiles. He grabbed my hand and asked playfully, "Let me shake the hand that just shook the hand of our famous General!"

"Oh, sir!" I explained, "Thanks a lot, but honest, it wasn't my idea, Colonel Marshall sort of made me do it."

"That sounds like George," he laughed. "Well, I'll tell him you did a fine job, and now, haven't you a grand experience you can talk about at school?"

I was the heroine of the evening and I reveled in it, but I

learned something, too. The way I figured it back in 1920 was that of all the crowd at 2400 who gave a hoot about Rose Page speaking to General Pershing, there was only one who really cared, and that was Rose Page. So why bother agonizing over what sort of impression I might make? Colonal Marshall was right: "Be yourself." Of course, General Pershing's initially unfriendly attitude had forced me into being myself and saying the "first thing that came into my head"; but it had all been so much easier than Lily and I had anticipated.

Actually, it was Major Marshall who was right, for he was no longer a Colonel at the time I went through that little scene with General Pershing. When I met Colonel Marshall in 1919, he still held the temporary rank of Colonel he had received during the war, but in June 1920, he reverted to his permanent rank of Captain, and on the following day, was promoted to Major. When I first heard about this reverse action, I refused to believe anything so grossly unfair could happen. Naturally, I was prejudiced by my affection and admiration for Colonel Marshall, but I also knew from the consensus in the lobby that he was considered a man marked for success, a sure bet for Chief of Staff.

As soon as I saw him, the first thing I blurted out was, "Oh Colonel Marshall, I'll never call you Major, you are really truly a Colonel and you're going to be Chief of Staff! I know that for a fact, so don't worry."

He smiled and stooped down to kiss my forehead. "You and Lily are my biggest boosters," he replied; "if it were up to you two I'd be Chief of Staff day after tomorrow. Thank you, Rosie, you go right ahead and call me Colonel, and if I ever am Chief of Staff, you just keep on calling me Colonel."

Then I started to cry. In an outburst of rage and indignation I poured out vitriolic abuses against the President, Congress, the Chief of Staff, the whole United States, and was just getting around to God when Colonel Marshall told me unceremoniously to shut up.

"I deeply appreciate your concern," he started off gently, then, switching to a sterner voice, admonished me, "but you're hitting out wild and haven't landed a blow."

He cautioned me as he had many times before against letting my heart run away with me. He admitted nobody was worth a tinker's damn without a heart, but there had to be a proper ratio between how strongly a person felt and how ably his thinking directed his feelings into useful channels. He pointed out that my reaction to his drop in rank was a good example. "All your heartfelt objections," he said, "are strong feelings but pretty weak stuff for marking up any plus signs."

Colonel Marshall restricted his little lecture to barely more than five minutes. Perhaps that's why his lessons made such a lasting impression on me—they were short, potent, and direct. He ended this one by saying, "It might make you feel better to know that if the war had lasted a little longer I would have been a General, but neither of us would want to be a General at that price, would we?"

One spring day in 1920, Colonel Marshall, that is, Major Marshall, appeared at the door of my schoolroom a few minutes before the dismissal bell. I never saw Major, Colonel, or General Marshall enter a room without everyone in it shifting their attention to him and that one day was no exception. We children sat hypnotized as our autocratic old teacher, usually immune to the protests and pleas of worried parents, took one look at Colonel Marshall and fell apart. Nervously, she pulled at her skirt, patted her hair, and, smiling at him self-consciously, asked if she could be of any service. I had an eerie feeling she was about to curtsy. Colonel Marshall replied with clipped businesslike courtesy that he had only come to observe her teaching for a few minutes and did not care to disrupt the class. He stood at ease, looked her straight in the eye, and told her to continue with the lesson. It was a dirty trick. Colonel Marshall knew perfectly well that we were not having a lesson because I had told him the teacher ended every single day with a general bawling out that lasted anywhere from five to fifteen minutes.

"The lesson?" she murmured, jerking her head upward and staring at the ceiling. She cleared her throat and started to speak, decided against it, walked to her desk, sat down, and busily shuffled a few papers. The room was deathly still; not a child stirred.

"Class dismissed!" she screeched in an unnaturally high-pitched voice.

It was five minutes before the dismissal bell and, as I ran toward Colonel Marshall, I saw him move quickly away from the door to avoid the stampede.

As we left, Colonel Marshall did not even mention the teacher but hurried me out of the building and across the playground. He was in exceptionally high spirits, talking all sorts of foolishness about what a pretty day it was, and what a shame I was too tired to walk home. I protested I wasn't too tired and why would he think I was? We walked faster and faster, breaking into a sprint as we neared the street. There, parked at the playground entrance, was a brand-new, shiny, black Model-T Ford with Lily sitting in the back seat, beaming out at us. Colonal Marshall opened a door, and with much hammy bowing and scraping, said, *"Entrez, Mademoiselle,* in other words, get in."

"Oh my gosh!" I shouted, "Is it ours? Oh boy, Lily, isn't it peachy?" Lily agreed it was indeed peachy and wasn't it a grand surprise? Colonel Marshall drove off merrily down the street, every now and then beeping the horn at nothing. Well, it wasn't really beeping; the horn didn't have a siren call or the long, insulting blast that horns have today. It grunted, "Ugah—ugah, ugah."

Between "ugahs" and Lily's and my happy babbling, Colonel Marshall interposed, "It might not be a fancy limousine, but this tin Lizzie is all paid for, cash on the line, and it's a good enough car for our motor trip."

"Motor trip?" I asked, beside myself with excitement, "What motor trip?"

He told me Lily was going to visit her mother in Lexington for ten days or so and when it was time for her to come home, he and I would drive down through the Shenandoah Valley and fetch her back. He said he'd already talked to my mother and the plans were all made. I had never been on a motor trip in my life—in fact, very few people took motor trips—so I looked forward to a grand adventure.

It was the first of several trips Colonel Marshall and I took to pick up Lily, and Mother made elaborate preparations for it. Our seamstress was called in to make me a pretty nightgown and dressing robe, which turned out to be the prettiest I had ever owned. Mother, herself, embroidered the little white batiste nightgown with a wreath of pink roses surrounding my initials; and the pink wool robe had matching embroidery on the buttons. I remember that finery very well, but the trip is merged in my mind with other trips we took later. However, Colonel Marshall repeated an incident of that first trip so often and to so many people that, although I do not remember it myself, I record it here, since he thought it was so amusing.

When we checked in at the hotel, Colonel Marshall engaged only one room because he was uneasy about leaving me alone in a strange place. After dinner he sent me up to bed while he stayed downstairs to read the paper and smoke a cigarette. (Incidentally he used to be a chain smoker—Chesterfields). When he assumed I was asleep, he came upstairs and went to bed himself but as soon as the light was turned off I called, "Colonel Marshall, Colonel Marshall—may I have a drink of water? I'm terribly thirsty."

He switched on the light, whereupon I leapt out of bed and danced around and around the room. He immediately caught on, said Colonel Marshall, that I had no intention of not showing off my gorgeous new nightgown. He made all the hoped-for comments on how exquisite my gown was and then suggested maybe it was time to go to sleep.

Again the light went out and again I called, "Colonel Marshall, Colonel Marshall, I'm scared, I've never slept in a strange place before, and Sister's not here." This time he knew I wasn't playing possum, so he switched on the light again and I ran over and jumped in his bed, forcing him to tell me stories and sing to me until I went to sleep.

The next morning he awoke, dressed, and went downstairs, leaving word with the floor maid that she was to wake me in a half hour and tell me to get dressed right away and come down for breakfast.

A half hour later the maid came down, and, shaking with laughter, beckoned to Colonel Marshall. He went over to her and she told him she'd awakened me as she had been instructed, saying, "Your father says you're to dress right away and come down for breakfast."

"My father!" I replied.

"Why yes," she answered, "Isn't that gentleman downstairs your father?"

"Oh mercy, no!" I objected haughtily. "He's just a friend!"

And that's how Colonel Marshall told the story.

💛 CHAPTER IV 💛

NEW YEAR'S EVE IN 1920 WAS A MOMENTOUS ONE FOR ME, BECAUSE IT was Colonel Marshall's fortieth birthday, and the first New Year's Eve on which I was allowed to stay up past midnight. I was nine years old, and considered myself an old-time nursery alumna; nevertheless, my two years post-graduate course at the *2400* school of correct deportment and worldly wisdom hardly qualified me as a candidate for honors in sophistication. Consequently, that first celebration remains the *ne plus ultra* of all my New Years' Eves.

It was a closed party at *2400,* and those closed parties throw a revealing sidelight on the novel management of that supposedly public apartment house; every year several dances were held there exclusively for the residents. Ordinarily, outside guests were welcomed if they were personally invited by tenants of *2400;* but because of the large attendance expected on New Year's Eve, just as in a private club, no outsiders were allowed.

Ever since Mother had told Tom and Celeste that they could accompany her to watch the festivities, Sis and I had been discussing various ways to persuade her to let me come, too.

"No, I'm not sure Rose had better come this year," was all Mother would say when my sister asked about me.

Finally, we decided that perhaps the best plan would be to appeal to Colonel Marshall, who, we agreed, could fix anything.

It was a rainy Sunday afternoon when I definitely made up my mind to ask him for his help. We were in the Marshalls' apartment, one of 2400's small, two-room, furnished suites. Lily was napping in the adjoining bedroom, and Colonel Marshall and I had just finished playing a couple of games of Russian Bank, which my father, in a rare expansive mood, had taught me to play, and which I had taught to Colonel Marshall. He had won both games with very little effort, and, chiding me that I wasn't "half trying," he suggested we stop playing. He won so regularly anyhow, that it always bothered Lily. She used to tell him not to work so hard to beat me, it wasn't "nice."

"Heavens, George, she's only a little girl!" Lily protested.

Sometimes he would laugh and say, "Little girl or not, she's the one who taught me in the first place, and it's her hard luck if I beat her at her own game." Or other times he would remind Lily he knew perfectly well I was a kid but that was a "bum reason" for throwing me the game.

"What's the point of playing," he'd ask her, "if we both know it isn't a fair contest?" Colonel Marshall was absolutely incapable of losing on purpose. I used to win just often enough to want to play again, something like blasting out of a sand trap into the cup, and about as rare.

That rainy afternoon, however, I didn't have my mind on the cards and was glad when we stopped playing. Colonel Marshall knew something was bothering me. I was never able to conceal any of my inner feelings from him. He often told me I should try to master the technique of a poker face.

"It doesn't matter with me," he'd say. "But for your own protection, it isn't always appropriate or wise to let the other fellow know how you feel."

40

I waited impatiently while he took his time clearing the cards away, replacing the packs neatly in their boxes, and arranging the boxes meticulously in the desk drawer. All the while he whistled a little tune through his teeth—a tiny little whistle I never learned to imitate. At last he settled himself in an easy chair, lit a fresh cigarette, and, smiling amiably, waited for me to speak.

"Colonel Marshall," I began anxiously, "I'm dying to go to the New Year's Eve party and I don't think I'm going to make it."

I started off telling him the truth—I didn't want to miss his fortieth birthday. I thought forty was much more important than being thirty-nine or forty-one, and went on to explain I didn't think I was enough younger than Sis for Mother to decide I'd have to stay upstairs and miss all the fun. "I'm not even sure," I added, "that it's because I'm younger. She hasn't actually said why I can't go."

Avidly pleading my case, I built up an elaborate Rube Goldberg structure of justifications teetering on top of explanations with complaints and opinions sticking out haphazardly in between. Every now and then I would pause briefly, hoping he would agree with me or offer a suggestion, but he lounged comfortably in his chair, silently smoking his cigarette, so I racked my brain for still more convincing reasons.

As I talked, I watched his eyes, which I always did when I wanted a clue as to how he was thinking. His face was perfectly calm and his attitude as attentive as ever, but instead of the concern I was looking for, his eyes unmistakably betrayed evidence of growing amusement. Obviously, I wasn't getting across the vital importance of my request, so I made one last desperate try. Tremulously, I launched into a melodramatic characterization of myself as a pitiful, rejected child, a combination of Oliver Twist and The Little Match Girl. By this time Colonel Marshall was laughing out loud, so I gave up in disappointment.

"What's so darn funny?" I asked plaintively.

He told me he wasn't laughing because I wanted to go to the party. "Your plight is real enough," he said, "but your presentation of it was hilarious." He looked at his watch and commented dryly, "You took twenty-five minutes to tell me something you could have said in forty seconds."

"Why didn't you stop me, then, instead of just sitting there not saying anything?" I asked indignantly.

"I was curious to find out how long you could keep going," he replied, his eyes full of amusement, "and I'm surprised that your imagination gave out in twenty-five minutes."

"Shucks!" and I laughed a little defensively myself, "I could have thought up a lot more things; I only stopped because you were laughing. But it really isn't funny—I want to go so *bad!*"

"That's obvious enough," he replied. "But you made your point in the first two sentences—all the rest was eyewash."

"Well, will you help me, then?" I asked directly.

He did help me, but forever after that afternoon's fiasco, if I wanted to ask him something specific or explain a problem, I would say, "This is a forty-second question," or "Here comes a two-minute problem," and believe me, for a talkative female, those condensations required strenuous preliminary editing.

Never one to put things off, Colonel Marshall and Lily stopped by our table on their way in to dinner that same Sunday evening following my lengthy petition. I remember that my father was dining at the Cosmos Club, and although he would have deferred to Mother's dictum in any case, his absence made the situation less complicated. After a brief but amicable "Good evening," Colonel Marshall dispensed with further amenities and asked Mother if she would allow me to attend the New Year's Eve party.

"I know she will enjoy it," he said smiling. "I would also like to have Rosie there to help celebrate my birthday." He glanced briefly at me and told Mother very firmly that if she had specific reasons for my not coming, he would withdraw his request "on the spot."

Mother replied casually that if he wanted me to come, she didn't particularly object; and she, too, was sure that I would enjoy the party, but had been somewhat wary of giving me permission.

"Under excitement, as you've probably noticed," she said, "Rose is apt to become pretty obstreperous."

Oh, I thought, so that's why! But what does it mean? Before I could ask, Colonel Marshall explained, "Obstreperous means trying to stand on your head like you insisted on doing in our living room the other day when Lily was trying to write a letter." He ignored Mother's unhappy frown of disapproval. He looked directly into my eyes and told me that if I wanted to come to his birthday I must promise "right now" to behave properly.

"Cross my heart!" I promised fervently.

Colonel Marshall turned to Mother and said that he honored my word, and that if she did too, perhaps they could agree I should come to the New Year celebration. Mother's loyalty did not allow her to withhold sanction from her child's given word, so the matter was settled. It may be she had intended all along to take me to the party. I never knew. But I still believe Colonel Marshall tipped the scales in my favor. When I joined the Marshalls for dessert that evening, I thanked him, but added he'd nearly spoiled everything when he told Mother he was willing to withdraw his request. He straightened me out on that one in a hurry!

"I will never attempt to overrule your mother's wishes under any circumstances," he told me, and added that he had not done so in this case. He had only helped to clarify the issue, and the "rest is up to you."

Lily burst out impatiently, "Oh she'll be good, and let's stop talking about it. I think the important thing is to have a wonderful time."

"And by the way," she said to Colonel Marshall with her most engaging smile, "Obstreperous also means holding up somebody's feet while she's trying to stand on her head."

"Lily," I interrupted hastily, "Is New Year's Eve as marvelous as they say it is?"

"Oh yes, honey," she replied, and using a French word which was one of her little affectations, said, *"Magnifique!"*

The first surprise of that New Year's Eve was finding out the party didn't begin until nine o'clock; infuriatingly, I was beginning to get sleepy by the time Mother assembled us to go downstairs. Nobody was surprised that my father had declined to join us; but when we trooped into the living room to kiss him goodnight before we left, he paid us courtly compliments on our finery, and sent us off with wishes for a pleasant evening and a happy New Year.

It was close to nine thirty when Mother, Celeste, Tom, and I marched into the ballroom and seated ourselves in a row on the uncomfortable little gold chairs arranged around the walls. Sis and I, dressed alike as always, were resplendent in black velvet dresses with bright-blue embroidery, and patent-leather slippers, but Mother was wearing her old beige lace she had had made over for the occasion. I thought how pretty she looked and felt an unwelcome twinge of guilt that my dress was new and hers wasn't.

This troubling sentiment, however, was rapidly benumbed by delight as I gazed, enraptured, at the gaudy decorations which transformed the ballroom. A great golden bell was suspended from the central chandelier, colorful streamers festooned the others, and clusters of balloons bobbed from the wall fixtures. A big jazz band—the players, I thought, looked like princes and kings in their maroon jackets with silver-sequinned lapels—blasted out a frenzied foxtrot as blithe tenants of 2400, laughing and talking together, began to fill the ballroom. Wide awake now, I was astonished to observe that nobody seemed the same as they did in the lobby. Of course, they were in full evening dress, but everybody acted as if they were telling each other jokes, and some of the men's faces looked unusually red above their white ties and stiff white shirts.

I kept looking for Colonel Marshall and Lily, but the Burnettes, special friends of Mother's, arrived first and joined us, so we children moved down to make room for them next to her. They told Mother that the cocktail party had been a lot of fun and asked her why she hadn't come too. Mother laughed and replied that liquor only made her sick and depressed, especially bootleg stuff.

This was no news to me because she often told my father the same thing. Whiskey never seemed to have a noticeable effect on my father, but I knew he always had some on hand because I was the one who usually opened the door when his bootlegger rang. Although I had never seen an example of it, I had heard plenty of lobby talk about so and so's having had "too much to drink." It suddenly dawned on me why everybody looked different.

"Gosh!" I whispered to Sis, "They're all kinda drunk, aren't they?"

"Naturally, dummy!" was her cryptic reply.

Still Colonel Marshall and Lily hadn't come. Colonel and Mrs. Gasser showed up, and after talking to Mother a while, Colonel Gasser invited her to dance. Mother blushed and thanked him but declined, so he gallantly invited Sis. I sat and watched them, half proud, half envious, as Celeste skillfully followed Colonel Gasser without making a single misstep.

My sister and I had attended dancing school in the 2400 ballroom all fall, but she was in a more advanced section than mine and always had more partners than I. She and Marian Barkley even had beaux. Marian was the daughter of Congressman Alben Barkley who later became the famous Veep, but in those days, we knew him only as that nice Mr. Barkley who liked children, made up funny jokes, and could play "Chopsticks" faster than anybody else.

As I sat marveling at my sister's dancing, I was startled by a voice that said, "Let's see if *your* dancing lessons took. You and I will have the very first dance on my birthday night."

"Oh Colonel Marshall!" I cried. "Happy birthday, I thought you'd never get here!"

I jumped up, hoping to prove that I'd progressed further than the dancing teacher had led me to believe; but Colonel Marshall didn't take the three steps forward, one sideways, and two back that I'd been taught. He didn't count out loud, either, "One, two, three *forward,* and *side* one, now, one, two *back."* He danced with all sorts of fancy steps I'd never encountered before.

"You're going so fast!" I shouted above the music.

"You'll get the hang of it in a minute," he encouraged. "My left arm and hand will guide you; anybody can follow a good leader, and I'm *good."* He pushed me expertly around the floor, using his left hand to cue me into his next maneuver until I began to feel confident, even cocky. His shoulder was too high for me to reach, so I clutched his jacket and hung on to his left hand with an iron grip. I huffed and puffed, broke out into an unladylike sweat, and began to get dizzy.

"Up on your toes, Rosie!" he'd remind me from time to time; "you can't dance flatfooted; or, "Listen to the music, you've got a good sense of time, it'll help you. That's *fine!"* Every now and then he'd caution, "Don't weigh me down, a man isn't supposed to hold up his partner, just lead her. Loosen up, my left hand's getting numb in that vise you've got it in. That's right, Rosie, now you're dancing like a whiz; I'll bet we're the best-looking couple on the floor."

I learned more about dancing that night than I had at dancing school all fall. For the first time, I got the point; dancing wasn't as silly and boring as I'd thought. It was fun!

When the music stopped, he took me back to my seat, made a

fine bow, flashed a smile at me, and was off to ask a grownup for the next dance. Mother was engrossed in her friends, Sis was dancing, and Tom had left the party to see if he could pick up something interesting on his radio, so I went to sit by Lily. A disconsolate gentleman sitting beside her rose to offer me his chair, and when I took it, the gentleman on the other side of her burst out laughing.

"How'd we look?" I asked Lily proudly, oblivious to the joke. She assured me I'd done very well but added tactfully she thought maybe I was a little short for George. Lily didn't dance because of her weak heart, but she sat there looking like a Titian goddess, dressed in beaded gold satin with a mist of goldish tulle about her shoulders. More and more gentlemen came up to talk with her. Finally, I realized I'd better leave, but when I stood up Lily fluttered her hand and gave me a little wink as a sign for me to stay.

At the time I thought she didn't want me to be lonesome at the party, but as I look back on it, I suspect she also wasn't taking any chances on my getting into trouble, to say nothing of using me as a chaperone. No insinuations or provocative talk could go on with a nine-year-old glued to her side. She talked to me a great deal that evening, interrupting her admirers' sallies to call my attention to an especially graceful couple or a particularly lovely dress.

As for me, I was transported by the glittering, swirling dancers. Everything and everybody looked beautiful to me. There was only one brief bad moment, when a Lolita-inclined gentleman asked me to dance. I squirmed and blushed, and told him I couldn't dance well enough. Lily, mistaking my discomfort for diffidence, dismissed "Humbert Humbert," telling him pleasantly I wasn't a very experienced dancer and that I'd better stick to dancing with George until I'd grown up a little more.

Colonel Marshall danced every other dance the whole evening, sitting out the odd ones with Lily and me. How he loved to dance in those days! Lily and I played a little game, watching the dancers and selecting which lady we thought would make the best partner for him. Once, when he was sitting with us, I suggested he try Celeste.

"She's real good," I bragged.

More to please me than anything else, Colonel Marshall invited her to dance, but after their first dance he asked her for three more because she really was remarkably graceful.

"Like dancing with a feather," he told Lily. "To tell you the truth, I'd rather dance with Celeste than with three-quarters of the women here."

He meant it, too. Dancing for Colonel Marshall was a pleasure in itself. He did not use dancing as an excuse for making time with some seductive female. Not that he was a stiff Puritan moralist—far from it. All his life he admired attractive women, but vulgarity disgusted him and the substitution of raw sex for personality and intelligence bored him. As I grew older, I noticed that the women whose company he enjoyed were charming as well as chic, and anything but unsexy. He was not immune to the lure of the opposite sex, only to a bold and wanton use of it.

As I sat by Lily that New Year's Eve, I thought all his partners were lovely, although, of course, not as gorgeous as Lily.

I'll never forget what a good time Colonel Marshall had on his fortieth birthday! He whirled his partners around the ballroom, laughing and talking to them, and when he swept past our seats, he'd wave at us and nod approvingly if his partner happened to be one of our choices. He was tall and slim and graceful—so full of life, so animated, so sparklingly gay!

One of Lily's admirers commented in amazement, "I do believe George is a little high tonight."

"Why shouldn't he be?" Lily answered shortly. "It's New Year's Eve, and bless his heart, he's starting a new decade."

In all the years I knew Colonel Marshall, this is the only instance about which I can personally testify that he was even slightly tight, and I wouldn't have known it then if I hadn't been eavesdropping. Certainly he wasn't boisterous and red-faced like some of the other men who were laughing too loud and, as Mother put it, "pawing every woman they could get their hands on."

As midnight approached, Colonel Marshall joined Lily and me just as Sis came to fetch me to spend the great moment with Mother. As I left with Celeste, Colonel Marshall thrust a tin horn into one of my hands and a whirligig noisemaker into the other.

"Here," he said, "take these and let loose with all the racket you can make while the New Year comes in." When the lights went out at twelve o'clock, the uproarious clamor was beyond my most hoped-for expectations. I jumped up and down, swinging the raka-kak noisemaker, tooting the horn; and in between toots, I yelled my head off until Celeste clapped her hand over my mouth and shouted:

"For Pete's sake, shut up; remember your *promise!*"

Always solicitous, always in perfect control, my sister said in the next breath, "Where's Mother? I can't see her in this dark."

Just then the lights came on, the band struck up "Auld Lang Syne," and there was Mother, a few paces away. She rushed over to us smiling; her eyes were brimming with tears. Embracing us both in one big hug, she wished us a happy New Year and called us her darling, wonderful little girls. I returned her embrace and wishes wholeheartedly, but I wondered why she was crying at such a marvelous party.

Colonel Marshall materialized out of the throng, and, lifting me high in the air, his eyes shining and happy, said, "God bless you Rosie, joy and happiness to you all the days of your life!" Then he put me down quickly and swept me out onto the floor to dance the last bars of "Auld Lang Syne."

I had forgotten to prepare a special New Year's wish for him beforehand and now, excited, happy, and breathless, I spoke to him straight out of my heart: "Happy birthday again, Colonel

49

Marshall, and happy New Year to you, and I know some year you'll be Chief of Staff!"

"Auld Lang Syne." Oh well, it's easy enough now to understand Mother's tears.

CHAPTER V

DISCOUNTING ALL OTHER BENEFITS DERIVED FROM MY CHILDHOOD AT *2400,* the fact alone that I met Colonel Marshall there outweighs the sundry disadvantages—a certain amount of which are inescapable by anyone, anywhere, any time. All of mine stemmed from a stifling feeling of constraint. I had come to *2400* fresh from an informal country environment, so that the unremitting restrictions circumscribing my life at *2400* oppressed me the moment I entered the building.

I missed our rambling country home in Virginia, and, although our apartment was adequate and attractive, it was painfully small and confining compared to the roomy house that I was used to. I missed the large sunny nursery—playroom in modern verbiage—with its untidy accumulation of books and toys. I missed the airy, screened sleeping porch, the big fireplaces, and many other attributes which, in reality, were probably not half so Elysian as a child's nostalgic memories made them out to be. Worst of all, there was nowhere in our compact apartment to be alone. I can remember crawling under Mother's bed, away back in a far corner, where I would huddle, shut off from reality, in a glowing make-believe world of my own. But it never lasted long. Mother would come looking for me, calling in exasperation, "Rose, Rose, come out from under the bed, you'll get dirty there on the floor. Why on earth do you insist on crouching in that dark corner like a sick puppy?"

It seemed absurd to tell her I was playing a useless game with myself, so I'd scramble out obediently, looking silly and acting stupidly, because I was never able to think up a plausible explanation.

There was no need to make excuses when I lived in Virginia, because our house there had plenty of nooks and crannies where I could retreat without causing irritation. Besides, there was the wonderful wide outdoors: the garden, lawn, orchard, meadows, and our beloved oak grove. In summertime that shady grove was a favorite place to play, especially to play Indians, since it offered the added excitement of harboring a plentiful amount of Indian arrowheads. Tom, Sis, and I scuffed up so many arrowheads in the grove that we were sure fierce, savage battles had once bloodied our lovely woods.

"Before the white man came" my wise brother told me, "because we never find empty gun shells."

The country had so many delights to offer, that, by comparison, the concrete city playgrounds and manicured Meridian Park across Sixteenth Street from 2400 seemed a very boring substitute to me. Tom and Celeste also grumbled at first about city living, but they adjusted much faster and more easily than I.

Unfortunately for me, and more unfortunately for Mother, I never worked off enough steam in those fenced-in recreation areas. Nor could I rush into the 2400 lobby as I could have bounced through the door at home. It was strictly taboo to run in the lobby or to raise my voice above "the cultured, modulated tones suitable for a lady."

"Lower your voice," Mother would say, to quiet me down if my excitement mounted while I talked to her.

Be neat; stay clean; be quiet; change for dinner; never, never relax company manners—all forged into the Damocles sword, "Be a credit to your parents." It was a demanding role.

Colonel Marshall understood the pressure and, without ever rescinding maternal orders, provided avenues of escape as often as he could. When he took me to Rock Creek Park we would abandon the traveled paths, striking out into the woods where tall trees and thickets shut out the city, and then my lost sense of freedom would return with a surge of exuberance. Knowing also how homesick I was, he'd spend whole afternoons helping me look for arrowheads. They were fruitless searches, but he entered into them with such enthusiasm and interest that he kept the hope alive that on some future afternoon we might really find one. Sometimes we had races. I'd run shouting joyfully after him until my lungs nearly burst with the effort of whooping and running to catch him as he leapt over fallen logs and dodged agilely in and out through the trees.

"Had enough?" he'd call back to me, and after I'd caught up we'd throw ourselves down in the leaves, laughing and panting.

I did not belabor Colonel Marshall with vexations about the general prohibitions laid upon me or the perfection Mother expected of me, not so much because I wanted to spare him, as because I reasoned vaguely that such revelations would be disloyal, unfair to Mother when she tried so hard to make "a lady" out of me. I did tell him, though, about the innumerable scrapes I was incapable of avoiding, because he appeared to enjoy hearing about them. Actually, I got along pretty well within home boundaries except for Mr. Clay, an ogre disguised as the manager of 2400. No matter when, any time I was in a hurry and had to run through the lobby, Mr. Clay would appear out of nowhere to bear witness to my crime which he never failed to report to Mother.

"He's an awful man, the very worst, a tattletale!" I said to Colonel Marshall one day. "And every time I see him, even if I'm not doing anything wrong, he acts as if I am, and says something hateful."

Comparing him with Eugene, the lordly 2400 Negro head-waiter, I observed that even though Eugene frequently scolded me at breakfast when my parents weren't there, I liked him, because he didn't say mean things the way Mr. Clay did. Not only that—Eugene never tattled on me, either.

"You've hit on one of the basic differences between people," Colonel Marshall told me; "one of the determining factors that divide the sheep from the goats."

The difference between Eugene and Mr. Clay, he observed, could be multiplied to include practically everybody in the world, because Eugene represented secure self-respect while Mr. Clay represented insecure self-importance. My reaction to both of them had been perfectly normal, he mused half to himself; and, after a little silence, he said out loud:

"A normal reaction isn't good enough." He explained that self-respect almost always engendered respect and reasonable behavior from others, but self-importance met not only with lack of respect from others, but with an unreasoned response from the unwary. The unwary, he said, is the norm, and the norm usually means "half-thinking off the top of your head." He warned that I would run into a lot of Mr. Clays all my life—disagreeable, picayune, opinionated bullies who could seriously harm me if I persisted in antagonizing them. He advised me to avoid such people whenever possible; and if I couldn't do that, my own self-respect should never allow me to harrass or ridicule a troublesome but intrinsically unhappy fellow.

"Because,'" he concluded, "an insecure man is an unhappy man."

"In other words," he said, laughing, "don't bait Mr. Clay."

I hedged and replied it wasn't as if I always tried to make Mr. Clay mad—lots of times it just happened; and I recounted my most recent run-in with him.

"This time it wasn't just me," I said defensively, "but Tom and Sis were in on it too, especially Tom."

It was a mild enough incident. One Saturday morning Celeste and I had found Tom reading in the Smoking Room, which was deserted at that hour of the day. On an impulse, I grabbed my brother's book, ran to hide it, and, as he gained on me, passed it to Sis who disappeared into the Palm Court. In hot pursuit after me, Tom rounded the corner by the reception desk, hurtled headlong into the ubiquitous Mr. Clay, and knocked him flat on the floor. The result was severe punishment for all of us, but for me, the added discomfort of being ostracized by my brother because I'd been the instigator of the whole mess.

"All your fault—punk strategy." Colonel Marshall commented. "Why didn't you go the back way to the Palm Court instead of tearing out into the lobby?"

It wasn't my misdemeanor he criticized but the execution of it! Inspired by this rather unexciting episode, he composed a corny little poem. It was one of many he made up for Lily or me, and one of the few I remember in its entirety, probably because it had a tune of sorts. We often used to sing, or rather, shout it:

MY BROTHER. TOM

(*vivace*)

"I gotta brother and his name is Tom,
  He ain't very wide and he ain't very long,
  He talks through the air on a wireless tree,
  And gets mighty mad at Sis and me.

One day we went and hid his book,
  You ought to see him look and look,
  Chased us all around the way,
  And ran bang into Mr. Clay.

CHORUS
(*presto*)
Whoopee, my brother, Tom,
Whoopee, my brother, Tom,
He ain't very wide
And he ain't very long,
Whoopee, my brother, Tom!"

Obviously, when the many facets of Colonel Marshall's genius were cut and polished, the poetry Muses neglected to cut theirs.

"A poem," Archibald Macleish wrote, "should not mean but be." If MacLeish's view is taken as correct, and if one could call Colonel Marshall's rhymes "poems"—they shouldn't even *be*. We enjoyed them, though, he, Lily, and I. He made them up at the slightest excuse: to commemorate, tease, warn, praise, or, often, to reduce some exaggerated worry to absurdity.

"Oh George!" Lily would laugh, "Not another one." But she'd stop worrying about letters she had to write, or fussing about what she'd wear to tomorrow's tea.

There was another "poem," much longer than "My Brother Tom," which poked fun at my misbehavior in school, but I can't remember it beyond the first four lines:

What does Rosie do at school
She cannot do at home?
She's a tease and a pest
And all the rest . . .

Then followed a long list of fantastic pranks, real and imagined. He and Lily laughed so hard as the list grew that I felt very devilish; in fact, I considered myself quite the nimble-witted rascal. It is true that my behavior at school was far below par compared to my behavior at home, because I didn't give a hoot what the teacher thought of me, whereas I cared very much for Mother's approval. I never thought it appropriate to disclose my mischievous school doings to Mother, but it entertained

Colonel Marshall to hear tales about spitball battles and other such foolishness. He laid down only two rules; never overstep the boundary into maliciousness, and under no circumstances do anything dishonest.

He did not, however, laugh about my grades. I was a miserable arithmetic scholar and I used to tell him it was an inherited weakness because I had an uncle who was poor in math too. This had no effect on him. No excuse was acceptable and I thought up plenty: the teacher didn't explain it properly, there was too much homework, it was a boring subject, and I *hated* it.

"It all boils down to hating it," he said one day, "and that's the weakest excuse of all. It means you're lazy and won't work at something because you don't like it. If you fail, it'll be because you haven't got any guts."

"That's right," I repeated cheerfully, "No guts at all!"

He cocked his head a little to one side and, fixing his eyes sternly on mine. warned, "Just you look out!"

✿ CHAPTER VI ✿

How obstinate the human mind can be when it rejects sensible advice; how impermeable when it shuts out undesirable truths! Every day I confronted self-importance in Mrs. Swift, our unpopular fourth grade teacher, but ignoring Colonel Marshall's counsel, I subjected her to the most embarrassing indignity. Indubitably, when "I was a child I thought as a child," and I conveniently forgot Colonel Marshall's rule—never overstep the boundary into maliciousness.

Every evening I hurried through arithmetic assignments, smudging the paper with illegible figures I made no attempt to understand. Pushing arithmetic aside to concentrate on more agreeable subjects, I fell further and further behind, blithely unconcerned with Colonel Marshall's warning, "Just you look out!" Alas, I had occasion to regret the intractability of my hard little head!

My downfall was brought about by a plan I had conceived and put into effect whereby the whole fourth grade would have an opportunity to express its true sentiment for Mrs. Swift, under the guise of supposedly paying a tribute to her. Every year it was customary at our elementary public school for each class to give its respective teacher a fruit shower as a token of esteem and affection. The previous year I had been chosen Fruit Shower Chairman, and had proudly presented to the kind and dedicated third grade teacher a large basket of fruit, painstakingly arranged from contributions my classmates had brought to school.

Elected Fruit Shower Chairman again in the fourth grade, I suggested a change in the manner of presentation which met with enthusiastic agreement from a majority of the girls and with unanimity from the boys. We gave Mrs. Swift a real shower. We *threw* the fruit at her! In deference to a nagging conscience, I had specifically extracted a promise from each classmate not to aim for a direct hit, but the luckless teacher was unaware of this vital prohibition. With every fruit in season sailing toward her, she dodged, leapt, slipped, ducked, and whirled, waving her arms in spasmodic circular motions in a desperate effort to protect her head. Her frenzied dance to avoid that macédoine would make the frug look like a minuet. Bunches of grapes whizzed past her face to burst against the world globe and scatter pulp from pole to pole; squashed bananas and split oranges smeared the blackboard behind her; bruised apples littered the floor; and an impromptu punch trickled down from her desk to make a small puddle in the seat of her chair.

The uproar was deafening; the holocaust appalling. I stood paralyzed with horror, until the boy next to me cried, "Rose, Rose, hurry up. Throw your apples quick or it'll all be over!"

Automatically, I raised my arm, apple in hand, and was standing in a perfect Statue of Liberty pose when the principal rushed into the room.

"Rose Page!" he shouted, "put that apple down at once!"

Suddenly, my apple weighed a hundred pounds. My arm dropped abruptly under that awful weight, as an ominous silence, broken only by Mrs. Swift's hysterical gasps, enveloped the room.

"Who is the leader of this outrageous performance?" the principal asked.

No one spoke but all eyes turned in my direction.

"Very well," he said, in the I'll-attend-to-this tone used exclusively by school principals. "Mrs. Swift, put your pupils to work at cleaning up this mess. Rose, you come with me."

There followed a lecture which lasted a fraction over an hour and seventeen minutes; I know, because as the principal preached at and threatened me, I kept my eyes fixed on the big wall clock behind his head. I remember very little of what he said but I remember perfectly well how long it took him to say it.

Once he interrupted his harangue to ask impatiently, "What are you staring at?"

Incongruously, I thought of a grammar rule: Don't end a sentence with a preposition. But my Mother's training held fast. I replied politely, though evasively, that I was concentrating. He dismissed me at last, telling me to go straight home, as it was late—which, of course, I already knew.

On my way home, panic seized me as I speculated on Mother's reaction when news of this fearful day reached her. Would the principal telephone, send a letter through the mail? When would Mother hear about it? All the while, a vision of Mrs. Swift's terrified face and ridiculous dance kept rising up to haunt me.

She's an unhappy Mr. Clay, I thought remorsefully, walking home from school. Never, I swore to myself, would I tell Colonel Marshall about the fruit shower.

The school principal was conversant with the proper methods of torturing the tortured; not a word went home to my parents for a week. During that week I lived in a state of apprehension and humiliation. I had forced myself to apologize to Mrs. Swift, who had replied acidly that I was an evil child.

At the end of the week, when report cards were handed out, mine was sealed in a fat envelope. I, myself, was to bear home the bad tidings. There were two *F*'s on my report, one in arithmetic and one in conduct. Enclosed with this disgraceful record, which broke all family tradition, was a vituperative letter from Mrs. Swift, describing the fruit shower in graphic detail with heavy emphasis on my role as the blackguard who had instigated the offense.

When Mother saw my failures and read my teacher's letter, her unhappiness with me ranged from anger through mortification and despair and back again through the whole gamut to anger. She was an emotional and articulate woman, so that as the afternoon waned, I became exhausted beyond the point of feeling anything except a dull depression over what I felt was my inordinate stupidity, and an overwhelming sense of guilt that I had permanently wounded my mother.

When my father came home, Mother handed him the damning papers, telling him, "She's hopeless, absolutely hopeless. See what you can do."

This was very unusual; she rarely apealed to my father for help in dealing with me. He read the letter rapidly, refolded it, and commented in a rather detached manner, "What a vindictive woman!" He returned the letter to Mother and said haughtily, "Definitely inferior material for a teacher, I should say."

He then glanced at my horrendous report card, raised his eyebrows at the bad marks, and remarked to the ceiling, "I see she has an *A* in history."

My father abhorred unpleasantness, and if the family sea was even slightly ruffled, he would head at once for a secluded harbor, usually the Cosmos Club. Now finding himself caught in the midst of a storm, he grasped the only thing in sight—my *A* in history—which might possibly protect him from rough sailing.

"Look at her arithmetic, her conduct! Is that all you have to say about the letter?" my overwrought mother asked, and without waiting for an answer, implored, "*Do* something."

Daddy looked down at me. I was snuffling and hiccoughing

after hours of weeping, and he replied complacently, "After dinner, my dear. It appears to me that Rose has undergone sufficient chastisement for the present."

His calm indifference so frustrated Mother that she was on the verge of tears herself. She turned to me abruptly and said, "Take your bath and change for dinner at once. I want you to take this report card and letter and show them to Major Marshall. Now, hurry up!"

While I was bathing, I considered the possibility of drowning myself, but refrained, because it would get my hair wet and I didn't think it would dry in time to go down to dinner. That, I thought, would be an unnecessary offense on top of everything else. So I dressed, silently took the report card and letter Mother handed me, and walked out of the apartment with a breaking heart.

When I rang Colonel Marshall's doorbell, I prayed he wouldn't be at home, and if he were, that Lily would be there too. Neither prayer was answered. He opened the door himself, and when I hesitated to enter, hanging back, woebegone and frightened, he took my hand and gently pulled me inside.

"What a pleasant surprise!" he said affectionately. "I'm here all by myself—Lily's gone to a pink tea."

I loved him very much. "A pleasant surprise," he'd said. When I thought how disappointed in me he would soon be, I collapsed into a torrent of sobs.

He took me on his lap, and, stroking my hair, tried to calm me.

"My goodness," he said, "this is a regular monsoon." He didn't press me to tell him what was the matter but asked playfully, "Has the world come apart? I hadn't heard."

"Yes it has!" I wailed.

"Well," he replied, "let's see if we can patch it up."

He set me on my feet, took out his handkerchief and dried my eyes. I stopped howling and handed him my passports to Hell. After he read them, his first remark was, "Whew, you've really made an awful bust!"

But the important thing was, he went on, what did I learn from it?

It was difficult to tell him. If I was the numskull Mother said I was, he knew it anyhow. To admit that I was dumb sounded like an excuse which I knew from experience would be objectionable to him. I stood before him, trying to assemble all the impressions my "bust" had made on me. He sat quietly and waited, making no attempt either to prompt or to hurry me. If Lily had been there, she would have broken that heavy silence, but Lily wasn't there.

I made several abortive starts and finally stammered, "About arithmetic, I didn't work on it much, and I can see it's worthwhile to have guts."

"That's one good thing," he answered.

I was so grateful for that little bit of praise, I had no trouble continuing with what had really been bothering me about the fruit shower.

"Mrs. Swift looked so scared, and well, so kinda pitiful when we threw all that stuff at her. You know—real nutty in front of everybody. I told her I was sorry, Colonel Marshall, but it didn't do any good."

He told me apologizing might have helped me, but it wasn't so easy to heal Mrs. Swift's hurt feelings. This was the only lecture he gave me. He said as long as I understood what was wrong and why it was wrong, there was no point in talking about it any more.

He spent the next few minutes advising me how to establish a détente with Mrs. Swift for the rest of the year. He didn't admonish me to "be extra good" or to "study extra hard." He laid down a concise, matter-of-fact plan: "Show no emotion when she plagues you, neither distress nor resentment. This will be hard for you but it's important. Do your work as ably as you can, and cut out all small offenses—no tricks, absolutely no tricks at all. If your teacher is unable to arouse a visible reaction when she picks on you, and if you give her no excuse for criticizing you, she'll get no satisfaction from either, and will eventually leave you alone."

He stood up, reminding me it was time for me to go to dinner, leaned over and kissed me. "Good-bye for a while Rose," he said. "I shall have to deny myself the pleasure of speaking to you until you receive your next report card."

That was the first time Colonel Marshall punished me.

❦ CHAPTER VII ❦

COLONEL MARSHALL AND LILY WERE OUT OF TOWN FAIRLY OFTEN FOR a few weeks at a time. Colonel Marshall was usually off somewhere with General Pershing while Lily stayed in Lexington with her mother. I was used to their trips and accepted their absence well enough. It was dreadful, however, not to be able to talk with them, to be deprived of their company, when they were right there at 2400, especially since Colonel Marshall took a literal view of the oneness of husband and wife and had instructed Lily to go along with him in the silent treatment.

It was a long and lonesome time. I missed the Marshalls much worse seeing them every evening than I did when they were away. Of course, I couldn't join them for dessert, but went directly into the lobby after dinner with Mother and Celeste, as I always did when the Marshalls were not there. The painful part was having to watch them come out of the dining room without me. My insides rolled up like a tortured caterpillar, when they passed directly in front of our regular spot in the lobby, and bowed and smiled pleasantly to Mother and Celeste as if I were not even present. Everybody in the lobby knew what was going on, and a few people teased me mildly, calling me "Peck's Bad Girl" and like names.

One evening Colonel Marshall and I met alone in the elevator. How different it was from our first chance meeting, when his open, friendly smile had given me courage to speak to him! This time his expression was so aloof and withdrawn, I moved around behind him so I wouldn't have to see his face. I fixed my eyes on his back for the several hundred hours it took the elevator to reach the lobby floor, and although my first impulse was to dash out past him as soon as the door opened, I held back, standing resolutely in the rear of the elevator so he would have to turn around and speak to me. My tactic was a total failure. Colonel Marshall moved aside formally, looked straight through me, and silently motioned me to precede him as if I were a grown-up stranger.

Another evening, about halfway through the month, both the Marshalls rode up in the elevator with Celeste and me (we were on our way upstairs to do our homework). Colonel Marshall began an animated conversation with my sister about her Girl Scout work; but Lily, my ally, stood on tiptoe behind him, peering over his shoulder, smiling at me affectionately, and further reaffirming our fellowship with little surreptitious wavings of her hand. Colonel Marshall gave no sign that he knew what Lily was up to, but he was aware of her antics. I'm sure of that.

Meanwhile, Celeste, my champion, summarily broke off her conversation with Colonel Marshall to volunteer extravagant reports of my earnest labors and angelic behavior.

"Oh Colonel Marshall," she told him, "Rose is getting to be a positive genius in arithmetic, and she's so *good;* I even saw Mrs. Swift grin at her yesterday on the playground!"

"That's splendid news," Colonel Marshall answered. "Tell Rose I'm delighted to hear she's making such fine progress and I hope she keeps it up. It would be very tedious for all of us to continue another month like this one."

Thus, without relaxing one iota his intention to follow through on his original sentence, Colonel Marshall offered me encouragement through the two people he knew would be most willing to transmit it. He also left no doubt in my mind but that I was expected to fulfill the necessary requirements for the sentence to be lifted at all!

Although it seemed an eon to me, that month did not stretch out into eternity. My deplorable grades changed radically enough to give ample testimony to Celeste's enthusiastic claims. I had accomplished the impossible: an *A* in conduct and a *B* in arithmetic.

Needless to say, however, Colonel Marshall's advice and discipline did not strengthen me sufficiently to "hold fast to the good," nor, for that matter, did it transform me into a proficient student of mathematics; I have taken many a misstep since then, and I am still a very poor mathematician. What I did learn was the value of tenacity of purpose and the efficacy of hard work. Colonel Marshall forever denied me the luxury of pushing the blame elsewhere. This double lesson is a gadfly with a venomous sting!

The disquieting insect was hatched during one of the most dolorous months of my life, but after the month was over, Colonel Marshall, Lily, and I had a joyous reunion. Lily presented me with a tin of her favorite Sherry's candy, smothering me with jubilant embraces and lavish praise, so that once again, my heart swelled with the warmth of her welcome.

Colonel Marshall was not so demonstrative. He said simply, "I was counting on you, and you came through. Your mistake was planning a reverse strategy, and it worked to everybody's disadvantage, including your own. Aim your aptitudes for worthwhile results and we'll have no more trouble."

Neither he nor I ever again referred to that unhappy month.

When our little celebration was over, I suggested, "Colonel Marshall, let's do something unusual. Think up something that's real fun we've never done before."

"Yes ma'am," he replied with mock servility. He thought a moment, then snapped his fingers and said, "How would you like to go to see General Pershing?"

Of course I wanted to go, and besides, I thought it an especially good idea because it was something Lily could do with us; so we three drove out to Chevy Chase where General Pershing had rented a house.

His house is somewhat hazy in my memory. I think it was fairly old, not historic, more "middle-aged." It was white clapboard, quite large, with a wide veranda stretching halfway around it. I remember the veranda because we sat on it at the end of the afternoon to have cookies and lemonade. The house was set back from the road on an extensive lawn, hemmed in by trees and shrubs. There must have been a stable, because the highlight of the afternoon was when General Pershing ordered his famous horse, Jeff, to be saddled and brought out.

I stood stroking and patting the "First Horse of America," admiring his glossy coat and superb conformation, while in my mind's eye I pictured him stepping proudly forth, neck arched and head high, bearing his heroic master through the Arc de Triomphe.

General Pershing stood holding Jeff's bridle and watching me, a pensive half-smile gentling his austere, handsome face. Quite suddenly, he said, "Let's give Rose a little ride."

I was overcome. Even Colonel Marshall wouldn't suggest such a treat, for it was common knowledge that no one was permitted to mount Jeff except his master. It flashed through my mind that perhaps in those few moments, General Pershing hadn't actually seen me caressing his horse, but instead, might have envisioned one of his own little dead daughters standing there beside him. Colonel Marshall had told me about Pershing's tragedy. His wife

68

and two small daughters were burned to death five years before, in 1915. A flash fire had raged through their house one evening when General Pershing was away from the Post. Pershing's striker had tried desperately to save all of the General's family, but the fire was so fierce and so rapid that the Sergeant could only manage to rescue Pershing's young son, Warren, who was sleeping on a first-floor screened porch.

I was thinking to myself about this sad catastrophe as General Pershing and Colonel Marshall began adjusting the stirrups, but I attempted to assume the poker face Colonel Marshall recommended—it seemed a singularly inappropriate time to look mournful. Mine was a short-lived poker face at any rate, for although my sympathy was real enough, I had had no experience of personal grief. General Pershing's tragedy had happened a very long time ago to me, and I couldn't even imagine the depth of his sorrow. Consequently, I was diverted very shortly by the men's conversation and my own happy anticipation of riding Jeff.

Colonel Marshall was saying, "Shorter, General, shorter. At least two more notches."

"Two more yet?" asked Pershing. "They look ridiculous!"

He motioned me to come stand beside him, and, looking down on the top of my head, he shrugged and smiled.

"I guess you're right," he said. "Well, we're all set."

"Now, Rose," Colonel Marshall instructed, locking his hands together to make a step, "up you go!" And he heaved me onto Jeff's back.

Pershing led Jeff at a walk around the lawn while I sat on his back, shouting, "Advance, men! Courage!" and other soldierly commands out of my story books, and each time we passed Lily watching from the veranda, I gave her a smart military salute.

General Pershing, Jeff, and I made three or four wide circles around the lawn before we returned to Colonel Marshall.

"We won the battle," the General reported and they both laughed.

Colonel Marshall helped me dismount, reminding me in a low voice that it was a great honor to ride Jeff.

I whispered back, "I know, Colonel Marshall, I know it was something wonderful!"

"General Pershing," I said with genuine enthusiasm, "thank you ever and ever so much. I'm real proud I rode on Jeff and I know I'll remember it all my whole life." I have remembered so far, which is a pretty good indication that my prophecy was accurate.

"That's a thank you for posterity," Colonel Marshall observed. "It's a darn sight better than your usual"; and he tried to imitate the honeyed, company-manners voice in which I customarily spoke the polite adieu I'd been taught: " 'Thank you, Colonel Marshall, I had a *lovely* time.' " Colonel Marshall was about as good a mimic as he was a poet.

General Pershing didn't occupy his house in Chevy Chase for long, because he was made Chief of Staff in 1921. He succeeded General Peyton C. March. I'd heard a lot of gossip among the Army people at 2400 about a feud of some sort, unpleasantness between General March and General Pershing; so one day I asked Colonel Marshall bluntly what it was all about. He told me that General Pershing was a higher ranking General than General March, but that technically General March was General Pershing's boss.

"It's a difficult situation for them both," he said, "and that's all you have to know."

"Well, that's not much," I answered. "Can I ask just one more thing?"

"No," he said.

"Just one more!" I persisted. "Whose side are you on?"

"Oh Lord!" Colonel Marshall said, laughing. "What a question! Rose, I won't take sides."

It was an unsatisfactory answer to me, but I knew that any further questions would only bounce back at me unanswered.

70

General Pershing's appointment as Chief of Staff was important to me solely because it meant that Colonel Marshall, as General Pershing's senior aide, was assigned quarters next to the "big" house, perennially occupied by the incumbent Chief of Staff, at Fort Myer, Virginia, which is just across the Potomac River from Washington.

I missed seeing the Marshalls every day at 2400, but I loved their house; it was almost as good as having a house of my own again. Lily loved the house too. When Colonel Marshall brought me out to see it for the first time, Lily was standing out on the front porch waiting for us, and as I jumped out of the car, she called,

"Hurry up, come see our house!"

"Come on, Colonel Marshall!" I cried, and without waiting for him, dashed up the steps to greet Lily. We exchanged excited hugs and kisses, and were about to enter the house when I hesitated, turning around to look for Colonel Marshall who had not followed me.

"Aren't you coming, Colonel Marshall?" I asked. "Why are you just waiting there?"

I can see him now as vividly as I saw him on that far-off day when I looked back to call him. He had gotten out of the car and was leaning against it, looking up and smiling at us; his expression, a little amused by our feminine display of emotion, was at the same time full of love and happiness and contentment.

Even then, it touched my heart to see him thus, so I stood quite still and said, "We'll wait for you, Colonel Marshall, come with us!"

"Here I come, ladies!" he replied, bounding up the steps to join us.

He put one arm around Lily, one arm around me, and the three of us squeezed happily through the front door.

Lily, ebullient and talkative, led me through each room, commenting on almost every piece of furniture.

"This was my grandmother's chair," she said proudly, pointing to a delicate mahogany piece.

"Don't sit on it, if you want to save your own bottom and Lily's precious antique!" Colonel Marshall warned. "It looks very handsome but it collapses like a Girl Scout drinking cup."

Lily protested indignantly that it wasn't so, she'd had the chair redone. "There's not one thing in this house that can't be properly used," she assured us.

Indeed, the house had a casual, lived-in look from the very first—that is, the downstairs did.

The floors were covered with thick Chinese rugs in soft colors, blues and yellows predominating, and Lily's living-room color scheme was planned to harmonize with her rugs. Excluding her antique chair, the furniture looked comfortable and pretty, although it was mixed in style. There was quite a lot of rattan furniture, purchased along with the rugs on their trip to the Orient before I knew them. I remember one large fan-back rattan chair which stood directly opposite the front door in the small entrance hall. Lily had draped its wide back with a colorful, heavily embroidered Chinese shawl, and I thought it was the grandest looking thing I ever saw.

Magazines lying on a round mahogany table in the living room were neither thrown down haphazardly nor lined up stiffly in precise rows. Fresh flowers were everywhere, not arranged according to garden club standards, but with colors and varieties mixed together as if they had sprung up right out of the vases.

Here and there were photographs of their friends and one or two of Lily's family—all in silver frames, except one picture of Lily's mother in an elegant petit point French frame.

"It came from Paris," Lily told me.

There were quite a few large, empty, brass shell casings polished to a high gloss, which were used for ashtrays. I think they were cannon shells, but I kept forgetting what kind of gun they were used for, and asked Colonel Marshall so often that he told me I'd never remember so he wouldn't ever tell me again.

My first look at the dining room made little impression on me, except that it seemed rather small, probably because I had become used to the large 2400 dining room. The room was about standard; the table, chairs, and sideboard were in some traditional style. There was nothing particularly distinguished about it. Later, it was the atmosphere of the dining room, the pleasure we had there, that endeared it to me.

I do remember a copy of John Marshall's portrait hung on one wall, because at dinner one evening, I expressed surprise when I noticed it and thereby caused the only slight friction I recall at any of our meals together.

"Gosh, Colonel Marshall!" I exclaimed. "Are you kin to the famous Chief Justice? He was a *Virginian,* and I thought you were one-hundred percent Yankee."

He replied gruffly, "The fact that John Marshall happened to be born in Virginia had nothing to do with his achievements." He admitted a remote kinship to the famous Chief Justice and continued, "If it makes you feel any better, I probably have at least a half dozen drops of Virginia blood."

I was confused, and sorry I'd said something wrong and tried to make amends:

"Oh gee, Colonel Marshall, I don't mind a bit your being a Yankee! A whole lot of nice people are Yankees."

"I am sure the American people living outside the South would be delighted to learn that good news," he answered.

Obviously, I'd said the wrong thing again, so I tried another tack. "Well," I commented gaily, "maybe one reason you're so smart is because you inherited John Marshall's brains."

"Don't *say* that!" he replied sharply with an unusual show of irritation.

Lily laughed and reminded him I had no idea why I was annoying him.

"She only meant it as a compliment," Lily said, and tactfully changed the subject.

Later, when Lily and I were alone, I asked her why Colonel

Marshall hadn't liked what I'd said about Virginians and Chief Justice Marshall.

"You're a Virginian," I observed, "and I'm a Virginian; I thought he liked Virginians."

"Oh, he likes Virginians all right," she answered vaguely, and told me not to worry about it. He admired John Marshall too, she added, but explained that his father had harped on old John Marshall all through his childhood. "George wants to be himself," she said, "not a shadow of a man somewhere back in his ancestry."

"You know how George is," she said laughingly. "He does his own thinking and working, and when he gets to be Chief of Staff, it won't be because of Justice Marshall who died a hundred years ago!"

But I have digressed from our tour of the house; the dining room completed the downstairs circuit, and Lily led me upstairs, obviously impatient to show me their bedroom. I'll never forget my first sight of it—I was flabbergasted! After the pleasant, rather conservative downstairs, I was totally unprepared for that fancy bower.

Lily's huge dressing table gleamed with a bewildering assortment of bottles and jars, and a huge framed mirror hung above it. Colonel Marshall's bureau on the opposite side of the room looked stark and bare, with only Lily's picture, his military brushes, and a shoe horn resting on it. There were a few straight chairs, a rocking chair, and an enormous double bed with a high, straight back, rolled over backward at the top. The bed was flanked on each side by night tables laden with books and magazines stacked around pink-shaded crystal lamps. All the furniture was pale, some sort of wood finished in a *café-au-lait* color.

What most caught my eye were the rose-covered chaise lounge and the dozens and dozens of little pink, lacy pillows. They were piled up on the bolster of the bed and they bubbled all over the back of the chaise lounge. The whole room glowed in varying shades of rose and pink, and Lily's delicate fragrance hung in the air: a light, flowery scent, like a bouquet of fresh violets and lilies-of-the-valley.

"Lily," Colonel Marshall said, "really let loose on our room."

It was a bedroom which would probably give nightmares to a professional decorator, but that is not the effect it had on the Marshalls.

My astonished exclamations delighted Lily.

"Come along with me, there's more!" she cried happily.

I followed close behind her and was at her side when she opened the next door. She gave me a little push forward, saying,

"Here is your room, and over there is the door to your own private bathroom."

It would be appropriate here to record that I was over-whelmed with gratitude and surprise. Such was not the case; I had been secretly wondering all along where my room could be. I was, however, greatly relieved and very happy they did have a room for me, so that my exuberant expressions of delight and pride were genuine as I walked into the middle of it and looked about me. I remember only a small oriental rug, starched white curtains, and a couple of beds. I seldom used the room except for sleeping, because during my visits to Fort Myer most of my time was spent outdoors, and the time I did spend in the house, we were together—in the dining room, living room, or the Marshalls' bedroom. Of course, my room doubled as the guest room, but Colonel Marshall and Lily were careful to preserve the illusion that it was really mine.

"The So-and-sos are coming next week," Lily would tell me. "I'll have to put them up in your room if you don't mind."

As for my "own private bathroom," I couldn't have been less interested. When I first started going out to Fort Myer, the bothersome requirement of taking my daily bath was a nuisance to be endured only at the insistence of grownups. My lackadaisical attitude toward cleanliness was shocking to Lily. She used to march me into the bathroom and stand there, arms folded, until she was sure I'd scrubbed off—according to her standards, I complained—the entire outside layer of skin.

The Fort Myer house became my alternate home until the Marshalls left for China in July 1924. As I recall those early years at 2400 and at Fort Myer, it seems a short while indeed, but it was the formative period of my life, the very heart of my childhood.

CHAPTER VIII

THE YEAR 1921 MARKED A TURNING POINT IN MY YOUNG LIFE; THE
Marshalls moved to Fort Myer, and Celeste and I changed schools.
Mother effected the change, but in the end, it was my father who
made it possible. We were placed in the National Cathedral
School, an Episcopal school for girls adjacent to the National
Cathedral in Washington.

My family was Episcopalian. I knew this because Tom, Celeste, and I had attended Episcopal Sunday Schools, although
irregularly, and rarely on consecutive Sundays. Also, on the
delightful occasions I visited my father's three spinster sisters in
Virginia, I sometimes went with them to the Episcopal church,
Grace Church, in whose quiet, oak-shaded cemetery generations
of my relatives sleep. Grace Church is a lovely little stone edifice
deep in the rolling country of Albemarle County, about fifteen
miles from the University of Virginia, and half a dozen or so
from my father's ancestral home, Keswick, where my aunts lived
in shabby grandeur.

My aunts did not go to church regularly—it was an arduous

trip to get there over poorly kept country roads. But they held morning prayers daily, and whoever happened to be at Keswick was expected to attend: cousins, uncles, aunts, great-aunts, friends, and servants.

I cannot recall a single Sunday when my parents attended church, either in Virginia or Washington. My father frequently spoke of "the ethical life," of "excellence," and of "honor," treating them as abstracts of irrefutable merit. His student days at Leipzig lead me to guess that, like many intellectuals educated in Germany at the turn of the century, he was at least partially influenced by Neo-Kantian idealism. He heavily emphasized the supremacy of the mind, but he never taught his children that God was non-existent; he just never mentioned Him one way or the other. Mother did. When she was beset and upset by a particularly trying circumstance, she used to lament that if there was a God, He must have forgotten her. The "if" of her statement demonstrates her willingness to conform to the modern skepticism, but its implicit sense of loneliness indicates to me she had not entirely shaken off her early beliefs.

I do not think either of my parents were committed to atheism; they may have been agnostic, or, quite possibly, simply indifferent. Their attitude, however, was in no way an embarrassment to me. Religion was not a hot issue in the milieu where I grew up.

But my father and mother, although disinclined to assume the task themselves, considered it an essential part of their children's education to acquire a familiarity with the Christian religion and, more specifically, the family-inherited Episcopalian view of it. Besides, my father had a high regard for the *King James Bible,* and wanted us to be exposed to its magnificent literature.

In addition to these considerations, although our family income was small compared to the enormous wealth of the lush twenties, both parents were anxious that we receive the best academic training available that they could afford.

Having established this agreement between them, each one reacted in character.

My father haughtily decreed, "The children must be sent to a good school." But what school and how to pay for it, he left up to Mother.

Mother, with her usual efficiency, arranged for us to enter as day students in the National Cathedral School, which offered both sound religious training and academic excellence. Not only that, she persuaded the school that Celeste and I should receive scholarships as the daughters of a distinguished Episcopalian professor and public servant!

I liked the Cathedral School, although, I confess, one of the main reasons I liked it was because we stayed there all day. We left 2400 a little after eight o'clock in the morning and did not return until almost six in the evening. We didn't study all that time—I was not such an ardent scholar that my enthusiasm for the school could be attributed to so rigorous a work schedule. What I did enjoy was the outdoor play. The school, built in the shadow of the National Cathedral, was set in a spacious, well-kept park dignified by wide-spreading old trees. In addition to the attractive surroundings, there were two large athletic fields, a grass basketball court, excellent clay tennis courts, and a fine gymnasium for indoor athletics when the weather was bad.

In my day, the school subscribed to a policy of *mens sana in corpore sano* (one of the first Latin phrases I learned there), a policy I assume is continued today. It suited me fine. I enjoyed the competitive games, track meets, field day, and other kid stuff, and would return to 2400 tired and hungry.

The academic schedule was all my parents had hoped for, but the formal religious training was a bore, and to me, actually upsetting—at least the biweekly Bible classes were.

Not so bad was the daily morning worship when the Upper and Lower schools joined together for the service led by Miss MacDonald, the formidable Head Mistress. The best part about morning prayer was the music, particularly the *Jubilate Deo.* Every girl was instructed to sing, and woe unto those recalcitrants who did not comply. The result was a melodious "concord of sweet voices" which never failed to thrill me. I, myself, sang lustily—off key. Like Charles Lamb, "sentimentally I am disposed to harmony. But organically I am incapable of a tune."

Our Bible classes were conducted by a professional pious Deaconess whose religious primping, impatience with questions, and lack of imagination almost succeeded in turning all of us into militant little heathens. When Confucius wrote, "goody-goodies confuse us with virtuous people," he forgot the glaring insight of the very young; we children were not fooled by the Deaconess. But I, for one, was confused about God.

In spite of the religious unconcern at home and among most of my parents' and my friends, and although the Deaconess came close to convincing me that God was a status symbol for goody-goodies, I still clung precariously to my totally anthropomorphic conception of a "Big Daddy" up in Heaven who really cared about what happened to me.

I was too shy to ask my parents to straighten me out. My father's erudite dissertations meant nothing to me, and Mother was so scornful of the few openly religious ladies we knew, whom she referred to as weak women who couldn't face up to responsibility, that I was afraid any questions to her would discourage me further.

As usual, I took my problem to Colonel Marshall. After I'd been going to Cathedral School for several months, he picked me up one Friday to take me directly out to Fort Myer for the weekend. Friday was a Bible-class day, and that Friday the Deaconess had been particularly obnoxious. Every time she pronounced the name God, she had rolled her eyes Heavenward, her voice trembling with dramatic resonance, a performance which had struck me as ridiculously hammy.

"How are things going?" Colonel Marshall asked as I climbed into the car.

"Pretty good," I replied as a starter, knowing that wasn't enough of an answer. Once I'd made the mistake of answering, "Oh, nothing happened." It was only once, because he had subjected me to the most merciless teasing.

"Some lost day," he'd chided. "Nothing happened? You didn't learn anything, see anybody, play any games? You didn't laugh, get mad . . . ," and on and on.

So I gave him the afternoon's basketball score, conjugated a French verb, and reported that Miss Templeton must be the best history and English teacher in the world. I wasn't so keen on geography, I told him—all those trade winds and currents—but at least I understood it. The geography teacher was very patient.

"How about arithmetic?" he continued.

"Oh, all right," I answered and changed the subject abruptly. "Colonel Marshall, do you believe in God?" I asked anxiously.

He took his eyes off the road and glanced at me with a surprised smile. I was glad he was not in a position to give me one of his scrutinizing x-ray looks, because the minute I asked the question, I regretted it. My face burned with a raging blush. Gosh, I thought, he'll think I'm an awful dumbbell; nobody smart believes in God.

His answer was instantaneous. "Yes, I do," he said, not dramatically or emphatically, but quite simply, in a matter-of-fact, conversational tone.

Encouraged by his easy response, I questioned eagerly, "Well, what about Him? I mean, like what?"

"It seems to me," he replied, "you should be telling me. Didn't you say you had Bible classes every week?"

"Yes," I replied, disappointed. But thinking that to complain about how frustrating they were would annoy him, I fell into a dejected silence.

Colonel Marshall was quiet too as we drove along for a few blocks. Then he began speaking casually, exactly as if he were telling me a story.

"God," he said, "is Commander in Chief, and any good soldier, even if he doesn't understand his Commander in Chief's overall plan, obeys him. Now then, God is the Commander in Chief who never makes mistakes, and because I try to be a good soldier I obey Him even though I don't always understand what He's up to. What I am sure of: no matter how good a soldier actually is, or wants to be, he can't accomplish much without help and guidance from his Supreme Commander."

"Oh boy!" I replied, an expression which carried the sentiment of reverence, however infelicitous. "Can I ask one more thing? The Deaconess is always harping on 'Love thy neighbor as thyself.' I think that's about the most impossible thing in the world."

He laughed and said, "All it means is, don't expect the other fellow to do all the adjusting to make you happy. That's the hitch that throws most people. You want to be understood and appreciated? That's natural, but it doesn't matter so much to God if people understand *you;* it does matter to Him if you try to understand *them* and make allowances accordingly."

Mr. Clay and Mrs. Swift, I thought uncomfortably, and now that old Deaconess too.

His explanations were suitably elementary but the basic precepts were there. He may have told me more; the little I have set down here, however, suffused me with such a welcome sense of comfortable reassurance that whatever else he might have said was blotted out. I distinctly recall thinking that if Colonel Marshall believed in God, it was all right if I did too. There must be a God if Colonel Marshall said so.

He had told me the answer, but when I was old enough to deliberate more independently, I rejected it as shallow and insufficient, a make-believe palliative to ease the discomfort of an insecure child. Consequently, I passed through shifting stages of doubt, agnosticism, disbelief, despair, hope. The way back was circuitous and long, and I have never recovered my "Big Daddy"; but who ever recovers childhood? Who wants to?

As for the second great commandment, I merely struggle with it, whereas Colonel Marshall came as close to achieving it as any man could.

❦ CHAPTER IX ❦

ALTHOUGH MY VISITS TO FORT MYER LASTED ONLY A FEW DAYS AT A stretch, it was inevitable that living in the same house, the Marshalls and I were drawn into a closer relationship than was possible when our time together was more curtailed.

I was never considered a "guest," but as far as I remember Colonel Marshall assigned me only one regular chore when I stayed with them. I took over his nightly job as Chief Hair-brusher for Lily.

It was in their fabulous bedroom that I used to brush Lily's hair before we went to bed. Lily, wrapped in a beribboned, chiffon negligee, would seat herself in a rocking chair and lean back so that it would tilt slightly backwards. Then she would lift her long, heavy hair up and over the chair back, to let it cascade down toward the floor. I would take my position on her dressing table stool pulled up behind the rocker, where I'd sit to brush, and brush, and brush.

While I was brushing, there was always some light banter going on. Once, I told Lily I wished she would bob her hair because "my arm aches so bad it's about to fall off." Colonel Marshall wisecracked that if Lily had bobbed her hair, it would have destroyed his invincible tennis serve, because his years of hairbrushing had developed his strong right arm.

I winced and made a face, because Colonel Marshall had a ludicrous puff-ball serve! He would wind up for it with a great show of form, and then tap the ball sky-high over the net to his crouching opponent, poised for a whizzer. Startled, his timing off, the opponent would leap up flailing his racquet at the ball soaring gently far above his head. When the poor fellow finally connected and slammed the ball back, Colonel Marshall would return it easily and softly, placing it where it would bounce up like a bubble on the far side of the court from the running, sweating, exasperated player. I never watched funnier volleys: Puff-wham, puff-wham. Then, just as his opponent was adjusting to this curious game, Colonel Marshall would send over a hot ball which barely skimmed the net and skidded along the court leaving a little trail of dust.

"Good ball!" the fellow would shout, happy to have missed a decent tennis shot at last.

I complained to Colonel Marshall it embarrassed me to watch him hit those cottony balls, but he replied, "What difference does it make how they look; I usually win, don't I?"

"Let 'em hit their hard, fast balls," he said. "It's the unexpected, the element of uncertainty that gets 'em. I use my head and they use their brawn and that's how I win, so stop criticizing my game."

When he bragged about his serve that night at the hairbrushing, I teased him, "Some tennis player, some great soldier! Boy, if people could only see you now!"

"I think I look beautiful," he replied calmly; "pink is my favorite color." Colonel Marshall was lounging on the chaise lounge with his head framed by a froth of Lily's pink pillows.

When the Marshalls were ready for bed, their gorgeous appearance never failed to bedazzle me. Lily's filmy décolleté night-gowns embarrassed me at first, but I got used to them in time. I remember a wide expanse of neck and chest with her firm round breasts clearly outlined beneath her nightgown. Her skin was flawless, and so delicate and transparent that the fine blue net-work of veins across her chest was clearly visible.

When I commented on her veins showing through she assumed I was paying her a compliment. She told me never never to get sunburned.

"It will ruin your skin," she warned. "The sun and wind will make your fair skin as tough and thick as George's boot leather and nearly the same color."

"Well," I answered indifferently, "I don't get sunburned any-how, just millions of freckles."

Before she went to bed, Lily floated around the room straight-ening a chair, folding the bedspread, arranging her bottles and jars—performing these homely little chores with an innate rhyth-mic elegance. Gosh! I thought, what a swell dancer Lily would be if only her heart were stronger. Even when she got into bed, her decorous grace gave the impression she had rehearsed this simple act. Childlike, I would make believe Lily was Queen of the Fairies as I gazed at her reclining against her rosy cloud of pillows, her dark auburn hair, braided into a thick coil, rippling in a silken stream across her shoulder. (You can bet it shone after all my brushing!)

Unlike his elegant Lily, Colonel Marshall would hustle into the bedroom looking like a too-tall, wholesome elf; his homely face gleamed from rigorous scrubbing, his thick sandy hair was wet and meticulously combed, and his fresh pajamas were care-fully pressed. He smelled of toothpaste, Ivory soap, and bay rum.

"Holy smoke, Colonel Marshall!" I exclaimed on my first visit. "Do you have sharp creases down your pajama pants too? Gosh, you and Lily look so grand just to go to bed."

I had outgrown the pretty embroidered nightgown I had contrived to show off on our first motor trip, and felt very plain in my simple cotton print pajamas.

But Colonel Marshall paid me a compliment which immediately restored my aplomb. "Why," he said smiling with admiration, "you look very fetching yourself with those bright little daisies blooming all over you."

Then he went through a kind of ritual which recurred almost every night I stayed with them. He raised his arms high, straining to reach the ceiling; hunched his shoulders this way and that; and sat down on his side of the bed, stretching out his long legs stiffly in front of him. Then he threw his feet into bed, pulled up the covers, leaned over to kiss Lily, and, with a prodigious yawn, cried out, "Oh Min!" Then he exhaled, relaxed, and smiled.

"What do you mean, 'Oh Min!' " I asked.

"Don't you ever read the funnies?" he asked in turn.

This was a touchy question; my parents did not allow their children to read "that trash." The family newspaper was censored, so I never saw the comics unless I was at a friend's house, where of course, I read them avidly.

I hesitated a moment before admitting part of my transgression.

"Well, I sometimes read *The Captain and the Kids*."

"*The Gumps* are my favorite," he answered. "That's where I got 'Oh Min!' It's part of what Andy's always saying to his wife when he goes to bed."

He went on to tell me he thought *The Gumps* were consistently funny and that the whole expression was, "Oh Min, this bed feels good to I!"

"That's exactly the way I feel when I'm bone-tired," he said, smiling; " 'this bed feels good to I!' " Then he shouted at the top of his voice, "OH MIN!" burst out laughing, buried his face in the pillows, and pretended to snore.

I picked up one of his bedtime habits, for I still find myself sighing with delight, "Oh Min!" when I get into bed after an especially fatiguing day.

I hardly ever went to bed in my own room at the Marshalls'. Most of the time, they would make room for me between them in their outsized double bed. Sometimes, they would give me a *National Geographic* to look at while they read. Lily usually had the latest novel, and Colonel Marshall, a detective story or a biography of some figure in American history. Sometimes Colonel Marshall would tell me stories, but no matter what the program was, I'd fall asleep leaning against Lily's soft shoulder, my nostrils full of the pleasant combination of Lily's delicate perfume and Colonel Marshall's clean man-smell. Colonel Marshall would carry me sleeping into my room; I always swore I'd wake up some night when he was carrying me, but I never did.

Mealtime at Fort Myer was always gay. We dined by candlelight, which, as everyone knows, can magically soften and beautify the features of the plainest women. Lily looked positively ravishing.

One evening Colonel Marshall broke off in the middle of a sentence to say in that special tender voice he sometimes used for his wife, "Ah, my lovely Lily!"

She arose immediately with her leisurely measured grace, and, walking around the table, she kissed him and exclaimed, "How lucky we are!"

They had been married nearly twenty years but they were still very much in love. This time I thought with pleasure of the remark of the lady from 2400 which had so upset me two years before; "Oh, how George adores her!"

Perhaps what I most enjoyed about mealtime with the Marshalls was the feeling of isolation in their smallish dining room: the dim lighting at dinner, the sun streaming in at luncheon, the opportunity to laugh out loud as much as I wanted, the intimacy, the closeness of three congenial people laughing and talking together privately. I liked Lily's cobwebby, crocheted place mats with the dark wood of the table showing through, the flowers on the table, her silver and crystal—all the pleasing appointments which transform a simple meal into a small fete. It was a delightful contrast from the hotel fare at 2400. I so obviously enjoyed dining off a pretty table, that often, Lily very kindly got out her best porcelain and finest table linen when I was there. I appreciated that. I still do.

At Fort Myer, we didn't have story time at dessert as we had at 2400, because the whole night lay before us; we just talked. Our conversations were of nothing memorable. It was the atmosphere of relaxation, pleasure, and levity that remains in my memory.

I recall that Colonel Marshall or Lily would sometimes ply me with questions, drawing me out to tell them about my friends, studies, athletics, things about my everyday life. Frequently they would smile or laugh, when I didn't know what it was I'd said that amused them. Anyone accustomed to children can understand that I didn't have to be witty to make them laugh; a child's frank point of view and naïve wisdom are often quite enough to amuse an adult.

I do know that my appetite amazed them. I used to complain myself that I was so plump, an unfortunate condition emphasized by Celeste's dainty figure and Tom's slender build. I hated being fat but only between meals; it never bothered me when it was time to eat. Colonel Marshall plied me with food and Lily rarely interfered, but one day she exclaimed, "Rose, you'll burst!"

It was a remark perfectly suited to set Colonel Marshall to composing one of his "poems." He worked at this one intermittently during the afternoon, and that night at bedtime, after he'd jotted the verses down on four little squares of scratch paper, he proudly read them to Lily and me. We laughed and complimented him, but Lily objected to a part of his second line.

"Rose isn't shy," she criticized.

"Well," Colonel Marshall replied, "everybody's shy at one

time or another, and that's the only word I could think of that scanned. Don't be such a perfectionist!"

Twenty-one years later, I received a letter from Colonel Marshall enclosing those same little squares of paper with the half-forgotten poem he'd written on them.

> A little girl I strive to please,
> Is very shy but likes to tease,
> And tell all sorts of funny jokes
> About all kinds of curious folks.
>
> She likes to ride, and dance, and coast,
> But better still to butter toast,
> And smear it deep with honey sweet
> And sit and eat, and eat, and eat.
>
> I think sometime along in Spring
> She'll eat so much of everything,
> Her dresses all will spread and split,
> And open out to make a fit.
>
> And then perhaps, she'll look right thin
> With strips of dress and streaks of skin.
> I think she'll look real odd like that
> With nothing whole except her hat!

Colonel Marshall's verses were light and trivial, but when I was a child, his lapses into foolishness delighted me. He never lost his sense of fun, and in later years I realized that without it, he would not have been the whole man that he was. His brilliance, decency, kindness; his continual efforts "to understand rather than be understood"; his strict adherence to honor in total disregard of vicious criticism; his utterly selfless service to humanity; and all these virtues leavened by his humor—that was George C. Marshall, the whole man.

It does seem a pity though, that of his many worthwhile qualities I should have picked up two of the most inconsequential. One is "Oh Min!"—some earthshaker. The other is a downright inconvenience: since Colonel Marshall's death, I am the fastest eater extant.

With no hint of grossness, he consumed his food with unbelievable rapidity. The hottest soup would disappear in a matter of seconds (but quietly!), and he would polish off his entrée in a trice. Meanwhile he'd make pertinent comments on the flavor of this or that dish and carry on an animated conversation. I would race to keep up with him and soon developed the trick of eating like a steam engine without sacrificing the amenities of good table manners or withdrawing from the table talk.

I tried to break Colonel Marshall from eating so fast, and you can see with what results. Lily warned me that it was no use.

He and Lily enjoyed informal entertaining, and on winter Sundays there were often guests for luncheon; they rarely gave a formal dinner, and when they did, I was not present. When guests came to share the Marshalls' board, Colonel Marshall never showed his impatience at having to wait for them; but I always sat next to him, and I knew he was nervously drumming his fingers on his knee under the table while his guests munched their leisurely way toward dessert.

The Marshalls and my parents shared at least one characteristic: all four were inordinately tidy. My brother and sister were also very neat. As for me, something of mine was always where it shouldn't be; it was uncanny that no matter how I scurried about our apartment picking up things, there was always one of my books, or a shoe, or some damn thing out of place.

It was not so tedious keeping my belongings in order when I was at the Marshalls. I had a whole bureau to myself, and only the few things I brought with me to put into it. Also, Colonel Marshall designated a special place for my books, which was always cleared for me when I came directly to Fort Myer from school.

At home, Celeste and I made our own beds, or were supposed to. It usually ended by Celeste's making mine as well as hers, not only because I was almost always running late, but also because we shared a room and she disapproved of my bed-making. I made my bed at the Marshalls once or twice, but Lily said it looked so awful, she'd rather have the maid make it.

Quite probably, the short duration of my visits with the Marshalls had much to do with the continuance of our friendship! I stayed with them often enough and long enough to create a sense of belonging, of being a child in a childless family. On the other hand, they did not have to cope, month in and month out, year in and year out with the continual responsibilities of prodding and admonishing a careless, oversensitive child.

It may have shocked Lily that I hated to take a bath, but it amused her too, and Colonel Marshall thought it was downright funny. For Mother, however, it was a boring, unending struggle seeing to it that I was properly clean. If I tore my dress or lost my barrette, the Marshalls thought it an unfortunate accident, but at home, the annoying regularity of such heedlessness tended to inflate each small offense out of all proportion.

In short, when I went to visit Colonel Marshall and Lily, I was more than tolerated—I was the big cheese, and the whole visit would be devoted to having a good time. No wonder I behaved the best I knew how; nobody would have been fool enough to spoil a deal like that. More to the point, I made a special effort to behave well because I was extremely fond of them.

❧ CHAPTER X ❧

UNLESS THE WEATHER WAS EXCEPTIONALLY DISAGREEABLE, ONE THING Colonel Marshall and I were sure to do at Fort Myer was to go horseback riding. Colonel Marshall had his own ideas about what constituted bad weather; we ignored cold, wind, drizzling rain, or heat except to dress suitably. Snow and ice or a downpour were about the only conditions he considered severe enough to keep us from riding. If the day promised to be excessively hot, we rode at dawn; on pleasant days, we would start out around seven or seven thirty; and on cold days, we'd wait until as late as ten o'clock.

Horseback riding was far and away Colonel Marshall's favorite sport and he was determined to make a good rider out of me. He advocated riding as the most delightful form of exercise, but explained to me that the real pleasures of riding could be fully enjoyed only through mastery of the various techniques of good form and proper handling of the horse. In conjunction with his plans for my enjoyment, he told me quite candidly that he wanted a riding companion with whom he would not be required to talk shop or make polite conversation. Furthermore, he disapproved of riding alone.

"It's poor business to ride alone," he warned me, "no matter how expert a rider a person may be. The horse might step into a hole and break a leg, or shy into a tree—too many unexpected accidents can occur. I've known two men, both excellent riders, who met up with accidents when they were riding alone, and they lay in pain for hours before they were found. One of them died, and I've always entertained the idea he might have been saved if he'd had a companion who could have gone for help."

During the hectic years of World War II, when Colonel Marshall snatched brief times for exercise—early in the morning or late in the afternoon—he often had to ride alone, but if he'd had an accident there was little danger of his waiting for help very long. It is highly unlikely that the Chief of Staff's failure to return within a reasonable time would have gone unnoticed.

I had never had riding lessons before I began to ride regularly with Colonel Marshall, although I was not unused to horses. Keswick lay in the heart of the Virginia horse country and my father assumed his children would learn to ride as naturally as they had learned to walk. He had long since given up riding himself, but told us he had ridden to the hounds all through his youth and nobody had taught *him* how to ride.

At Keswick, when I was almost six years old, I was turned over to a little colored girl named Cary, who was seven or eight years older than I. Cary and I had many amusing adventures, but the most fun we had was riding Nellie, a big, clumsy, gentle work horse. Cary, carrying a halter, and I, trailing after her, would tramp through the meadows until we found old Nellie. Cary would throw the halter over Nellie's head, lift me (dressed in my gingham rompers) onto the mare's broad back, and then somehow manage to scramble up in front of me. We would clump back through the fields, to the bottom of the driveway leading up a hill to the main house, where we'd stop; then, at

Cary's signal, "Ready?" I'd get a firm grip around her waist and she'd kick old Nellie into a gallop up the hill. After we reached the top, we'd turn around, walk back down, and cloppity-clop up again—over and over. It wasn't long before Cary and I took turns, chiefly because I begged her so persistently to let me ride alone that she finally gave in to quiet my exasperating ding-dong.

This was not a practice likely to train me for competition with the blue-ribbon set; but those bareback bridleless rides, even though Nellie was a docile old plug, forestalled any fear of horses I might have developed at a later age.

I had progressed somewhat beyond those elementary gallops on Nellie when I started riding with Colonel Marshall at Fort Myer, because by the time I was a little older, my father had provided saddle horses for Celeste and me when we were visiting at Keswick.

On my first ride with Colonel Marshall, he hardly mentioned my seat or how I handled my horse except to warn me that I was riding a polo pony with a very sensitive mouth. He talked instead mostly about his own mount, Duchess, a beautiful, very high-spirited chestnut mare. I am not sure whether Duchess was a Government mount or belonged to Colonel Marshall, but he rode no other horse during the three years he was at Fort Myer, and no one else rode Duchess except a groom who exercised her when Colonel Marshall was out of town. I rode many different horses; they were all Government polo ponies, and I rode whatever pony was available. Colonel Marshall would never under any circumstance ask a special favor for himself, although he did select the horse he thought best for me from among those not in use on the days we rode.

My first lesson from Colonel Marshall was indirect. He told me that he'd taught Duchess to respond to a slight shifting of his weight and pressure from his knee.

"I barely use my hands at all," he said. "Watch this."

I watched closely but I could not see that he made a single

movement and yet Duchess turned abruptly to the right. He asked me to try the same thing with my horse and I had to admit that I hadn't observed anything to try.

Obviously pleased, he grinned, and patting his horse fondly, said, "Oh Duchess and I are a sometime pair. Aren't we, old girl?"

Then we started to trot. We trotted and trotted and trotted. After what seemed an awfully long time to me, I suggested, "Gosh, Colonel Marshall, let's canter some, it's more fun."

"No," he replied. He said that both of our horses had a good smooth trot, and that trotting was the best exercise for the rider and the least tiring gait for the horse. Finally he asked me if I was tired, a consideration I thought due me in spite of his concern for the horses. But I knew Colonel Marshall well enough by then to suspect that he was putting me to some sort of test, so I lied breathlessly, "Oh no, I'm not tired a bit; I've been posting for years."

He burst out laughing and replied, "Good for you! But your face looks pretty red to me so let's walk a while."

When we returned to the stables, Colonel Marshall made a big fuss over Duchess, unsaddling her himself, patting her, and calling her foolish little endearing names. He loved his horse. Lily told me that lots of mornings he would get up early enough to go to the stables before work so that he could carry sugar and carrots to Duchess. She always referred to Duchess as "George's beloved pet."

During the Marshalls' first year at Fort Myer, Colonel Marshall taught me something new on each ride. For one thing, he completely changed my English seat to the military forward seat. He said a lot of people complained that the forward seat was not stylish-looking, but it had been developed through long years of cavalry experience and was undoubtedly the safest seat for the rider and the easiest on the horse. He taught me how to post low in the saddle, an indispensable skill for the miles and miles we used to trot. In short, he gave me lessons on all the essentials which I practiced every time we rode. Over and over he instructed me how to stop a horse if he should ever run away—lessons I did not have an opportunity to practice. Toward the end of the year, as I learned most of the fundamentals, our rides became longer and longer.

In the early twenties, Fort Myer was surrounded by farm country and wooded areas with numerous lovely country lanes for riding. Just as on our walks we would leave the paths in Rock Creek Park for the freedom of the woods, so on our rides we would often leave the lanes to ride through the open fields. I began to believe I was nearly as good a rider as Colonel Marshall. That was the trouble with me; I always jumped the gun.

One fine morning Colonel Marshall tipped into my room to awaken me, warning me as usual not to wake up Lily. I dressed hurriedly and ran down to the kitchen where we would have a bite to eat before we went for our ride; when we rode in the early morning we would always wait for our real breakfast until we returned home. That morning, Colonel Marshall poked around the kitchen and came upon the remains of last night's cake.

"Want a piece of cake?" he offered as he poured himself a small bowl of cornflakes.

"Sure!" I replied, and downed a large hunk of chocolate layer cake at six thirty in the morning. I gag to think of it now!

Thus fortified, we rode happily out into the country until we came to a wide, flat meadow which Colonel Marshall decided was a good place for a brisk canter.

"Always be on the alert," he had told me again and again. "Never forget that an animal can be unpredictable."

Soon after we began to canter, a rabbit jumped up suddenly in front of my horse, startling him so that he shied violently and took off at a full gallop. He stretched himself out and flew! Of course I hadn't been on the alert; my reins were lax, and I had been sitting so casually to the horse's even, pleasant canter that when he shied, I lost my stirrups.

"Grip hard with your knees!" Colonel Marshall shouted after me as we sped away from him.

The pony got the bit in his teeth and I couldn't stop him although I tried desperately to follow the instructions Colonel Marshall had drilled into me for just such an eventuality. After all my efforts had failed, I gave up trying to halt the runaway and concentrated on staying in the saddle. We were clear across the field and about to head into the woods when Colonel Marshall galloped up beside me and grabbed my horse's reins.

"Are you all right?" he asked when we'd stopped, and in the next breath, said, "You didn't do what I told you."

I was livid with rage; I've never been madder in my life before or since! Nothing is more infuriating than to know you're wrong and to have it pointed out. Added to this ignominy was the equally infuriating humiliation of knowing that the horse had bested me.

"I did too so!" I screamed at him. "This is a stupid fool horse, and you stop hollering at me!"

Colonel Marshall regarded me steadily and without perturbation. "It appears," he replied evenly, "that you're the one doing the hollering." Then with a twinkle in his eye he added, "I believe that chocolate cake went to your head. Now, put your feet back in your stirrups before you blow yourself off the horse."

I replaced my feet in the stirrups and began to bawl. "Oh, Colonel Marshall!" I blubbered, "I'm real sorry I talked so ugly, and why am I so dumb?"

"You weren't mad at me," he answered, smiling, "only at yourself."

Then he stopped smiling and spoke very earnestly; "If you were dumb, you wouldn't be riding with me, so never offer me the cheap excuse that you made a mistake because you're dumb.

It's a weak pretense; feeling sorry for yourself is always objectionable to other people, and especially so to me. It's a form of cowardice."

I made no reply, but that little lecture burnt into me like a flame. As for his opinion about self-pity, I knew he was right about that—but a cheap *excuse,* I thought, a weak *pretense?* Good gosh, Mother told me practically every day how dumb I was. Maybe she didn't really mean it!

"Rose, do you understand what I'm trying to tell you?" Colonel Marshall asked gravely when I didn't answer him.

"Oh, yes sir," I said, "I was just thinking about it."

He changed the tone of his voice at once. "Well then," he continued brightly, "your horse got away from you because you didn't really believe my warnings that he could or would; what happened was due to lack of experience and overconfidence. You're not hurt and you've learned something, so dry your tears and we'll finish our ride."

When we returned home and told Lily about our exciting morning, I didn't know which horrified her more—the horse running away or Colonel Marshall giving me chocolate cake for my preliminary breakfast.

Colonel Marshall and I rode mornings in all sorts of weather, but when the weather was really fine, we'd almost always have a picnic too. The Marshalls and I had a strong predilection for picnics. We didn't start out on our excursions until after the customary lunch hour, because breakfast was late and substantial after our ride; and the actual picnicking was further delayed by certain habitual procedures which always took place first. We rarely settled down to eat until an hour or so before sundown.

The first item on our agenda was to buy food for the picnic, this being a major contribution to the fun. We would drive all the way into town to patronize our favorite Greek delicatessen at Eighteenth Street and Columbia Road. Leaving Lily in the parked Ford, Colonel Marshall and I would go into the store to select the food. Actually, I picked it out, and no matter how ill-chosen my selections might be, Colonel Marshall bought everything without a word of suggestion or criticism.

"Half the enjoyment of a picnic," he maintained, "is eating stuff you'd never ordinarily eat. One stomachache a week won't kill us."

Curiously enough, our outlandish picnic fare never made any of us sick, not even Lily.

After we had purchased our mess—in both senses of the word—we'd walk down the block to the "Parisian Bakery." There fat cream puffs, glossy fruit tarts, or chocolate-covered gingerbread still warm from the oven presented me with a fascinating problem of choice. Once in a while we would go to "Budds' Confectionary Shop" on the corner, where Colonel Marshall invariably bought Turkish paste for Lily, her favorite candy next to Sherry's.

Lily rarely objected to my odd menus; on the contrary, she assumed an attitude of pleasurable suspense as she curiously inspected each package. Before opening one, she'd shake it gently, giving it little ladylike sniffs and making guesses as to what delicacy might be inside. I recall only one occasion when she failed to pretend delighted surprise.

"What's this?" she asked apprehensively as she opened an odoriferous pasteboard carton.

"Oh," I replied, "that's pickled herring out of a big barrel."

"Ugh!" she grimaced. "I can't possibly eat that horrid smelly stuff."

"Well, never mind," I comforted her. "We have lots of other things, and besides, Colonel Marshall got some Turkish paste today and you can have my share to make up."

"Ugh, Turkish paste!" Colonel Marshall mimicked Lily, wrinkling up his nose, "I'd just as soon eat solidified spit!"

"Oh, Colonel Marshall!" I exclaimed, horrified. "That's awful!"

Lily, continuing to open the other packages, told him frigidly that his analogy was disgusting, but before he could reply, she changed her tone and said gaily, "Oh good, macaroni salad and salami; we're saved!"

Nevertheless, from that day onward, Colonel Marshall always referred to Turkish paste by that revolting term.

"Well, let's go to Budds' and buy some solidified spit for Lily," he'd say.

Eventually, we got so used to his nasty name for the candy that it ceased to bother Lily and me, nor did it diminish Lily's taste for it. I, however, could never again bring myself to eat—ugh—"solidified spit."

After the ceremony of buying our picnic, we would drive far out into the country, sometimes in Maryland, sometimes in Virginia. We would make a big to-do about the location of our picnic site and we'd never settle for one unless all three of us agreed it was the perfect place. There were only two criteria: it must be near enough the road for Lily to reach easily, and it had to offer some particularly attractive feature.

When we came to surroundings we considered picnic territory, Lily would concentrate on watching for "the place."

"Stop here, George!" she'd cry.

"Hey, Colonel Marshall, how about over yonder?" I'd shout.

"All right, ladies," Colonel Marshall would say laughingly, and stop the car. "Don't throw a fit. I can hear you."

Occasionally we'd have good luck on our first try, but more often some little thing or other would be wrong: maybe there were too many brambles we hadn't noticed from the car, or perhaps a previously undetected house showed up nearby. Sometimes we would stop in a promising environment so that Colonel Marshall and I could get out and reconnoiter. We always knew when we'd found the ideal spot. Returning to the car, we enthusiastically described it to Lily: a charming glen hidden a short way back in the woods, a field of blooming wild flowers just around the bend, or an especially good vantage point from which to watch the sunset.

What delightful times we had! Throughout his life, Colonel Marshall never lost his felicitous gift of being able to remove himself and anyone with him from the agitating encumbrances of daily life. Even during the strenuous years that were to come, when his leisure times were cut to mere minutes, he relaxed with as complete abandon as he worked with total concentration. Unpleasantness or allusions to troublesome responsibilities were taboo on our picnics. Colonel Marshall's capacity to shift his whole being, mind and body, from fulfillment of the relentless duties laid upon him to the enjoyment of undemanding, simple pleasures, helped immeasurably to fortify him in his future trying times.

CHAPTER XI

LILY, AS I HAVE MENTIONED BEFORE, STAYED WITH HER MOTHER when Colonel Marshall was traveling. She was very fond of Mrs. Coles and wrote to her every day, a practice which led me to guess that, in addition to affection, she also felt an obligatory responsibility for the welfare and happiness of her elderly mother who lived alone in Lexington. I rarely saw Mrs. Coles. I remember her as a bent, rheumatic old lady swathed in black, who would smile at me wanly and address me pleasantly enough, but as briefly as courtesy would allow. I think she was bored stiff with the very idea of me and only tolerated me grudgingly as a somewhat tiresome whim that amused Lily and George. At any rate, Mrs. Coles seldom visited the Marshalls at Fort Myer and not at all when they lived at 2400. Nor did I ever see her in Lexington, because Colonel Marshall never took me there. Back in the twenties, when we motored to pick up Lily, the mountain roads leading to Lexington were poor and dangerous, quite impossible for our little Ford, so Lily always took the train to meet us in Staunton.

The occasions of those meetings were exuberant and happy, but slightly flawed for me by a disturbing uneasiness.

Lily would embrace us both, chattering a mile a minute. "Oh, it's good to see you! I can't wait to get home! Did you have fun driving down? Did the car behave? Where did you spend the night? Oh George, I'll be glad to get home! What a lovely day! We're always so lucky about the weather. Oh, George . . . !"

A little worried frown would shadow Colonel Marshall's otherwise delighted greeting, and although always attentive to Lily, he would become even more so than ordinarily.

"You didn't overdo" he'd ask. "There is a limit to duty; your own health and well-being are of the utmost importance."

"Just reverse all you've said and apply it to yourself," she'd answer, laughing. "Did you overdo? Are you all right? Goodness, because I'm happy to see my husband doesn't mean I had a bad time."

Nevertheless, I worried about her too because I could see the blue smudges under her eyes, and see that in spite of her gaiety she looked wrung out and drained.

Lily never complained about Colonel Marshall's absences with General Pershing, but she did fret that he worked too hard—at home or away.

As Chief of Staff, General Pershing customarily spent months at a time in France, leaving Colonel Marshall (actually still Major Marshall) to "mind the store." This delegation of authority in fact but not in title was a situation which both pleased and displeased Lily.

"You're really Chief of Staff now," she'd say proudly, but sometimes she couldn't refrain from fussing. "You're running the Chief of Staff's show, doing all the brain work; it's absurd and unfair you're kept back as a Major."

Immediately she would sweeten her words—whether to excuse herself for complaining, or to comfort and encourage Colonel Marshall, I never figured out. It was probably some of both.

"Oh well," she'd add, "you're getting invaluable experience.

Anyhow you're the smartest officer in the Army, and the work you're doing will let everybody in the Army know it."

Colonel Marshall would smile and reply, "You're right about the experience, dear, but I doubt very seriously if 'everybody in the Army' will share your generous point of view that I'm 'the smartest officer in the Army.'"

Chief of Staff, Chief of Staff; I can't remember a time when Lily and I did not accept as a certainty that Colonel Marshall was destined to fill that office. "When he's Chief of Staff" colored all our private conversations about the future.

It was a natural ambition. Reaching that high office would verify the usefulness of his years of service in the Army. In retrospect, I believe also that Colonel Marshall wanted to be Chief of Staff because his head was full of ideas and plans for making the Army into a more efficient organization.

Colonel Marshall, it is true, advanced through circumstance beyond his own ambition, but he had the mark of greatness on him. Even as far back as the twenties, any child with a teaspoon full of sense, who was in as close and frequent association with Colonel Marshall as I, could have readily perceived his superiority. The confidence Lily and I had that he would one day be Chief of Staff was not by any means based wholly on wishful thinking or on our affection for him. I knew both intuitively and through the rudiments of immature reasoning that his star would rise bright and high. I knew intuitively because I invariably felt that his ideas and actions concerning my small affairs were not only perspicacious and right, but carried the weight of a completely impartial judgment, regardless of what his personal sentiment for me might be. Yet I felt as secure in his affection as I was confident in his fairness. Drawing on these feelings, I reasoned simply that his astuteness in handling my concerns justly and correctly would, on a larger and more complicated scale, enable him to handle grown-up situations with equal justice and correctness.

Colonel Marshall loved America passionately, and I use this

word advisedly. Only a passionate devotion to his country could have bolstered him to withstand the physical drain and mental demands that his country asked of him. He left the flag-waving and red, white, and blue rhetoric to the so-called "super-patriots." He not only scorned self-aggrandizement, but was incontrovertibly uninterested in public acclaim.

Colonel Marshall's heart was ever with the little people, the anonymous citizens.

A letter from him written in the summer of 1923 reached me at my summer camp. It so impressed me that I forwarded it to my parents. On the back of the envelope is my penciled note to them: "Dear Mother and Daddy, I thought you would like to read this."

August 4, 1923

My dear Rose,

This will be a hard letter to read for it is a hard letter to write because the train shakes a good bit. I left San Francisco yesterday, very suddenly, to accompany General Pershing on the President's special train taking Mr. Harding's body back to Washington. So this is a very sad journey, though a very impressive one.

At all the stations day or night the people, the very kind hearted and sympathetic people of America stand in long silent lines, bareheaded. The boy and girl scouts, the veterans of our wars, and the local military organizations, with their flags hung with mourning streamers salute as the train rolls by without pause.

In the observation vestibule at the rear, a guard of four soldiers, sailors, and marines stand motionless on guard around the casket. It is all very solemn and impressive and will grow more so as we reach the more thickly settled populated country east of Kansas.

The silence of the motionless throngs, the steady and uninterrupted progress of the train, and the bared heads of the humblest workers along the railroad, marks this journey apart from any I have taken. . . .

This is not a very cheerful letter, Rosey, but I think you will be interested in what I have written.

With much love, GCM

106

There is no hint in this letter of Harding's weaknesses, or of his scandalous administration, although Colonel Marshall was aware that I must have learned about them in the *2400* lobby. He did not write to me about a bad President, but about the deep-felt response of the American masses to the death of their fellow American who had held the highest office in the land.

CHAPTER XII

"COLONEL MARSHALL, PLEASE QUIT MAKING THAT AWFUL FACE! I keep telling you and telling you, it ruins your looks!"

Colonel Marshall acknowledged my reproof by relaxing his mouth into an absent half-smile, but in a couple of minutes he was at it again—drawing his lips back in a thin, taut line, and clenching his teeth in a fierce-looking grimace. I called it his "tiger smile," and sometimes I'd snarl "Grrrrrrr" at him to make him stop, but he'd have to be in a sufficiently carefree mood for this facetious tactic to have full effect.

Colonel Marshall ordinarily put on his "tiger smile" when he was concentrating on some physical activity, but it didn't necessarily have to be strenuous activity; he might be adjusting the hose to water his cherished little zinnia bed, or polishing the Ford, or pitching a tent—any insignificant thing.

That particular day, he had better reason to grimace than usual because we were running late and he was engrossed in steering the Ford from bump to bump over a mucky country road, trying to go as fast as he could without skidding into one of the deep, muddy ruts. I couldn't refrain from reminding him about his ferocious expression, which he knew I hated; but it was not a situation when a "Grrr" would have amused him.

Personally, although I was enjoying our wild ride immensely, I didn't see what difference it would make if we were ten minutes or so late, but I wouldn't have dared voice such a heretical opinion to Colonel Marshall. A few woeful experiences had impressed upon me that a mere half-minute's tardiness was a sin to him, so I gave myself up to the rare pleasure of jouncing about in the bucking Lizzie, and shouting "Thank-you-ma'am" when I flew up out of the seat. We were racing over that wretched road to keep a rendezvous with Colonel Marshall's good friend Colonel Lewis, and his daughter Ann, whom we were joining for an overnight camp-out, and Colonel Marshall was driving like a *Grand Prix* contestant to get there on time.

Even though Colonel Lewis and Colonel Marshall were congenial, it was by great good luck, plus Colonel Marshall's tact, that Ann and I liked each other too.

Nearly everyone's parents (and Colonel Marshall was my "sort-of" parent) have admonished their offspring at one time or another, "My dear friend So-and-so's lovely child is coming today. Do make an effort to be nice; I want so very much for you two to be friends." I don't know why parents expect their friends' children and their own to "catch" a friendship automatically, but it's apparently a universal mistake recurring from generation to generation. Such is the complexity of genes, however, and the perversity of children, that this timeless parental hope is rarely fulfilled.

At any rate, Colonel Marshall had apparently had first-hand experience with this commonplace misfortune, and consequently avoided making any biased comments about Ann before he brought us together. The first time I met her, he was taking me to the circus, and remarked off-handedly that we were going to stop by for Ann Lewis.

"Who's Ann Lewis?" I asked, immediately on the defensive.

"She's a little girl with dark, straight hair," Colonel Marshall answered.

"What's she like?" I countered.

"Well," he replied, "she has two arms, two legs—"

"Oh for Pete's sake, Colonel Marshall!" I interrupted in annoyance. "I mean what's she really like?"

"That's for you to decide," he replied.

When Ann got into the car, she regarded me with such poorly masked hostility that I naturally surmised her parents had exhorted her to "be nice" to me. This posed something of a challenge, so I knocked myself out to be amiable and to prove to her that I wasn't the least bit qualified to fulfill any parents' idea of a "lovely child." It worked, and from that day on, Ann accompanied us from time to time on special excursions: parades, the White House Easter-egg roll, and like occasions. She, her father, and Colonel Marshall and I joined forces for overnight camping trips—extra-special, favorite, looked-forward-to treats.

So that's where we were speeding on a bright Saturday May morning—to meet the Lewises. Of course, we had started in plenty of time, but two overventuresome little boys had delayed us.

A short while before, we had been driving unhurriedly through a thickly wooded area when all of a sudden—ping!—a rock hit the Ford just below the window on Colonel Marshall's side; then in quick succession—clink, clunk, pow!—a shower of small stones and mud clods bombarded the car. Colonel Marshall had immediately slammed on the brakes and looked in every direction at once. He could do that—he had those proverbial "eyes in the back of his head." In a split second, he spied the two boys running away through the woods, jumped out of the car, took off after them, and was at least a hundred feet ahead of me by the time I could scramble out of the Ford.

I knew that those kids didn't stand a chance; I'd raced too

often with Colonel Marshall in Rock Creek Park not to know how fast he could cover ground with those seven-league boots he wore. He caught the boys all right, collared them, and was hurrying back before I'd been able to run any appreciable distance.

He was giving them hell in a chillingly severe voice, a voice which unmistakably meant business but was unrelieved by hot, emotional variations—a firm, forceful tone held to a deadly calm level.

"What you did was stupid, dangerous, and wrong," he rebuked them. "I am warning you now, don't you ever again throw rocks or anything else at a moving car. You are very fortunate that my windshield was not shattered, or that I didn't have a wreck."

He released the boys and they stood before him as if he'd nailed them to the ground.

"By what right do you damage another person's property, endanger another person's life?" he continued. "What pleasure do you derive from hiding in the bushes and attacking a complete stranger with no earthly reason except to do harm?"

The boys were paralyzed with fright and I didn't blame them; it even scared me to see Colonel Marshall so coldly furious. If he had shouted and ranted like most angry adults, he would not have been half so fearsome. As it was, those rough tough kids froze to attention under his sure, low-keyed, authoritative manner.

When he stopped speaking, there was a tense, vibrant silence. Finally, the larger boy exclaimed, "Jeez, Mister, we never thought about it thatta way!"

And the smaller one added, "I ain't never gonna do it no more!"

"Whatcha gonna do to us?" the big one quavered, full of apprehension.

I think they both expected to be drawn and quartered on the spot.

Colonel Marshall ignored the boy's question and asked,

"What are your names, and where do you live? Where do your fathers work?"

They said they were brothers, and gave him their names. They told him that their father was dead, and they lived with their "ma" about a quarter of a mile from where we stood.

"That's where we're going," Colonel Marshall ordered.

All of us about-faced and marched rapidly down a wagon road through the woods toward the boys' home, Colonel Marshall with a boy on each side of him, and I bringing up the rear. Not a word was spoken until we reached their shabby little house where our silent parade ended in a ragged yard brightened here and there by golden glints of dandelions. I remember how relieved I was to look at those shining dandelions, because it embarrassed and disturbed me to see those boys standing like limp puppets waiting for Colonel Marshall to pull the strings. He brought them to life in a hurry by directing crisply,

"Call your mother."

"Ma, *Ma!*" they shouted with an urgency that implied that if she didn't show up right away the whole place would go up in smoke.

An emaciated old-young woman came running out of the house. She stopped short when she saw our little group, clutched her hands together, and asked in a voice shrill with fright, "What in Gawd's name's the matter?"

Colonel Marshall said quietly, his voice still calm but now warm and friendly, "Don't be alarmed. You have a couple of sturdy sons here who will very likely grow into fine men, but they've made a serious mistake I think you should know about."

Briefly, he recounted what had happened and added something else he hadn't mentioned to the boys. He pointed out the dire consequences that might have befallen them if another victim had caught them and decided to turn them over to the police, or, if not that, had physically maltreated them.

The woman reacted hysterically, cuffing her offspring and screaming at them.

"Just a minute," Colonel Marshall said firmly, interrupting the din. "I didn't bring them here for you to beat them; I brought them home so that you, yourself, would understand the nature of their mischief and impress it upon them."

She stopped hitting her children and regarded him curiously.

He spoke to her earnestly, as if she and her sons were the most important people on earth, as indeed they were to each other.

"As their mother," he said, "I am certain you work very hard to see that these boys have enough to eat and warm clothes to wear, and I know that to achieve those things alone is a back-breaking task. They look healthy and well-clad, and for this you can be proud. But they need another kind of looking after as well. I am suggesting (he did not say, "I am *telling* you") that you take a little time each day—five minutes is enough—to drill into these children a wholesome respect for other people's lives and property. That sounds pretty solemn, but if they learn that, they'll learn respect for honesty. Do you understand what I'm saying? Nobody goes bad if they get the habit of honesty."

The woman had listened to Colonel Marshall with close attention and obvious interest. After a moment's pause, she replied, "Yes sir, I understands clear. I guess I works so hard around the place, I just lets 'em run wild, but I can spare five minutes in a day. I'll try to do what you says, Mister, I'll shore try."

"Good—and good-bye!" Colonel Marshall said, saluting her politely.

As we turned to leave, the elder boy, to my astonishment, asked wistfully, "Mister, you reckon we'll git to see each other again sometime—maybe sometime when things is better?"

"There's always a chance of that!" Colonel Marshall reassured him gaily. "So long for now!"

I looked up at Colonel Marshall and smiled; I was proud to death of him. He smiled back at me, slapped my rear-end, and cried, "Let's go, we're late!" And we took off for the car at a run.

CHAPTER XIII

In spite of his speeding, Colonel Marshall and I were close to fifteen minutes late when our exhausted, besmeared, but plucky little Ford rolled sputtering into our camp site. Colonel Lewis was already beginning to be alarmed; George Marshall was never late. Even before we'd pulled to a stop, he and Ann came rushing over to our pock-marked, mud-splattered car, crying, "What happened? Where were you? Are you all right?"

Colonel Marshall gave them a quick résumé of our experience, shooting off the bare facts in a rapid staccato: the "attack," catching the boys, the approximate distance to their home, and the time we spent taking them there. But he omitted the psychological qualities of the episode which had infused it with poignancy and meaningfulness for me: his succinct, sensible advice to the overwrought mother; and more especially, his magical treatment of the boys, which had almost instantly transformed their recalcitrance into meekness, and in the end, had supplanted their fear with a piteous longing—an instinctive need felt by all children—for the security of a just and magnanimous authority.

"Mister, you reckon we'll git to see each other again sometime . . . ?" That little urchin's forlorn words ring across the years.

Colonel Lewis reacted quite naturally to the unadorned account he'd been given and suggested indignantly that Colonel Marshall ought to sue, but Colonel Marshall laughed and dismissed the suggestion, saying that he had never thought of suing, and besides, the woman didn't have an extra five cents anyhow. Then, characteristically, he summarily changed the subject, reminding us that it was a beautiful day, our best camp site yet, and that we had come to have a good time, so we should get about it.

Ann and I ran off at once to inspect the enchanting locale that Colonel Marshall and her father had found earlier in the week. Ann chattered about how scared her father had been when we didn't show up, and I blew up our recent experience into a dangerous "adventure" (but I did not expose my secret feelings about it).

The men had selected a secluded, woodsy area for our outing, and on that glorious spring morning, lavish sunshine poured through the tender young foliage of trees not yet in full leaf. Ann and I threw off our sweaters after the first five minutes of skittering hither and yon, examining the innumerable possibilities that revealed themselves to a couple of children looking for fun. Suddenly, we came upon an abrupt, short incline. Looking down, we discovered a noisy little brook riffling and dancing over a series of moss-covered rocks. Directly below us, it paused and gurgled in a small sandy-bottomed pool before it went sashaying off to lose its identity in the mingled waters of a hundred others like it.

Nothing intrigues a child more than the sight of water on a warm sunny day, and the little brook sang out an invitation for us to come and play in it right away. Delighted, we were sliding down the bank when a shout from Colonel Marshall diverted our attention.

"I know the water looks tempting," he called, "but it's too early in the year for wading. You may think it's a hot enough day, but summer's not here yet and the brook will be icy cold from winter snows."

Colonel Lewis chimed in that we certainly must not go wading—this was the prime season for catching a bad cold.

Disappointed, we climbed back up the bank and disconsolately started throwing sticks and pebbles in the water until the men summoned us to hold the tent stakes while they hammered them into the ground. After our camp was set up to everybody's satisfaction, and we'd had a cold picnic lunch, the men announced that they were going over to the field just around the bend for some target shooting.

"We won't be far," they told us, and Colonel Marshall suggested that we build a rock fireplace so that we could have a nice fire to cook supper and keep us warm after the sun went down.

We built the fireplace, we climbed two trees, we got very hot, then we went wading. We knew we wouldn't get caught, because we could hear the firing of the target shooting. But that tricky Colonel Marshall fooled us; he came back to the camp, leaving Colonel Lewis to keep up the regular bang-bang of the firing. He arrived to find us wading out into the deepest part of the little pool; to make matters worse, we were hollering at each other so loudly that we didn't hear or spot him until I chanced to look up and see him standing, hands on hips, at the top of the bank. I cut dead off in the middle of a holler, and Ann, turning around to find out why, saw him an instant after I did. He looked at least eight feet tall, as he stood there, motionless, just long enough for us to stare bleakly up at him for a few horrendous moments before he wheeled about and walked briskly away.

While we were putting on our shoes and socks, Ann nervously started to speculate on what our fate would be.

"Do you s'pose they'll take us home?" she suggested. "Or

maybe Daddy'll spank me even if I am practically grown up. Do you think maybe we won't get any of the big steak we're going to cook tonight?"

She conjured up many more unhappy possibilities; hers was a fruitful imagination. But I had only one idea of what would happen to me. In utter dejection, I looked forward to a second long isolated spell of silence.

We had a miserable wait, but as it turned out, our whole punishment consisted of self-torture by our own imaginations. When the men returned to camp, they greeted us with gay animation and completely ignored our disobedience.

Years later, Colonel Marshall told me with much amusement that he and Colonel Lewis had guessed that we had gone wading. They had been shooting for a good while when Colonel Lewis had commented on the excessive off-season heat, and then he added casually that it was too bad the kids couldn't go wading. Colonel Marshall had replied that the kids undoubtedly were wading—wouldn't he be if he was a kid on a hot day with little chance of getting caught?

Colonel Lewis replied, "Hell yes!"

When they decided that we had probably been at it long enough, Colonel Marshall had dreamed up his sneaky trick to get us out before time to cook supper.

"Not a bad idea either," he chortled when he finished telling me how he'd fooled us. "We got away with a minimum of unpleasantness for you and none for us. Who wants to mar an outing with scolding and punishing?"

By the way, neither Ann nor I caught a cold.

As is obvious by now, Colonel Marshall had a distaste for scolding and punishment. He was usually able to avoid both by not allowing a situation to get out of hand, or by not setting up such unreasonable standards that disobedience or mischief would be an almost automatic response. When punishment was unavoidable—the fruit shower, the boys' attack, our wading—he took great pains to point out the heart of the error if it was a serious one, and meted out his unique punishment at once. But when it was over, it was over for good; there was no long, drawn-out dwelling on the subject, no ad infinitum rehashing.

Besides, he loved and enjoyed children, he understood them, he had empathy for their shortcomings, he made allowances for their embryonic ethical values, and, above all, he strove to re-see through their wondering, inquisitive eyes the forgotten enchantments of a child's world. All his life, long after I had grown to the sober state of adulthood, wherever he lived, children were drawn to him and perennially frolicked in the sunshine of his extraordinary personality.

Colonel Marshall was born to be a father, which he never was except by "adoption." He was born to be a husband, which he was twice, both times happily married, but, as we shall see, to women entirely different in personality and appearance.

No man took greater pleasure in the blessings of home life. If Lily concerned herself with making their home an attractive place of happiness and contentment, Colonel Marshall delighted in indulging her in every way he could. Not that he gave her expensive presents; he was a frugal man—he had to be on his small Army pay. But he showered Lily with a hundred little attentions; he fetched and carried; he planned little surprises; he was ever solicitous about her health and comfort; he relieved her of mundane financial budgeting and any like chores or decisions; and if he teased her, he paid her innumerable little compliments. When she performed some necessary or even quite simple extra service for him, he praised her as if she had suffered immeasurable inconvenience for his sake—in short, he gave her his unremitting consideration, smoothed the path before his queen and led her by the hand.

He was a sucker for Lily and she unquestionably enjoyed it, but she was never tempted to take undue advantage of him, and indeed, often submitted to his attentiveness more to please him than to benefit herself. Once, when she asked me to run upstairs to fetch her embroidery scissors and I started to go, Colonel Marshall told me to sit down, he'd get them. After he left, Lily smiled and told me, "George just naturally has to look after me; it's his pleasure, bless his heart. You too," she added; "haven't you noticed how he absolutely has to take care of us fragile females?"

✿ CHAPTER XIV ✿

MOTHER USED TO SAY THAT BY THE TIME CHILDREN WERE TWELVE years old they had all the sense they would ever have. I don't know how she arrived at this curious conclusion or exactly what she meant by it. Perhaps she hit on twelve because it was generally considered the last year of childhood, although I suspect some of today's sophisticated nine-year-olds would dispute the point.

At any rate, if Mother held that the twelve-year-old brain had reached its peak of mental capacity, the Episcopal Church also attached (and still does) a certain significance to twelve years old. It is the age, Episcopalians maintain, when a child has reached a sufficiently advanced stage of mental development to understand the importance of confirmation into the Faith and into the Church.

Fortunately for me, I reached the magic age in September 1923; for 1923 was the last full year Colonel Marshall and Lily lived at Fort Myer. It is not mandatory for Episcopalians to be confirmed in their twelfth year, but it is the preferred age, and at the National Cathedral School, confirmation at an earlier age would most certainly have been frowned upon. If, then, I had been born a year later than I was, I would have missed my chance of asking Colonel Marshall to be my godfather. Indeed, the chain of circumstances lying behind that chance was as long and accidentally linked as the chain of events in "The House That Jack Built."

First of all, I wanted to be confirmed along with my classmates at school, but if I hadn't gone to the Cathedral School, I probably would not have been confirmed—at least, not then; I couldn't be confirmed unless I was baptized; if I hadn't been baptized, I wouldn't have had a godfather. Finally, since that lucky day I spoke to Colonel Marshall in the 2400 elevator, a bond of affection had evolved between us, and this was the determining cause for actually wanting him to *be* my godfather.

Religious training being a prime concern at the Cathedral School, it was not surprising that toward the end of the school year of 1923, the Deaconess reminded us eleven-year-olds that the next year would be our confirmation year. As students of the Cathedral School, she told us, anyone whose parents so desired would have the rare privilege of receiving confirmation instruction from the Bishop. This was a break for me because my family did not belong to a church and we had no parish priest.

I would have signed up for the Bishop on the spot, but I waited until the appointed day set for the following week in order to allow time for my classmates to consult their more orthodox parents. All of the other kids signed up for the Bishop's instruction too, although he had a reputation for being a dull teacher. I have a sneaking suspicion the parents thought the Bishop could set their children on a more direct route to the Kingdom of Heaven than was possible for a mere parish priest.

At any rate, after we had registered, the Deaconess cautioned us that we must have our baptismal certificates in readiness next year as evidence of our eligibility for confirmation. We should tell our parents, she warned, that they'd have the whole summer either to locate the long-put-away certificates or to secure the evidence from the church where the rite had been performed. Meanwhile, I'd been thinking to myself that I would have the whole summer to get myself baptized before anyone found out that nobody had "renounced the Devil and all his works" in my name. I am bound to confess that my proximity to Hell's fire didn't bother me half so much as the acute embarrassment of being a maverick—or, more aptly in this context, a black sheep— among my peers. If there is anything common to the majority of children, a majority which included me, it is the determination to be like all other children.

My dismay, then, at not having been baptized stemmed from an anxiety of how, where, and by whom it could be accomplished with as little fanfare as possible. Paradoxically, my parents, whose religious views were and still are obscure to me, appeared extraordinarily amenable to my intention to be confirmed, and my father even came up with a perfect solution to my dilemma. He assured me he could arrange to have me baptized at Keswick by Dr. Robinson, the gentle, uncomplicated rector of Grace Church.

The next consideration was the question of godparents. As I sat listening to my mother and father talking over the pros and cons of whom they should invite, their discussion seemed more and more unjustifiable to me, until at last, I interrupted them.

"Don't you think," I asked, "I should at least be allowed to choose my own godfather, as long as you didn't have me baptized in the first place?"

"Fair enough!" my father laughed.

"Well then," I continued, "you can pick anybody you like for my godmother, but I want Colonel Marshall for my godfather."

For my godmother, they settled on my father's youngest and favorite sister, my aunt Rose Page, after whom I had been called, and for whom I was soon to be legitimately named. Mother told my father to write his sister and Dr. Robinson, and announced that she would write to Colonel Marshall. I asked her emphatically please not to, I wanted to invite him myself; but of course she did, for she would never have countenanced such a breach of etiquette. But I had anticipated that she would most certainly write to him and had already asked him before she got around to sending off her note.

I had planned to ask him the following Saturday when we went riding together, and had looked forward to it. But when the time came to my complete surprise, I was overcome with a painful shyness. As we rode along, the awful thought occurred to me that Colonel Marshall's enthusiasm for being my godfather quite possibly might not match my own; so I kept turning over in my mind various ways to broach the subject, so that he wouldn't have to accept "just to be nice." Every time I was about to start, my shyness increased, because I worried if it was presumptuous to ask him at all; and when I thought he might decline, a panicky feeling of desolation blotted out whatever little speech I'd made up.

At last I began tentatively, "You're an Episcopalian too, aren't you, Colonel Marshall?"

It was a sorry opener. I knew perfectly well he was an Episcopalian, but I'd hoped somehow to work around to mentioning baptisms and confirmations in general, then mine in particular, and from there, lead into the godfather invitation. But to ask Colonel Marshall a question when he knew I had the answer only put him on the alert. Furthermore, as he had often pointed out, I was a poor hand at beating around the bush; so his reply to my nonsensical question was hopelessly uncooperative.

"Why?" he said.

"Oh gosh!" I exclaimed, caught off balance, and giving up all hope of a subtle and gracious approach, I seized the bull by the horns and blurted out, "Colonel Marshall, will you please be my godfather?"

He showed no surprise at my sudden invitation and asked for no explanations. Without hesitating an instant, he leaned out of his saddle, kissed me, and replied, "It would be a high honor and a great privilege to be your godfather. Thank you for asking me."

In all truth, that was one of the happiest and most thrilling moments of my life.

When we got home, that is, home at Fort Myer, I rushed into the house, calling to Lily at the top of my voice that Colonel Marshall was going to be my godfather, and didn't that make us sort of kin, like a real family? Lily's response was warm and enthusiastic, but later, when we sat down to breakfast, she tactfully raised a point of order. She began by saying we were already like a "real family" even though George had not been my godfather, and continued gently that no one could be baptized twice, so I mustn't be disappointed if the minister refused me.

"Baptized twice," I asked; "who, me?" Then all at once, I understood what she was driving at, and hastened to explain I'd never been baptized before.

"Because," I hesitated, trying to think up a plausible excuse that would not reflect unfavorably on my parents, "well, because Mother and Daddy are different from just anybody."

Lily laughed and assured me she was very happy and relieved to learn that George could really be my authentic godfather.

She looked at Colonel Marshall and said defensively, "Get herself baptized twice, it's just like something Rose would think up. You know it is."

He agreed, and said, "The possibility occurred to me too, but I had decided to do my checking on the q.t."

"Even if she had set her sights on a second baptism," he continued, smiling at me, "it would not have diminished the fine compliment of her invitation."

"Oh thank you, Colonel Marshall!" was all I said, but I was filled with gratitude and pride that he considered it a compliment to be my godfather.

My actual baptism was anticlimactic as far as it related to

Colonel Marshall, though in every other way it was lovely. My father arranged for the ceremony to take place at Keswick after my return from summer camp in September—a time when Colonel Marshall happened to be away with General Pershing and couldn't come. My father proxied for Colonel Marshall. I was happy that he did and I was inspired by the dignity and reverence with which Dr. Robinson conducted the simple ceremony. Of course, I was secretly disappointed that Colonel Marshall was not able to be there. But as he told me later, "It wasn't necessary for me to be present. The good Lord and you and I know that I'm your godfather."

☙ CHAPTER XV ☙

COLONEL MARSHALL'S PHENOMENAL MEMORY WAS ONE OF HIS attributes that never failed to amaze anyone who had occasion to observe it. Of the many tales about his uncanny ability to instantly grasp and retain great masses of facts, there's an especially illustrative anecdote about a large press conference he once held at the height of World War II. The press conference opened, so the story goes, with the first reporter asking a long, complicated question to which Colonel Marshall did not reply at once. Instead, he passed on to the next correspondent who asked another involved question, then the next, and so on down the line. Each reporter's different and complex query required serious consideration. After the entire group had fired some twenty or more double-barreled questions, Colonel Marshall came back to the first man, answered him concisely and in detail, then proceeded to reply to each one in turn until every newsman there had received a clear answer to the specific information he sought. Not one correspondent had to repeat his question!

This tale is not surprising to me, for Colonel Marshall used to try his untiring best to impress upon me the importance of a good memory. He repeated over and over that a sound *selective* memory demonstrated the ability to concentrate; and concentration, he firmly maintained, was the key to making full use of the mind.

"Don't clutter up your noodle with useless trivialities," he warned. "Learn to decide what is important to remember and what isn't."

Once, to please and surprise him, I learned Coleridge's "Rime of the Ancient Mariner" from beginning to end. When I'd finished reciting it, he didn't say a word about my stupendous feat of memorizing the whole of that lengthy ballad; instead, he commented on the way I had recited it.

"You really like that poem, don't you? It really stirs you up."

It did "stir me up;" at least, the poem's vivid imagery, harmonious aural patterns, and enthralling story fascinated me. I was too young to understand the underlying significance, or even to be aware there was any, so I replied naïvely that of course I liked the "Ancient Mariner"—that was why I'd picked it out of Daddy's poetry books. Besides, I said, everybody liked great poetry. He corrected me, saying that some people didn't like poetry at all, while others, although they wanted to enjoy it, didn't have the knack for getting much out of it.

"Always keep up your enthusiasm for poetry," he told me emphatically. "Never let it get away from you. *That's* what I want you to remember."

Thanks to Colonel Marshall's insistent training, I have a pretty good memory. But unlike him, I retain only those things which have had a deep intellectual or emotional impact on my mind and heart. In other words, what I remember is not necessarily worthwhile to anybody but me. Unlike him, too, my head is crammed full of miscellaneous superficialities. Colonel Marshall's genius lay in his unerring accuracy for holding on to whole bodies of information shorn of insignificant detail and entirely remote from any personal consideration.

Certainly, I have never been able to sort my recollections with anything like his precision; so that apart from those I have catalogued, there remains a disarray of remembered experiences and conversations with the Marshalls, which, though vivid in themselves, are all jumbled up in my "head file."

Drawing haphazardly from my own mishmash department, I recall one rainy Saturday afternoon when Colonel Marshall was working at his office and Lily took me to the movies. I thought it was a lousy show, and such is my flair for retaining the unnecessary, I could tell you almost the whole plot. It was a torrid silent movie; Ricardo Cortez was the star; the plot was a second-rate, Faust-like melodrama; and the movie was replete with hot love scenes, wild parties, and slinky "vamps." We sat through the entire production because Lily's sense of the appropriate had temporarily succumbed to all that lavish Hollywood fantasy.

On the way home in the taxi, she was belatedly conscience-stricken and kept repeating that she shouldn't have taken me to that bad movie, George would have a fit. Oh, how she hoped I hadn't been harmed by watching such a sophisticated, grown-up show; and I mustn't believe, she interjected lamely, that people ever acted so indiscreetly in real life. Her worries were unfounded, I wasn't such a blockhead that I couldn't perceive the picture was supposed to be shocking; but I hadn't been constantly exposed to the mass-media vulgarity children encounter today, so I'd thought the show merely silly and impossible. My only reaction to Cortez' suave love-making was excruciating boredom—rootin', tootin' William S. Hart was my boy!

I reassured Lily I was positive I hadn't been "harmed," and as far as Colonel Marshall was concerned, at least they'd shown an *Our Gang* comedy.

"And you know," I said, to ease her anxiety, "Colonel Marshall is crazy about *Our Gang*—he's always talking about Farina."

Farina was a winsome, amusing little colored boy dressed in diapers, who always upstaged the rest of the gang—a motley group of "reg'lar fellers" and one insipid little blond-headed girl.

That evening at dinner, Colonel Marshall looked anxiously across the candles at his unusually subdued Lily and asked if she were feeling all right. She hastened to assure him she was quite well, but he wasn't satisfied and insisted she must be overtired.

"How did you and Rose spend this long, dreary afternoon?" he asked, probably assuming I'd worn her down.

"We went to the movies," she murmured unhappily.

Colonel Marshall raised his eyebrows, but before he could speak, I started jabbering about *Our Gang*—he really should have seen Farina, he'd been so funny and cute, he'd fed the dog an ice cream cone. . . .

He cut off my absurdly obvious effort to cover up for Lily with the cryptic observation that we both looked guilty as the devil.

"So, Rose," he said, "stop trying to pull the wool over my eyes"; and he asked Lily sharply, "What was the main feature?"

"Ricardo Cortez," she quavered, "in *Skin*" (or some equally ridiculous title).

"Oh good Lord!" Colonel Marshall remarked witheringly. Then he turned to me and instructed me to tell him everything I remembered about the picture.

I think my answer helped save the day, because he burst out laughing when I told him there wasn't anything in the movie worth remembering. Poor Colonel Marshall, I suspect he mistakenly believed he'd made some headway in teaching me to throw off the superficialities he'd warned so often would constantly assault my brain.

I only helped save the day, in any case, because Colonel Marshall, the frigid, reserved, impersonal public figure I've read about, could not bear to see his darling Lily unhappy. Undoubtedly Lily's conscience bothered her, but I know she was not as miserable as she made out to be. Except for his disapproving "Oh good Lord!" it ended by Colonel Marshall's comforting her that she mustn't worry so deeply, Rose was too young to be seriously affected by the show, and anyhow, she'd forgotten it already (!). Colonel Marshall's wilted Lily began to revive under the gentle shower of his tenderness, until after a short while, she bloomed forth in all her radiance to dazzle and delight him.

As I watched this touching tableau, a vague amusement gathered inside me. By chance, Lily's eyes met mine, and in that brief, loaded glance, I became consciously and acutely aware for the first time that the female of the species (*The Feminine Mystique* notwithstanding) is endowed with a special gift of magic which is far removed from the intellect. Mere males are powerless to withstand it, and when Lily cast the spell, Colonel Marshall was no exception.

Another isolated memory that flares up in my mind brings back a fearful occurrence when Colonel Marshall narrowly escaped death one fateful day between 1921 and 1923. We were on one of our motor trips to meet Lily, and Colonel Marshall had been explaining to me in exhaustive detail the mechanical mysteries of an automobile. He opened his discourse by confessing that he was not at all mechanically inclined. "About as interested and proficient in mechanics as you are in arithmetic," he'd laughed. But it had bothered him, he said, to be completely ignorant about something he needed and used frequently, so one day he'd taken a car engine apart to find out what went on inside. When I tried to tease him, asking if he'd been able to put it back together again, he'd replied indignantly that of course he had; the whole point had been to overcome his ignorance. He lectured me about how electric current travels from the ignition to the battery to the coil, then sparks the plugs; how gas and air fumes mix in the carburetor; about explosions pushing the pistons up and down; about intake manifold; crank shaft; cylinders—oh woe, on and on ad infinitum! It is the only occasion I recall when he truly bored me, although I politely, gallantly, arduously tried to pay attention. Nevertheless, however hard I struggled to blow up my interest, it kept seeping away like air out of a faulty balloon. I was on the verge of falling asleep when he summarily broke off in the middle of a sentence.

Abruptly, quietly, urgently, he ordered me, "Get down on the floor!"

We were driving up a long hill on a narrow, shoulderless macadam road, from each side of which steep cliffs dropped dead away. At Colonel Marshall's command, "Duck down!" my sleepy eyes flew open and I had just barely time enough to glimpse a big truck bearing down on us backwards at breakneck speed. I dove to the floor; Colonel Marshall jerked into reverse, kicked me *wham* on the side of my head, and as I dizzily moved further away from his feet, I felt the Ford race downhill in reverse as fast as Colonel Marshall could make it go. Suddenly our can swerved sharply and came to a bumpity stop.

"Whew!" Colonel Marshall exclaimed. "Thank God we made it!"

I had not been very frightened. I was a child and incapable of imagining that anything could go wrong as long as Colonel Marshall was near to take care of me. From my position, I couldn't see how rapidly the truck was gaining on us, besides, I was half groggy from the fierce kick Colonel Marshall had landed on my head. I eased back onto the seat, holding my throbbing head and looking over at Colonel Marshall, I was astonished to see sweat pouring down his face.

He leaned back in his seat, lit a cigarette, inhaled deeply, and said, "I'm glad I noticed this little side road when we passed by. I'm glad I knew it was here," he repeated. "I might not have spotted it in the rush and strain. I couldn't have outrun that truck all the way down the hill; it was only a hair's breadth away from us when we backed in!"

He was visibly shaken, and suddenly, unexpectedly, he gave me a big bear-hug and cried, "Oh Rosie, life is a beautiful thing!"

It was a sentiment I shared (and still do most of the time), but insensitive as I'd been to the reality of our danger, only smiled a polite agreement, because my immediate concern was the big knot growing on my head.

"What did you have to go and kick me so hard for?" I asked plaintively.

He replied, laughing, "There wasn't a half second to lose. We'd both be splattered over the highway right now if I had taken the time to ask you politely to please remove your head from under my foot."

"I told you to duck down," he continued, "because if we'd been hit, you would have been better protected."

After we'd taken time to find out that the truck driver was okay—his "brakes busted," he said—we proceeded on our way. It was while we were retracing our route uphill that I observed the sharp inclines on either side of the road and also saw again our little side road to safety. I saw it because I was looking for it— otherwise I'm sure I would have missed it—and I marveled aloud to Colonel Marshall that he had noticed the road when we'd driven by the first time.

"However did you see it?" I asked. "Do you mark down every single little cow path we pass?"

"I guess I must," he answered. "I didn't realize it though. I suppose it's because I did a lot of surveying when I was a young Lieutenant. It's habitual for me to scan the surroundings. I do it almost unconsciously and I suppose the lay of the land is automatically photographed in my mind. Lucky for us—eh, Rosie?"

No wonder I wasn't scared when Colonel Marshall was around to take care of me.

✿ CHAPTER XVI ✿

IN THE EARLY TWENTIES WHEN I WAS A KID, WASHINGTON WAS scarcely more than a big town, or at most, a small city. Not anymore. The national capital is now a people-packed traffic-jammed metropolis, and the lovely open country which used to surround it is a teeming network of freeways and burgeoning real-estate developments which, together with endless gas stations and sprawling shopping centers, extend for miles outside the city limits. This is hardly surprising. Since my childhood, the extensive growth of the Government has required an extensive addition of people to operate it.

Although a good part of the swollen population, either living in Washington or in the surrounding suburbs, is still transient, the number of year-round residents at that time was miniscule compared to what it is today. My father was destined to be a perennial member of the nonpartisan Tariff Commission, so our family numbered among the few long-term residents of Washington. By 1924, I had lost all conception of what life would be like growing up with the same people around me year after year—except for Colonel Marshall and Lily.

The Marshalls had lived in Washington for a longer unbroken period than almost anyone I knew. During those years
they became such an integral part of my life that I could not
bring myself to face the thought of their leaving. Although I was
accustomed to my friends moving away, and was aware that
Service personnel regularly changed posts, I indulged myself in
wishful thinking that somehow it would be different with Colonel Marshall and Lily. But I aways knew in my heart that the
sorrowful day of their departure would surely come. As for
Colonel Marshall, never one to darken his personal life with
useless plaints about the inevitable, he did not drop hints that
would darken mine. I cannot remember a single instance when
the subject of his leaving was discussed between us until the
afternoon he told me he had received his orders to go to Tientsin,
China. It was a numbing blow.

We were driving out to Fort Myer in the new Oakland he'd
bought a short while before, and I'd been having a great time
putting on airs and feeling swell in the big automobile. When he
told me the news, all my fun melted instantly away.

"Going to China, to *China!*" I cried in utter dismay. "Oh,
Colonel Marshall, oh, Colonel Marshall!" was all I managed to
say.

He pulled over to the curb and stopped the car. "Come on
now, don't throw a fit," he said, half joking, half severe.

Gently but firmly, he reminded me, "You've known all along
that Lily and I would be leaving some day. Don't act like a
dumbbell. You have sense enough to understand that few things
last, good or bad."

He went on to explain that this didn't mean that our affection
would not last, or that he and Lily would not miss me, but only
that I must accept with courage and equanimity the fact that all
my life situations would shift and change. Finally he sternly
advised me not to spoil our time left together with "pouts and
tears and yammers."

I promised him I wouldn't fuss and wail, not because I didn't want to but because I knew it wouldn't do any good. Secretly, I thought poorly of his argument, about having enough sense to understand the relentless certainty of change, and having to accept it well; I felt that there was little to understand about this change, which had hit me smack in the face, and which I was forced to accept with good grace. Later in life, however, there were so many occasions to recall his little homily that it was eventually absorbed into my consciousness, and I almost forgot it was he who first planted it there. I am sure the expectation of and reasonable reaction to change was all that Colonel Marshall intended to prepare me for when he coupled his warning and advice with the abrupt announcement of his coming departure.

When he'd finished his stiff little lecture, he started up the car, and as usual, did not refer to the subject again. For the rest of the way, he talked about China in general, about the unbelievable antiquity of Chinese culture, and something or other about the Great Wall. He made only one concession to my crushed feelings.

"I will tell you honestly, Rosie," he said, "Lily and I would like very much to snatch you away and take you with us. You would love China and I'm sorry you can't come. That being impossible," he continued, using a favorite expression he'd coined in reference to my growing up, "I expect you 'to jell' very well without us."

After I'd calmed down, even I realized it would be absurd to contemplate the possibility of the Marshalls burdening themselves with a thirteen-year-old girl, to say nothing of separating me from my family. Many nights after I'd gone to bed, I used to guess how I might have felt if they had invited me, and lying there listening to my much-loved sister's even breathing, I was glad they hadn't. How could I have refused? How could I have gone? It always came round to the same old dilemma: I wanted to go with the Marshalls but I wanted to stay with my family too!

One weekend in that long ago spring of 1924, before the Marshalls left for China, Colonel Marshall and I took one last trip through the Shenandoah Valley to fetch Lily. We planned to make it the most momentous of all our trips, and, thank God, we were spared the knowledge we would never have another.

The countryside appeared more beautiful to me that day than ever before. The velvety mountain backdrop was deeper and bluer; the undulating hills rising up from the valley seemed breathing and alive in the vivifying warmth of the caressing spring sunlight; and the apple trees, at their peak of bloom, rained down showers of pink petals when little breezes played through their boughs. The rich-red clay of spring-plowed fields, the fresh, new-green meadows, and the blooming orchards formed enchanting geometric patterns, stitched together with Virginia "snake fences," and sprinkled all over with wild flowers.

I was feverishly gay, and Colonel Marshall responded to my keyed-up mood with indulgence and good humor. He laughed uproariously at my corny jokes, agreed enthusiastically with my every ecstatic observation on the extraordinary beauty of the valley, and joined in lustily with my off-key renditions of the lengthy repertoire of songs I'd picked up at camp and school.

"Let's sing the one about 'Awake, awake, ye dreamers,'" he suggested when I'd finally given out. "Have you forgotten that one?"

I hadn't forgotten it; I had omitted it on purpose. It was the song I had sung to him on our very first motor trip, though it had been displaced by later songs and we hadn't sung it for a long time. He'd loved it, and always doubled up with laughter when I got to the last line. The thought of that little song already filled me with nostalgia, but when he asked me I sang it readily rather than crack the glossy veneer of my gaiety.

> Awake, awake, ye dreamers,
> The cuckoo loudly calls!
> The sun shines o'er the tree tops
> That wave on mountain walls.
> Awaken, awaken,

The cuckoo loudly calls,
Awaken, awaken,
The cuckoo loudly calls,
Cuckoo, cuckoo cuckoo!

As usual, my three final "cuckoos" jagged up and down a musical scale known only to me, but instead of guffawing this time, Colonel Marshall only smiled absently and patted me on the head. I thought then with a twinge of heart that he, too, might be a little sad.

By the time the sun had reached its high-noon position in the sky, I was exhausted and grew quiet. Colonel Marshall reduced our speed, telling me that we would stop for lunch as soon as I'd located "the place." It was a good suggestion, for in spite of my emotional turmoil, I was beset with the voracious animal hunger of a disgustingly healthy twelve-year-old. I spied "the place" in less than ten minutes, and it was a gem. Carrying our picnic gear, we slid down a steep bank to a tiny grassy vale cut by a lazy little creek and almost entirely curtained from the road by the graceful, drooping green of a big willow tree.

Colonel Marshall had brought a fine sirloin steak, a delicacy usually reserved for our camp-outs, and while he found wood and built a fire, I spread out the picnic cloth and dishes (we never carried paper plates—he and Lily didn't like them). After we had finished lunch, Colonel Marshall leaned back against the willow tree, stretched out his long legs, and lit a Chesterfield, but I lay down in the warm sun and immediately fell asleep.

Sometime later, I was awakened by a not too gentle prod in the ribs; I sat up listening to Colonel Marshall chiding me, "Your Highness, arise and make it snappy; I've washed all the dishes while you rested your royal carcass."

"You did? Oh how sweet of you, I do appreciate it!" I cooed, oozing charm and favoring him with an ingratiating smile. I was trying very hard to imitate Lily but the effect was not the same. All the reaction I got was a horselaugh and the mocking rejoinder, "You'd better appreciate it, I'm not in the habit of washing dishes for able-bodied little girls."

Nevertheless, he knew that I knew he had purposely indulged me as a show of affection on our farewell excursion.

Throughout the years we occasionally joked about how he had waited on me during that trip, and the subject always came up in connection with his first tour of duty in China. Twenty-two years later, in 1946, I received a letter from him written in China at the height of his exhausting labors during his second ill-fated tour there.

The letter concluded:

> . . . My desires focus on Leesburg and Pinehurst and my wants are very simple. It's too bad you and I cannot go picnicing again down the Shenandoah Valley, this time you doing all the work while I loaf selfishly and delightfully! . . .

We hurried more than usual that long-ago afternoon, because this time we were going to pick up Lily before we spent the night, so that we could start back for Washington very early the next morning. We spent most of the time composing a comic French poem to spring on her as a joke.

Lily, unlike my college-graduate mother, had received the conventional "genteel" education of her time, with heavy emphasis on French and music. If my formerly studious mother pushed and prodded me to excel at school, my less broadly educated friend Lily did her share by urging me to become proficient in French.

"I cannot abide a fool!" Mother would storm.

"French will be invaluable to you when you're grown," Lily would preach. Then, more often than not, she would add some derogatory remark about Colonel Marshall's soldier French and terrible accent, both of which I agree were pretty bad.

I can't remember what our poem was about or how it went, except that Colonel Marshall asked me to insert a tricky fake line that only sounded like French. His plan was to get back at Lily for making fun of his own bum French.

My contribution was *pas de la rone que nous,* which rhymed with the line before it. I was so proud of it and bragged so much that Colonel Marshall told me to be quiet; he was tired of hearing how great I was.

On the way home the next day, he warned Lily to listen carefully, because we had composed a French poem together and he wanted her to find out how well I'd progressed and how mistaken she was in her snooty ideas about his lack of linguistic talent. He fired off the poem in his clipped Yankee accent with the same staccato rapidity with which he spoke English.

"Absolutely impossible to understand you," Lily laughed. "You've already flunked on your accent. Rose, you recite it."

Paying close attention to all Mademoiselle had taught me at school, I carefully spoke the poem. Lily translated the lines until she got to *pas de la rone que nous* which she stoutly maintained didn't make any sense. I thought she'd won the day for sure, but Colonel Marshall insisted it made very good sense, and said he was surprised she was unable to understand it.

"Not of the 'something' that we? Step from the 'watchama-callit' that we?" she asked hesitantly. "Maybe if I knew what *la rone* meant I could figure it out."

After she puzzled over it a while and made some pretty wild guesses, I asked Colonel Marshall to let me tell her what the line meant.

"It means: 'paddle yer own canoe'!" I burst out triumphantly.

We spent the night of our last go-to-get-Lily trip in the best hotel in town, but Colonel Marshall, practicing his customary frugality, engaged only one room.

Let me emphasize here that Colonel Marshall was frugal, not penurious. For example, he offered to give me a small Prayer-Book-and-hymnal set to commemorate my new estate as his goddaughter. I haven't seen a set like that for years. They were designed to carry to church: little leather books fitted together with a pocket arrangement on one binding. Somehow I'd learned they could be ordered in violet-colored leather instead of the usual black or white, and I was dying for those violet books. They were somewhat more expensive, and my fancy for them was both frivolous and unnecessary, but Colonel Marshall bought them for me, all gold-edged and gold-engraved to boot.

It was the same sort of thing with Lily and the Oakland. She didn't need a bigger car than the Ford, but she was crazy to have it. By the way, for that segment of the population born after 1923, which according to mass-media advertising is practically everybody but me, an Oakland was a medium-priced automobile in no way comparable to a Stutz. Oh dear, a Stutz was a big, sporty car.

The point I'm trying to make is that whenever he could Colonel Marshall indulged us in things we genuinely wanted very much, so long as we did not overstep the boundary into absurd extravagance. His frugality was a considered use of money which did not exclude pleasure, whereas penury idolizes money on the one side as fervently as profligacy does on the other. Lily and I, therefore, went along with the one hotel room as a matter of course, ordering up a cot for me. Lily had it placed in the only available spot—at the foot of the double bed which occupied the major part of the room. She said that she absolutely refused to sleep with their feet practically in my face, and she made me help her remake the bed so we would sleep head to head.

We were all pretty tired that night. Lily was always tired after her Lexington visits, and this one had been particularly strenuous. She had had to make arrangements about closing Mrs. Coles' house, as the Marshalls were taking Lily's mother to China with them. Colonel Marshall had driven all day, and I was both physically and emotionally fatigued.

We finally went to bed, after a good deal of banter over our close quarters and the resultant traffic jam when we ducked in and out of the bathroom to get undressed. There was a temporary calamity when Lily discovered she'd forgotten her toothbrush, followed by a hilarious debate, which ended when she was finally persuaded to borrow Colonel Marshall's.

"It's a real proof of true love, when I agree to use your toothbrush," she'd told him, giving up.

Nobody read that night; we were all too tired. When the lights were turned out, I settled down to go right off to sleep. But instead of sleep coming, the cold hand of an unexpected, inexplicable panic lay upon me and pressed and pressed until the chilling weight became unbearable and I cried out in terror, "Colonel Marshall, I'm scared!"

"That's ridiculous," Lily said sleepily, "we're packed in here like a tenement house and our heads aren't a half-a-foot apart."

"I don't mean I'm that kind of scared," I answered. "It's an awful feeling, way down deep."

"Here, take my hand," Colonel Marshall comforted me, "there's nothing to worry about." I reached up and clung to his hand as he talked to me.

"You've heard of growing pains kids sometimes get in their legs?" he asked me. "Well, you've got growing pains in your heart and head. Maybe I've made a mistake. Maybe you've become too dependent on Lily and me, but I don't think so. Your trouble, Rosie, is that you're frightened because we're going away. China's not the end of the world, you know; we'll be back. Believe me, you will be all right; I know you well, better than you know yourself, and I'm sure.

"You are perfectly able to stand on your own two feet; you've had a good start in life and the natural equipment to make the most of it. Remember that, Rose, and remember that nobody's worth his salt who can't face up to a crisis, who can't depend on himself and the grace of God to help him."

Warmed by his reassurance, but inarticulate from nervous exhaustion, I only replied, "Thank you, Colonel Marshall, I'll remember."

He held onto my hand until I fell asleep.

The Marshalls and I saw each other only twice more during the brief intervening time between our Shenandoah trip and their departure. They were busy with the innumerable details involved in moving to the other side of the world for three years, and I was occupied with the examinations and festivities that mark the end of the school year.

On Colonel Marshall's and Lily's last Sunday in Washington, Colonel Marshall came and fetched me so we could spend the day together. We had a picnic on the front porch at Fort Myer because all the furniture had been packed up except for one old canvas camp chair. It was a bright sunny day, and on an impulse, Lily said she wanted to take a picture of Colonel Marshall and me for remembrance's sake. He sat in the lone camp chair and I sat at his feet, smiling a big smile, because he and Lily told me they wanted a cheerful-looking picture. As a matter of fact, I behaved very well that day—no "pouts, tears and yammers." I'm glad of it, because later I disgraced myself.

They were to leave on a Tuesday or Wednesday, I'm not sure which, and Colonel Marshall promised they would drive by 2400 to tell me good-bye.

"If you telephone me before you come," I said, "I'll meet you on Crescent Street. That'll save you and Lily the trouble of coming upstairs." Crescent was a posh, seldom-traveled residential street alongside 2400. It wasn't really to save them the trouble that I'd made the suggestion, but rather because I wanted to tell them good-bye in privacy without my family gathered about us.

"I'll call you," Colonel Marshall had replied without further comment.

It was early evening when they came. The sun had gone down and Crescent Street was shrouded in the beginning dusk. I stood on the curb waiting as they drove up and stopped, but when Colonel Marshall got out of the car I just stood there looking up at him, unable to speak.

"Good-bye, Rosie," he said. "We're all set to go."

I threw a frantic glance at Lily sitting in the car, and saw that she was smiling her closed-lip, unbelievably sweet smile, but that tears were streaming down her cheeks.

I fell apart. "I can't say good-bye, I can't say good-bye, Colonel Marshall, " I wept. "So long for now, I'll see you when I'm sixteen."

I turned away from him and leaning through the open car window, I hugged and kissed Lily again and again. Then, sobbing uncontrollably, I ran back to Colonel Marshall and threw my arms around his neck.

Stroking my hair, he said, "I wish with all my heart I could spare you this hard time. I wish I could spare you hard times always. God bless you, Rosie."

He untwined my arms, quickly got into the car, and drove off into the gathering night without once looking back.

CHAPTER XVII

FROM THE SUMMER OF 1924 WHEN THE MARSHALLS AND I PARTED until the summer of 1927 when Colonel Marshall and I met again, contrary to my childish forebodings, and as Colonel Marshall had predicted, I continued "to jell" quite normally. That is to say, I blundered through the giddy maze of early adolescence, absorbed by the peculiar interests that characterized the special, kooky world of my peers. Oh lucky Marshalls, to be spared my company during those hectic, awkward, groping years!

I was not so far out in orbit that I forgot Colonel Marshall and Lily. I thought of them often. I missed them; sometimes vividly, when a chance remark or fleeting scene brought them to mind; sometimes painfully, when I longed for the warmth and security of their companionship; and sometimes vaguely, like a remembered happiness that floated formless and elusive on the edge of consciousness.

I missed them, but I seldom wrote, for the most boringly commonplace reason—procrastination stayed my pen. Actually, I recall writing only three letters, although for decency's sake, I

145

hope there were more. Of the three I remember, one was a plaintive note written on my thirteenth birthday; another, a feverish reply to a letter from Colonel Marshall demanding my version of "raising the flag," about which General Pershing had written him; and my last long letter mailed to reach the Marshalls before they left China.

The subject of my second letter, raising the flag, concerned a humiliating affair I had not intended Colonel Marshall to hear about, and my gratitude to General Pershing for helping me out at the time was shaken by the agitation of learning he'd spilled the beans to Colonel Marshall.

The flag-raising incident took place during an Armistice Day function at the Cathedral School. I was president of the freshman class (ninth grade it's called now) of the Upper School—elected, incidentally, as a dark horse compromise, a fact my best friend candidly pointed out to me immediately after my victory. At any rate, my first public duty in office fell on Armistice Day. Together with the president of the sophomore class, I was delegated to share the honor of raising Old Glory and thus introducing the patriotic doings immediately following the Bishop's opening prayer.

There was a sizeable crowd present, many of them parents, although my own mother and father were unable to come. I felt very grand, but was disappointed not to have a personal sponsor among the onlookers. It was one of the times I badly missed Colonel Marshall and Lily. They had always made a point of attending the school festivities in which I took part. I was always proud to have them there—except for the occasion in the fifth grade when Lily had collapsed into helpless laughter while watching me gallop about in a folk dance. She had tried to cover up by waving at me with wild enthusiasm whenever she'd spied me looking up into the stands, but she hadn't been aware of my surreptitious glances.

When we met afterwards, I told her indignantly I'd seen her

laughing; she immediately made up all kinds of excuses but none of them fooled me.

"It's because I'm fatter than the others," I'd sulked. "That's why you thought I looked funny."

Finally, Colonel Marshall interrupted bluntly, "Well, you're right. You are pretty round, and all that folk prancing and kicking up is not the sort of choreography best suited to your present physique."

Right away he started composing a verse. All I remember about that one is that he conjured up a very funny spectacle of me, without a trace of ridicule, so that in the end I was laughing at myself and forgave Lily.

As for Armistice Day, with no parents and no Marshalls present, I was delightfully surprised when General Pershing, flanked by a hand-picked military guard, strode across the lawn and seated himself on the front row directly opposite the flag pole. He looked very handsome and distinguished with the two soldiers standing on either side of him, and I thought proudly to myself that I had someone special there after all—and the biggest cheese, to boot!

Affecting an ostentatiously military pose for General Pershing's benefit, with the enormous flag folded in my aching, outstretched arms, I stood rigidly at attention while the Bishop advised God of the best course the Almighty should pursue. Meanwhile, a lusty wind buffeted me mercilessly, but when it capriciously lifted up my new beret and carried it off into the wide blue yonder, I never blinked an eye in spite of the sophomore president's suppressed giggles.

By the time the Bishop had completed his rhetorical invocation, the weight of the flag and the irritation of the wind, combined with my forced, ramrod posture, had so unnerved me that I recklessly over-hurried my co-partner into getting on with the raising. The result was that we affixed our national banner to the ropes the wrong way round and started it aloft unaware of

147

our mistake. We had it running smoothly up the pole when I momentarily relaxed my grip to peek at the audience for a quick reading on the stunning impression I was creating. Instantly, that wicked wind caught the heavy flag, whipping and lashing it about while we two girls pulled and tugged at the writhing, vibrating ropes, which twisted into such an appalling tangle that we couldn't move the flag. It stuck tight at half-mast, and only then, when I looked up, did I realize that the Stars and Stripes were flying upside down. It was an unorthodox but authentic distress signal all right—mine. My great moment had turned into a fiasco, and in desperation and despair I looked squarely at General Pershing. He replied to my SOS with a reassuring smile and immediately dispatched one of the soldiers to help us.

The poor guy was furious. He struggled frantically with the jerking, tangled ropes, and in spite of my burning embarrassment, his big, white-gloved hands had a hypnotic effect on me. They looked like some sort of curious mythological birds, flexing, curling, and twitching, spread-fingered around the ropes.

I came to my senses abruptly when he muttered out of the corner of his mouth, "How the hell *could* you make such a mess? I'll probably get court-martialed for not being able to raise the American flag, all on account of a couple of dumb kids."

"It's not my fault, it's hers!" the sophomore indignantly whispered back with considerable justification.

It took the soldier fully ten minutes to straighten out the lines and restring the flag, whereupon, not taking any chances, he raised it himself, to the spontaneous cheers of the relieved crowd.

General Pershing, to my regret, must have been hard up for news to have written Colonel Marshall about that miserable performance, and thus force on me the distasteful task of defending myself. I labored hard over my letter and wrote a true enough account, though heavily glossed over with colorful prose and imaginative exaggerations which I hoped would distract Colonel Marshall's attention from the unpleasant reality that I had goofed. The thousands of miles between us and our many months' separation, however, had in no way affected Colonel Marshall's sensibility to the quirks of my character.

He wrote back that he'd never heard of such a violent gale in Washington, and that based on my effusive praise, it might be a good idea to recommend the soldier for a medal of honor. Finally, he advised me to reserve my dramatic talents for use at the proper time and to pay attention to business when called upon to exercise a solemn public duty. All this he put into one short paragraph, switching abruptly to write about the remarkable endurance and speed of tough little Mongolian ponies in China. But that flag-raising stuck in his craw, for he teased me about it throughout the years, the last time only a very short while before his death.

But in general, our correspondence was sparse. I recall a long, interesting letter from Colonel Marshall reminiscent of his story-telling, in which he described the countryside around Tientsin in fascinating detail, and gave an amusing, sprightly account of the pleasant aspects of their life there. Both he and Lily sent post cards, and from time to time I would receive little gifts. But toward the middle of the second year, after an extended silence on my part, Colonel Marshall wrote a stern note warning me to pick up on my letter writing. Then, sometime during the third year, Lily sent an urgent note telling me to hurry up and write, as she was running out of excuses for me.

My affection for Colonel Marshall and Lily remained un-diminished, but I was so *busy:* going to the movies, playing on the class basketball team, running to little parties, struggling with Latin and algebra, reading anything and everything, improving my tennis, discovering Boys! And when I wasn't involved in a frenzied round of activities, or studying, or reading, I occupied myself with such useful pursuits as learning the words to the latest song hits.

When I put off writing to the Marshalls, I salved my conscience by telling myself I'd write soon; and relying heavily on the questionable merits of mental telepathy, I hoped they got the message every time I thought of them. As for the little matter of good manners, of a show of appreciation for all they had done for me—ah well, my sins of omission found me out, and I brought down on my head Colonel Marshall's third and last punishment.

Lily had promised to bring me a fur coat from China—a luxury I could hardly imagine being mine—and during the years they were in China, she had assembled a collection of fine skins that she intended to have made into my coat. Colonel Marshall encouraged her at first, but as the months went by with no word from me, he withdrew his support. He told me later that during their last year there, he advised Lily to drop her plan of bringing me a fur coat; if I was so lazy and inconsiderate, he announced, he'd be damned if he would be a party to giving me such a fine present. I suspect it was this severe decision that prompted Lily's futile tip-off to me, because Colonel Marshall reported she'd wept and told him all adolescents were careless and unconcerned and that he was hard-hearted and too strict. He reminded Lily that he had given me fair warning some time ago, and that was the end of it—no letters, no coat.

So he had warned me, but letters compare poorly with the spoken word, with face-to-face communication. For my part, correspondence, at least personal correspondence, though convenient, is never more than a partially satisfactory substitute for conversation. The revelations which occur when people talk together—the expression of the voice, eyes, and face—generate a clearer understanding and produce more effective results than is possible on paper. The personality that does come through a letter is canned, and regardless of how distinctive it may be, its full, true flavor is missing.

Months passed after I received Colonel Marshall's warning, and weeks after I received Lily's, before I finally wrote back. The nearer the time approached for the Marshalls to return home, the more forcefully they occupied my thoughts, and I wrote simply because I wanted to, not from any sense of obligation or contrition. My letter was blithely free from apologies or excuses, and because the mood had struck me, I spent a lot of time and had a lot of fun composing it.

My efforts paid off in some measure, because Colonel Marshall praised the letter and told me that it was so entertaining he'd read it aloud at a dinner party. My masterpiece, however, didn't turn the trick in regard to the fur coat. Colonel Marshall enjoyed the letter, but although he forgave my negligence, his judgment on it held firm. I didn't get the coat.

The point of Colonel Marshall's retribution was not lost on me. But although I never told him, the loss of the fur coat didn't really matter much, probably because I never saw it. It was like a pleasant dream, nice to think about but not to be confused with reality. When the Marshalls returned, I never once thought about the coat. There were too many more pressing concerns demanding my attention.

First of all, Lily was ill and went almost immediately to Walter Reed Hospital. As her health had always been poor, I assumed that her sojourn in the Orient had probably taxed her strength and that she'd be up and around soon. Nevertheless, I was worried about her, and genuinely disappointed that she would not be with Colonel Marshall for our reunion.

Colonel Marshall came to see me one June evening, having previously telephoned that afternoon when I was out. On my return, Mother's announcement that he was coming so soon plunged me into a turmoil of conflicting emotions: an almost painful joy at the prospect of seeing him, and a terrible fear that he wouldn't like me any more now that I was practically grown up. Nervous and upset, but unwilling to divulge my secret feelings, I agonized and stormed about what I should wear until Celeste impatiently put an end to my histrionics with the obvious solution: "Dummy, wear your new blue-and-white-checked taffeta. You know it's the best thing you've got."

So I shut up and stewed silently for the rest of the day. After dinner, which I couldn't eat, we went out into the lobby to wait for Colonel Marshall who was coming directly from Walter Reed. My father and Tom went straight upstairs as usual, and I wished that Mother and Sis had gone with them. They made me feel even more uncomfortable and self-conscious, but to suggest that they leave was out of the question. It would most certainly have offended Mother and probably would have irked my sister. We sat down in our customary place, and Mother began talking about how surprised Colonel Marshall would be to see how much I'd changed when, to my great relief, she was interrupted by one of her friends who stopped by to chat with her. Churning with apprehension, I turned to my sister and finally admitted that I was scared to death. She said I was silly and began enumerating all of the reasons why I shouldn't worry, while I listened unconvinced and tried to compose myself by tracing the outline of the carpet design with my eyes.

All of a sudden, Colonel Marshall was there.

"Hello, Rosie!"

Almost numb, I managed to stand up and he bent over and kissed me.

"I'm so glad to see you, Colonel Marshall," I murmured stiffly.

The four of us started walking toward the elevator, Colonel Marshall talking animatedly to Mother and Celeste while I remained as silent and outgoing as a stone. Riding up in the elevator, he scrutinized me with undisguised frankness—how clearly I see him now—his head tilted slightly forward, his eyes amused, kind, inquiring, vigilant.

Oh Lord! I thought, he sees I'm scared, and I blushed, but forced myself to smile back at him because I knew he'd be disgusted if I pulled a shy lowering-of-the-eyes stunt.

"You've grown very tall," he said to me, and to Mother, "Ah, she's not a little girl any longer."

"Oh yes she is!" Mother assured him.

Ordinarily, I would have resented Mother's opinion that I was still a child, but at that moment I was relieved and grateful.

"No," Colonel Marshall disagreed, "she's almost a young lady."

I felt like a boob standing there while they discussed the degree of maturity I had reached, and before I knew it, burst out in annoyance, "Well gosh, Colonel Marshall, I'm still me, just a lot more jelled! Let's talk about something else."

"Well gosh!" Colonel Marshall replied laughing, "Hello, Rose! I was wondering how long you could keep up that demure silence."

We went to our apartment where my father and brother courteously greeted Colonel Marshall; then we all sat in a circle making polite conversation: "Did you enjoy China? Do tell us how Lily is. It's wonderful to have you back."

It was a strain for me, and in spite of the butterflies swooping around in my stomach, I was relieved when Colonel Marshall invited me to walk over to Eighteenth Street and Columbia Road for a milk shake.

We started walking up Sixteenth Street and I timidly ventured a few perfunctory remarks, but Colonel Marshall did not press me to talk. He talked himself, starting off with little jokes about how Lily would have to adjust to life without her Number One boy.

Half forgetting my self-consciousness, I asked curiously, "What's a Number One boy?"

He told me, then branched out into a description of their house and servants in China.

My shyness began melting by the time we'd reached the French Embassy at the end of the block. Colonel Marshall's behavior was so natural and pleasant, so identical with the Colonel Marshall I remembered, that I thawed rapidly; indeed, before we'd gone three or four blocks he had put us back on the old, warm, familiar relationship. I was completely at ease, which is not to say I wasn't still concerned about Colonel Marshall's predilection for children, and it continued to bother me that my own lost childhood might affect his interest in me. I wanted to know how I stood, one way or the other, so I asked him outright if he would still want me around as much now that I was so old, almost sixteen. I was confident he'd understand that my question was asked seriously, and I knew that he would answer me directly and tell me if our friendship was destined to fade.

He did not make fun of my assumption that I was "so old"; he merely agreed with me that I had left childhood behind. He went on to say, implying a lack of understanding on my part, that he and Lily had not considered me a toy or a sprite, but a human being; and laughing, he assured me they had no intention of dropping me because I was not a female Peter Pan.

"But joking aside," he said soberly, "personality doesn't change with the years, and yours is your insurance for a lively life. Character though," he continued, "deepens, expands, and develops with increased experience and broadening of interests and knowledge. At least it should, and I hope yours will, and in the right direction."

After our reunion, which turned out so happily for me, we had little opportunity to see each other during the rest of the summer. Colonel Marshall was working hard, which was not unusual, but Lily's condition did not improve. She stayed on in the hospital, which meant that Colonel Marshall divided his time between the office and Walter Reed. When he did have an hour or so to spare, he'd telephone me and I would meet him on Crescent Street to go for a brief drive. Each time, I asked if today he could take me to see Lily, but he always put me off, saying that she needed complete rest and quiet and I must wait a while longer. So Lily and I would send each other messages and Colonel Marshall and I would make plans for the happy time when she would leave the hospital.

We looked forward to the years ahead with pleasant anticipation. Colonel Marshall had been assigned as an instructor at the Army War College, and he and I enthusiastically agreed the quarters there were perfect for Lily. I knew how lovely those big white-columned houses were, because Mother's friends, Colonel and Mrs. Gilbert Stewart, had been stationed at the War College, and I had gone with Mother on several occasions to visit with the Stewart children. Lily would have a far more spacious house than the one at Fort Myer, where she could arrange to advantage all the oriental treasures she had brought back from China.

Sometime in August Lily underwent an operation for a thyroid disturbance. After her operation I stopped asking Colonel Marshall to let me see her or even how she was getting along, although I continued to send her messages. I didn't dare ask him how she was, because I'd heard repeatedly in the lobby that her illness was extremely serious. I didn't want to show too much alarm, because Colonel Marshall never admitted to me, or to himself either, I'm sure, that Lily would not get well.

One evening in September shortly after my sixteenth birthday, he telephoned in high spirits to invite me for dinner.

"It's a celebration!" he said.

At dinner he told me the good news: Lily had made such a splendid recovery from her operation, he'd been assured that in a week or so she would be released from the hospital at last. We had a wonderfully happy, though hurried time, and afterwards Colonel Marshall dropped me off on his way to Walter Reed.

"In a week or so, she'll be coming home!" he had rejoiced.

In a week or so Lily was dead. A blood clot hit her heart killing her instantly. In the midst of writing a letter to her mother the pen had fallen from her hand, and the last word she wrote was "George . . ."

When I first heard about her last word, it sounded too improbable and romantic to believe, but it was true—Colonel Marshall told me so. On reflection, however, the phenomenon, stripped of sentimentality though still remarkably suitable, did not appear so miraculous. The pervading interest of Lily's life was "George." She had no hobbies; she was unable to participate in sports, loathed bridge, had no interest in cats or dogs or any kind of pet, and possessed little intellectual drive. Even her interest and delight in the things she bought in China were George-directed. The furniture and nicknacks were not purchased for the embellishment of *her* home, but for *their* home. They had friends, plenty of them, but Lily didn't care a whit whether or not they admired her taste; she decorated their home exclusively for their own comfort and pleasure.

Dear, warm-hearted, loving, home-maker Lily, so utterly charming, beautiful, vivacious—and all these gifts she gave of extravagantly to "George." She died as she had lived, with George Marshall on her mind and in her heart.

❧ CHAPTER XVIII ❧

MOTHER TOLD ME ABOUT LILY'S DEATH. SHE TOLD ME GENTLY, MAKING a genuine effort to soften the blow.

"You mustn't feel too bad," she'd consoled. "In many ways Lily is fortunate. She died happy. She never suspected, had no inkling death was at hand; why, she was planning on going home soon."

"The next day!" I answered, dry-eyed and unbelieving. "I mean today, she was coming home today. Mother, I never saw her again."

Mother replied it was better I hadn't seen her again, that I would always remember her as she was before she went to China, beautiful and fresh "as a Lily." "Everybody will remember her that way; Lily will never grow old, never lose her beauty."

"But her *personality* wouldn't have changed!" I cried. "Oh poor Colonel Marshall, poor Colonel Marshall!" I repeated over and over, and turning away, walked to the window where I stood looking out at nothing. Mother wisely left me there alone.

No one close to me had ever died before. Lily was dead. I tried to think about her but I couldn't even remember her face. I tried to imagine Colonel Marshall without her, but I couldn't do that either.

Mother and I went to the funeral at Arlington National Cemetery; it rained; there were a lot of people standing around, many of them weeping; Colonel Marshall got out of the car holding Mrs. Coles' arm, supporting her; he stood bareheaded with his back to me; he had a fresh haircut—how inappropriate, I thought, to notice. Lily is dead. The graveside service ended; Colonel Marshall turned and escorted Mrs. Coles back to the car. He passed by me looking straight ahead, and when I saw his face, strange and expressionless, I wept for the first time since Lily died.

A few days after Lily's funeral, Colonel Marshall telephoned to ask me to spend the afternoon with him. While I waited for him to fetch me, I resolved that no matter how difficult it might be, I would not weep, because I hoped that for once I could help him. Always before he had been the one to help me.

He picked me up in a chauffeur-driven car, a Government automobile which he seldom used, and never before with me. He didn't smile or get out when he greeted me; otherwise he behaved quite naturally, explaining he was only using this car for a few days.

"Good idea," I replied, getting in, hoping my voice sounded normal.

"You all right?" I asked almost steadily as I sat down beside him.

"Yes," he answered evenly, "I'm all right, thanks."

That was all he said; he just sat there silently, looking out of the window as we drove down Sixteenth Street.

What could I say, what could I say to help? Better be quiet, I decided, than stammer out how sorry I was, how much I mourned Lily too. He'd known that without my telling him.

After a while, he turned toward me, unmasked, making no attempt to hide his wretchedness. His face was haggard and drawn with grief; his eyes lifeless, clouded by such desolate and utter sadness that my heart contracted, and I knew I was seeing in him a sorrow as profound and awesome as is possible for a man to bear.

The compassion and pain I felt were too deep for expression. Helplessly, I murmured, "Colonel Marshall, Colonel Marshall!" and impulsively took his hand and held it tightly in both of mine.

When he spoke, his voice was scarcely audible, on the narrow verge of breaking: "Rosie, I'm so lonely, so *lonely*."

No wonder I couldn't imagine him without Lily. Nothing in my whole life experience had equipped me to envision Colonel Marshall as I saw him that day.

If Lily were only here, I thought, she'd know what to do, and suddenly, it occurred to me it was good Lily couldn't see him now; it would make her miserable to know she was the cause of this ravaging unhappiness.

"Colonel Marshall," I began, trying to hit the firm, gentle note I'd heard Lily use when he'd been worried or discouraged, "I know how lonely you must be and I'm sorrier than I can possibly tell you, but don't you see, you mustn't be so awfully sad? All Lily ever wanted in her whole life was for you to be happy and have a great career. Somehow, it doesn't seem fair to give up when she's not here."

It was an inadequate attempt—worse than that, it was trite— but I didn't know it then. How many variations of that little speech I've heard since: "So-and-so wouldn't want you to such- and-such if he were alive." I know now no words can unlock the impregnable, lonely prison of a fresh and terrible grief. However comforting it may be to have the sympathy of others, in the end the prisoner must liberate himself.

About all I accomplished was to let Colonel Marshall know I was trying to help him, for I'm sure he understood I didn't realize I was singing a stale old tune.

"Thank you, Rose," he answered, his voice steady again,

"You're right and I appreciate your thoughtful lecture." He even smiled a little, and then abruptly asked me how I liked my new school.

Here was my cue—divert his mind from this new painful emptiness. For the rest of the afternoon I talked about the adventures and changes encountered in a different school. Daddy was right, I told him, to shift me to Holton Arms where I could be "me" instead of Celeste's younger sister, which had become my identity with most of the teachers at Cathedral. I described my new friends and told him we were going to play field hockey for fall athletics.

"Holton doesn't have its own athletic field like Cathedral, I rattled on. "We'll play in the park down near the Washington Monument. Why don't you come watch us one day after work ?"

By the time we returned to 2400 I'd told him more about Holton than I realized I knew myself.

The next weekend Colonel Marshall took me to some house to help him sort out Lily's clothes. It may have been their quarters at the War College, but I don't remember anything about the house, only the painful business of going through Lily's things. Her dresses were too mature for me, but Colonel Marshall gave me mountains of her exquisite Chinese hand-embroidered lingerie, ropes of cultured pearls, a floor-length white bunny fur stole, various other trinkets and accessories, and a short, orange, Chinese silk wrap with a printed border of bright blue flowers and blue butterflies scattered here and there. He was especially interested in the wrap, and made me try it on and hold out my arms.

"Lily designed it," he told me. "When you raise your arms the jacket looks like a butterfly. She used to wear it pouring tea." And smiling wistfully on remembering her little vanity, he added, "She always managed to reach for things so the butterfly sleeves would show."

I laid out Lily's dresses in neat piles, daytime and evening, summer and winter, and the room was filled with the familiar fragrance of her delicate perfume. It was a hard time for me, harrowing for Colonel Marshall. I was terribly worried about him and on the way home got up the courage to make a suggestion I'd been thinking about all week.

"Colonel Marshall," I began, "it seems to me you'd be better off away from Washington. I'd miss you something awful, you know that, but if you could get yourself transferred somewhere you and Lily have never been together, well, wouldn't it be better?"

"It's a good idea," he answered. "As a matter of fact, that's what I've already decided to do. It'll take a while to arrange though, so I'll probably be here most of the fall."

We saw a great deal of each other that fall. Colonel Marshall accepted my invitation to watch our hockey games, and showed up toward the end of the game nearly every time we played. Afterwards, we would drive around a little while until it was time for me to return to 2400. I knew he came for me because he dreaded going home to an empty house, so I made a special effort to be entertaining; it wasn't really too difficult for not once since the day we met after Lily's funeral did he allow himself another overt show of grief. But grief was always there, seeping through, even though on occasions we laughed together as we used to in the old days. During that fall I didn't dare mention Lily's name, nor did he, and this unnatural restraint was the clearest evidence of the sorrow that hovered over us. But Colonel Marshall set the pace, making it easier for us both, so that although I know he was never free from the pain of Lily's absence, I, who had grown used to her absence during the past three years, sometimes callously forgot.

One afternoon I nearly scared him out of his wits. I asked him to let me drive his car, and when he demurred, I told him with all the assurance of youth that I'd been driving for ages and he didn't realize how good I was.

"How long have you been driving?" he asked with disparaging skepticism.

"The first time when I was fourteen," I replied proudly, and bragged that I'd driven Robbie's old Model-T Ford out to the Chevy Chase Club when he and Sis had gone off in her car and left me. Robbie was my sister's heavy beau.

I knew how to drive the Model T because I'd watched Colonel Marshall drive so often, but I fibbed, "I knew exactly what to do because of that long lecture you gave me the time the truck backed down on us."

That did it. He moved over and said, "Go ahead, let's see."

All went well until we hit Dupont Circle. There was no underpass then as there is now, and cars came at us from all directions while I drove around the circle, blithely oblivious to horns blasting, brakes screeching, and infuriated drivers cursing at us.

"My God!" Colonel Marshall shouted, "stop the car, you'll kill us both!"

I pulled over and asked him indignantly what he was so nervous about. I'd never even gotten a ticket yet.

"That may be," he replied, "but you won't drive me again for a long time. Obviously, my fine lecture didn't get through! And your performance only proves to me further that traffic tickets are not necessarily an indication of a poor driver. If they were, you could paper your bedroom with 'em. Take an expert driver like me. Did you know I got a ticket the other day?"

"You!" I laughed.

I can't remember what minor violation he'd incurred, but I do remember the story he told me about the policeman who'd stopped him. Colonel Marshall said all the cop had to do was explain the violation and write a ticket; instead, he had poured forth a stream of insults and abusive language.

Usually, when Colonel Marshall recounted one of his adventures, no matter what its nature, whether amusing, exciting, or of great or minor importance, he didn't merely tell it—he was apt to act it out, relive it. So he did with the incident of the policeman, and as usual, I was his stooge.

I sat there playing the part of the luckless cop, while Colonel Marshall fixed his eyes on me and said, "Arrest me at once! Take me to the police station. I *demand* to be taken to the station now, this moment."

Oh boy! That withering, censorious, cold-fire look, that decisive, level, authoritative voice; needless to say, they went to the station then and there! Colonel Marshall paid his fine and, insisting that the policeman accompany him, went to his superior and reported the officer's outrageous behavior.

"Did the cop get fired?" I asked.

"No," he replied, "I argued against firing him. What good would that have done, bust a man's career, maybe a fellow with a family? Mine was the first complaint about him and unless he's a fool, I taught him a lesson. If he's a fool, he'll destroy himself anyway; if not, he learned something. I made it perfectly clear that a public servant can never, under any circumstance, abuse his authority to insult, intimidate, or threaten a private citizen."

❧ CHAPTER XIX ❧

ON WEEKENDS, COLONEL MARSHALL AND I WOULD EITHER GO HORSE-back riding or watch the football games at the Episcopal High School in Alexandria, Virginia. He delighted in those boys' games, and liked walking up and down the side lines where he could see the plays close up. I'd trail along beside him, listening to his running comments, for woe unto me if I was not qualified after-wards to discuss the game play by play. Colonel Marshall never lost his enthusiasm for football. Years later, he often used the game to illustrate the necessity for efficient teamwork.

"You can't win a war," he'd say, "if the quarterback doesn't call the right plays . . . We've got a strong dependable line . . . Only a fool would send in players when they're not in top shape, the game would be lost, and worse, the players too . . . It takes a whole team working together to win, no one man can do it alone. . . ."

On our horseback rides, Colonel Marshall started two discus-sions which we kept up for years. One was about poetry, and the other, of all things, was an argument about Alexander Hamilton and Thomas Jefferson. He began them, I think, because either one was a topic we could chew on for a whole ride without mentioning Lily, who had always figured one way or another in everything we said or did. He kept them going in later years, I believe, as a diversion, an antidote for the exhaustion brought on by the multitudinous problems he was continuously called upon to deal with.

One afternoon following one of our long trotting sessions, when we had slowed our horses to a walk, Colonel Marshall asked me straight out of the blue, "Do you still like poetry?"

"Sure, why?" I asked in return.

"Once I advised you to hold on to your regard for it," he said, and momentarily stopping his horse, he looked at me earnestly and demanded, "I want you to tell me what you like about poetry, tell me why you enjoy it."

What an elusive target to hit! I hesitated so long before replying that he asked impatiently if I were deaf.

"For Pete's sake, Colonel Marshall," I exploded, irritated and perplexed, "you've asked something almost impossible to answer and you know you've always got to have a capsule answer. I'm trying to figure out how to begin."

"Oh! In that case, take your time," he replied amiably.

Finally, I admitted helplessly, "I don't know why I like poetry, I just do."

"Very informative, a fine beginning," he observed derisively.

"It's honestly very hard to explain why poetry appeals to me," I defended myself, "because it's a kind of feeling. Maybe I mean poets express what I feel better than I can myself and they make simple ordinary things not simple and ordinary; for example . . ."

I didn't know a lot of poetry by heart, but I'd been enchanted a few days before by Keats' sonnet "To Sleep," so I quoted the first four lines, which were not only all I'd memorized but all that were suitable to make my point.

Oh soft embalmer of the still midnight,
Shutting, with fingers careful and benign,
Our gloom-pleas'd eyes, embower'd with light,
Enshaded with forgetfulness divine . . .

"That's a peachy example of what I mean. It's Keats, and he's used a figure of speech in beautiful, rhyming, seeing-feeling language, lovely soothing sounds that say, 'Oh Min, this bed feels good to I!' In other words, everybody likes to rest and to go to sleep after a tiring or troublesome day—that's simple and ordinary; but the way Keats says it, the whole business means more or means deeper—well, it sinks in all through you."

That's all I recall of my first, stumbling, poorly articulated observations on poetry. Colonel Marshall listened attentively that day and on all subsequent occasions throughout the years when we, or rather I, talked about poetry, for he rarely contributed more than a brief question or neutral comment. Yet, when I'd make a move to change the subject, he would object. As I grew older and some poetry became more and some less meaningful, my "dissertations" became somewhat more profound and lucid, but not much. I am in no sense a knowledgeable critic.

Colonel Marshall had a reasoning, well-ordered mind; and poetry is the language of emotion, as distinct from emotionalism, which he abhorred, and of imagination, as distinct from imaginative planning, in which he excelled. Perhaps poetry never quite came into focus for him; I don't know, I'm guessing. I do know he never disparaged poets as dreamy kooks, or dismissed poetry as visionary nonsense, which is the contemptuous attitude of those who refuse to admit the value of something they cannot understand or enjoy. Although I can't say whether or not he was a "right reader" of poetry, certainly Colonel Marshall realized that it is "charged with meaning." Otherwise, why would he have shown so much interest in the aspects and attributes of poetry? Why would he have encouraged me as a child to foster my interest in it?

If Colonel Marshall did not see poetry in perspective, his view of history was sharp and clear—especially, but by no means exclusively, of American history. History was his preferred reading, and more particularly, biography. I believe that he would have been in agreement with Carlyle's premise that ". . . history is the essence of innumerable biographies . . . universal history, the history of what man has accomplished in this world is at the bottom the history of the great men who have worked here . . ."

As Colonel Marshall put it, "Biography often contributes to a clearer understanding of the period as well as of the man."

He knew that Jefferson was my hero, and he might have chosen to start a debate on those two founding fathers, Thomas Jefferson and Alexander Hamilton, because at sixteen the scope of my historical knowledge was limited. He was also aware that I had been nurtured on Virginia history in which my ancestors had played a creditable part, and he used our discussion to debunk any preconceived ideas of mine that through an accident of birth I could rest on someone else's bygone laurels.

"Your much-touted Virginia ancestors do not entitle *you* to any plaudits. You have to earn your own and don't you forget it!"

It would be tedious to rehash in its entirety our intermittent over-the-years' argument. A few samples, however, might be of interest insofar as they reveal Colonel Marshall's strict and logical adherence to facts (as they were known to us), and his patient effort to coax me away from a prejudiced attitude of unreasoning antipathy to Hamilton and idolization of Jefferson.

If I indulged in an impassioned speech on Jefferson's versatility of mind: his lofty ideals; his intellectual and artistic superiority manifest in his wide knowledge and appreciation of philosophy, literature, music, art, and architecture; or his remarkable understanding of science and agriculture, Colonel Marshall would reply, "Hamilton had a brilliant dynamic mind. He was a far-sighted realist."

When I extolled Jefferson's modest dignity and gracious manner, denigrating Hamilton as a conceited, power-happy, would-be
despot, Colonel Marshall would answer matter-of-factly that we
were not discussing personalities but how each man's genius,
though very different in brand, had left its mark on our country.

"But you must admit," I once cried in exasperation, "that
Jefferson is the central figure of American democracy! Surely his
ideas of self-government, his defense of the common man against
oppression—any oppression, economic, political, religious, intellectual—is what you and I stand for. We don't subscribe to Hamilton's government by 'the rich, the powerful, and the able.'
Abraham Lincoln wasn't rich or very powerful either before he
became President, but who questions his ability?"

"If it hadn't been for Hamilton," Colonel Marshall countered,
"the common man would have been oppressed in every area."

"What!" I exclaimed, "Hamilton help the common people,
the 'great beast'?"

"Certainly," he replied. "Without Hamilton's financial genius
the country would have gone bankrupt and fallen into chaos,
probably ruin. His fight to establish the bank of the United States
and his brilliant plan for paying off debts undoubtedly kept the
country from going under. Without Hamilton there wouldn't
have been a Republic where the common man or anyone else
could enjoy Jefferson's freedoms. The United States would have
been ripe for the picking."

"When you were a kid," he reminded me, "you'd get unreasonable and irritable if your lunch was late. What would you do
if you were ever downright hungry? You can imagine the effects
of threatened or actual starvation, and hunger is only a single
aspect of destitution, and destitution breeds desperation."

Once I tried to trap him, rile him up and shatter his everlast-
ing calm. I began by saying he was always harping on his
precious rule not to rely on what he called "Virginianism," and
followed it up with the snide insinuation that it was highly

probably his opinion about Hamilton was colored by his own ancestral connection with John Marshall. He did not get mad. He burst out laughing and ridiculed me, saying, "You must be getting hard up for arguments to throw a wild punch like that one."

"Oh course I subscribe to John Marshall's and Hamilton's interpretation of the Constitution," he announced emphatically. "Do you agree with Jefferson's strict construction of it?"

"Not really," I admitted sullenly, "at least not the way things have turned out. I know the 'implied powers' interpretation is more practical, more reasonable—oh dammit—essential!"

It was very frustrating. I admired John Marshall, and all that I'd accomplished was to fire up my own temper instead of kindling Colonel Marshall's. In addition, I'd struck a blow for the Federalists.

I could never win; it was worse than our Russian Bank games when I was a little girl. I thought that I surely had him when I denounced Hamilton's whiskey tax as a crafty device to expose the common people for the anarchists he claimed them to be. Triumphantly, I asserted that the Whiskey Rebellion had served to strengthen the chains of money and power Hamilton had forged between his rich cohorts and the Federal Government. But no victory here; Colonel Marshall countered that I'd ignored a pertinent fact. The Whiskey Rebellion, he argued, might also have proved the necessity for a strong central government, and it demonstrated that no group of malcontents who happened not to like a law could rise up and successfully defy governmental authority.

Thus, our debate went on and on, back and forth, touching almost every angle of the old Jefferson-Hamilton controversy. Colonel Marshall had unshakable patience, and he stubbornly refused to be led off-track by my repeated emphasis on Jefferson's moral superiority and diversified talents.

For instance, I depended on my argument that Jefferson was a man of his time and culture. Briefly, my contention was that Jefferson could not have anticipated the fantastic growth of population and technology, and after he had extended our borders from the Mississippi to the Pacific—an accomplishment I made the most of—he believed that there would be ample land to go around for literally ages to come. Hamilton, I conceded, caught on better to the significance of the Industrial Revolution, but I was not convinced he had promoted manufacturing for the good of the nation so much as for the glory of Hamilton.

"Jefferson was for a grand new experiment, a viable republic; for a great step forward toward a better life for all mankind. Hamilton was for Hamilton," I insisted.

"Hamilton for Hamilton or not," Colonel Marshall replied, "our economic growth has proved pretty successful. After all these years, I will remind you again we are discussing the marks left on our country by the genius of each man, no matter how disparate their genius was."

Of course I couldn't "win" the debate, because there was no question of win or lose. But I was frustrated by Colonel Marshall's rigid impartiality. Not once did he deny a single attribution of Jefferson, nor defend a single fault of Hamilton. His point throughout our debates was the fallacy of using subjective, biased standards in assessing the two men's different contributions to the country.

CHAPTER XX

In the fall of 1927, Colonel Marshall succeeded in getting himself transferred out of Washington to Fort Benning, Georgia. He arrived at his new post about two months after Lily died, and a few weeks before his forty-seventh birthday on December 31. Lily's death had terminated nearly twenty-six years of a marriage. Colonel Marshall had spent his entire adult life happily married to Lily, but there stretched out before him a whole new life crowded with unbelievable demands and undreamed-of achievements. In store for him too was a second wife who would give him the sympathetic companionship he so desperately needed. Colonel Marshall was not cut out for the bachelor's life; "home and hearth" was his natural habitat.

After he left Washington, I returned on a full-time basis to the pursuits customary for my age, and was soon absorbed in my friends and our activities. Colonel Marshall and I corresponded regularly, however, and in May he sent a letter inviting me for an extended visit with him at Fort Benning.

"Be sure to bring your riding clothes and bathing suit," he wrote, "and remember it's very hot down here."

Mother outfitted me with several pairs of new white riding breeches, new black boots, a couple of bathing suits, and enough suitable dresses to make a creditable appearance for Colonel Marshall. Thus equipped, I boarded the train for Georgia the first evening after school let out.

I remember that train ride vividly. Air conditioning had not yet been installed on railroad trains, so I lay in my berth with the window open to the soot sifting in all over me. But it was not the usual grime which marked that journey apart from any other I have taken. It was the fresh, sweet fragrance of new-blooming roses and honeysuckle wafted through the window on a balmy, early-summer breeze. Perhaps that lovely scent made a special impression on me because roses and honeysuckle had bloomed in profusion around the country house where I had spent the earliest years of my childhood. At any rate, half-asleep, half-awake as I was, it transformed my green-curtained cubicle into an enchanted garden.

My train was due to arrive in Columbus, Georgia, sometime the following morning, but we were held up by a minor wreck ahead of us some twenty-five miles or so short of Columbus. After several hours of sitting out in the middle of nowhere, I began to be nervous and impatient and could get absolutely no satisfaction from questioning the conductor. The delay had put him in a surly mood, inducing him to parry my queries with the indifferent double talk peculiar to harassed employees charged with answering questions when they don't know the answers, and with placating customers whom they aren't the least bit interested in placating.

"It won't be long now, Miss; at least, I don't think so, though I can't be sure. It might take two or three hours more, or then again, it mightn't be more'n a half hour."

172

I had finished my book and was reduced to scanning the ads in an unfamiliar small-town newspaper when I heard a little commotion in the car and looked up. There stood Colonel Marshall, all smiles.

"Here you are at last!" he exclaimed. "I've walked through at least eight cars and it took some doing to find the train in the first place!"

"Boy, am I glad to see you!" I cried jumping up and giving him a big hug.

"Well, let's get your bags and get out of here, and don't forget your hat and pocketbook or any other belongings you've strewn around. I know you, so check carefully, but make it snappy."

He grabbed my suitcases while I scooped up my other things —all except for one glove—and we hurried off the train. We alighted on the opposite side of the car from where I'd been sitting and looking around, I spotted Colonel Marshall's car parked some distance beyond a freshly plowed field. I was dismayed when we started cutting across the broken ground, because I was wearing brand-new shoes and Colonel Marshall, always a fast walker, chose to break into double time in spite of the fact that he was carrying my heavy bags.

"Hey," I complained, "have a heart! I've got on high heels and it's rough going on this old field."

He laughed. "Stop fussing," he said. "I didn't come all this way to listen to you holler at me." He was exuberantly gay, and inordinately proud of himself for having found his way over a maze of back country roads to the train stalled far out in the boondocks.

"Were you surprised to see me?" he called back as I hobbled panting after him.

"Not really," I replied casually.

He was piqued. "I didn't notice anybody coming for any of the other passengers. Why weren't you surprised?"

173

"Because you can do anything!" I cried triumphantly.

"Well, thanks," he laughed. "I haven't heard such extravagant praise for some time."

On our way to Fort Benning, he informed me that his sister, Marie, had arrived the day before. It hadn't occurred to him, he told me smiling, but Marie had reminded him "it wouldn't do" when he wrote her I was coming to visit him, so she was there to act as chaperone.

"*Chaperone* for *us*?" I asked in astonishment. "How silly!"

"Have you forgotten," he replied, "that in three months you will be seventeen? Wake up! You're grown up now."

Of course I hadn't forgotten my age, and I had the usual complement of beaux (boyfriends, how I hate that term) for a girl my age, but I thought the idea of a chaperone for Colonel Marshall and me was absurd, though I didn't press the issue.

As a matter of fact, I was curious to meet Marie, because I'd never met any members of his family. I knew that Marie had married a Mister Singer a year or so after Colonel Marshall and Lily were married, and that she lived in Pennsylvania. The Marshalls had sometimes talked about her, and my impression was that they were fond of Marie; but as far as I know, she never visited them during the time I knew them in Washington.

Colonel Marshall's mother had lived at the Grafton Hotel in Washington off and on, but I'd only seen her once, and then just her face framed in the hotel window; it bore a strong resemblance to Colonel Marshall's, or vice versa. Occasionally, I'd been in the car when Colonel Marshall visited her, but he never took me up with him. One afternoon when I was very young we were on our way to Fort Myer, when he said that he was going to stop by to take his mother a carton of cigarettes. Few ladies smoked back then, and no old ladies that I knew of; smoking was a pose affected mainly by "flappers." When I expressed surprise that his mother smoked, he told me that the doctor had prescribed smoking for her nerves, and I wasn't to say anything about it to anyone. I haven't until now when it doesn't matter anymore.

Colonel Marshall's father had died before I was born, and he and his elder brother were not on friendly terms; indeed, I never laid eyes on his brother. I had heard a lot of rumors about the falling out between them, so one day I asked Colonel Marshall, "Is it true you and your brother got mad at each other because he was in love with Lily too and you won out?"

"Certainly not," he answered coldly. "You know perfectly well we were never congenial, and that Stuart opposed everything I wanted to do, including my marriage to Lily which had absolutely nothing to do with him. I've told you before he thought I was too young and too poor to marry. He attempted to run my life and was unpleasant about it, but when he made unkind, unfair remarks about Lily, I cut him off my list."

We never mentioned his brother again.

When we arrived at Colonel Marshall's quarters at Fort Benning, the first thing I noticed was a gigantic magnolia tree near the house. It was in full bloom, laden with huge, creamy, heavily scented blossoms. The house itself was wood, one-storied and rambling, with a fairly large glassed-in porch, at one front corner.

Marie met us at the door and greeted me with informal, friendly directness. "Hello Rose," she said amiably, "I am Marie." She looked very much like Colonel Marshall—the same blunt nose and blond hair, except hers was beginning to gray. She was a little plump and considerably shorter than he; homelier too, I thought, or maybe she just looked homelier because I didn't know her so well. But I liked her face; it was intelligent, with crinkly smile lines around her eyes and mouth revealing her pleasant disposition. If we don't get along, I decided, it'll be my fault.

Colonel Marshall was keyed-up and gay, insisting on taking me all over the house before I could even take off my hat. How sharply I was reminded of my introduction to the Fort Myer house—of Lily showing me around just as he was doing now! Finally, like Lily, he threw open the door to my room. When he opened my door, such a wave of flowery perfume billowed out and flooded through the hallway that involuntarily I exclaimed, "Whew!" and peered curiously into the room. It was crammed full with vases of cape jasmine and magnolias; every table, the dresser, even the window ledge was adorned with flowers.

"George, do you think perhaps you've put too many flowers in Rose's room?" Marie suggested.

"Oh no!" I objected, and fought back the tears threatening to come. "It's perfectly beautiful. I love it!"

It was not only the "Grand Tour" which had reminded me of Lily, nor the innumerable pictures of her that were about; I saw her in the close imitation of her distinctive taste which was in evidence everywhere. It was not Colonel Marshall's house, but their house. And now I had arrived, his closest contact with Lily, and he had joyously prepared my room in memory of her. I glanced up at his happy, wistful face, and the touching poignancy of his loneliness went straight to my heart.

"It's not always suitable to show your real feelings," Colonel Marshall used to tell me. It was not suitable then, so I dispelled the pathos of the moment with excited expressions of lavish appreciation. "Oh thanks, Colonel Marshall! You can't imagine how thrilled I am with this lovely room. The flowers are gorgeous! How simply divine . . . !"

The next morning at breakfast, Colonel Marshall announced he had made arrangements with a lieutenant for me to take riding lessons.

"Riding lessons, what do I need riding lessons for?" I asked haughtily.

"Because you've never done any cross-country riding," he explained, and added that the setup at Benning offered a perfect opportunity to learn.

They were some lessons! Colonel Marshall would drive me over to the stable in the early cool of the morning and every day warned me to pay close attention so that I would progress rapidly. The Lieutenant worked me like a dog until a little before nine o'clock when a car would come for me. Routinely, the lieutenant would start me off every morning at a walk around the ring; then I'd trot my horse, then canter, and finally, urge him into a full gallop. While we galloped, I was instructed to lean forward and backward, slapping my mount on the neck and rump in rhythmic time; and every now and then I'd have to whoop and shout at the top of my voice. I felt perfectly ridiculous and asked the Lieutenant why I had to "yell like crazy."

"The Colonel's orders were to teach you the same as a man," he explained soberly, "and that's the way soldiers limber up before a hard ride."

"Yahooo!" I hollered. "O.K., teacher, just call me Cap'n Page!" I thought it might liven things up if I flirted a bit; the Lieutenant was so businesslike and formal, but rather cute withal.

After the "limbering up," which my instructor avoided for himself, we started out on the trails. At least for the first few days we went on the trails; later we rode everywhere but the trails. Fort Benning is a huge post, and in 1928 it encompassed miles of undeveloped territory. The Lieutenant and I dashed through woods, leapt over fallen logs, forded streams, and generally practiced "hard" riding. One morning he announced I was now prepared to ride down a steep cliff.

"There's not much to it," he said. "Just give the horse his head, hold on with your knees, thrust your feet forward, and lean back; but whatever you do, don't pull on the reins."

When we arrived at the cliff he'd chosen, we walked up to the brink for a look; as I peered down the precipitous incline falling away a hundred feet or more, I seriously doubted if any horse could make it. The Lieutenant, however, assured me our mounts were well trained and could easily do it. We turned around, walked back a little distance, then whirled and cantered straight toward the cliff, the Lieutenant riding ahead. Over we went; my horse, slipping and sliding on his haunches, pawed and scrambled for balance with his forefeet, while I leaned back as instructed, my head nearly touching the horse's rump. His head, directly below me, was almost out of sight, and I understood instantly how disastrous it would be if I tried to hold him back; he'd lose his balance and we'd both tumble down to the bottom. It was an exciting experience, and after we'd reached level ground I was exhilarated by our success. It was then that I remembered the postcard of the rearing white horse which Colonel Marshall had sent to me years ago.

"You're doing just fine," the Lieutenant complimented me. "The Colonel will be pleased at how well you're getting along!"

Alas, the Colonel's pleasure was short-lived.

The next morning I began with the usual workout in the ring, which by now had become a bore. Also by now, the Lieutenant was somewhat less solemn, and was leaning against the rails laughing as I clowned through the exercises. Inspired by his appreciative humor, instead of yelling war whoops on the gallop, I belted out snatches of popular songs and waved my "slapping" arm about in exaggerated ballet gestures. On the second go around as we whizzed by the Lieutenant, I made a comic little bow—and that's all I remember until I came to on the ground. The most vicious, venomous, enormous horsefly in all of Georgia had chosen that moment to sink his poisonous fang into my poor horse. The horse stopped dead and reared, but I continued on, somersaulting over his head.

When I opened my eyes, the Lieutenant was bending over me exclaiming, "Oh my God! Oh my God!"

"Uh—ow," I groaned.

The sound of my voice apparently relieved him considerably, because he broke off calling on the Deity and quietly instructed me not to move. To make a long story short, we tested my limbs for broken bones, he helped me up, and we staggered the short distance to the stable and sat down on a low step.

My most immediate and pressing concern was a frightful nausea rising in me, and I directed every physical and mental resource I could muster toward controlling the impulse to throw up. I positively could not bring myself to give in to such a revolting performance in front of the "cute" young officer.

The Lieutenant, unaware of my struggle, sat staring into space, wagging his head in astonished disbelief. "I've seen a lot of spills in my time," he mumbled to the atmosphere, "but this is the first time in my life I've ever seen anybody take a *double* somersault over a horse's head!"

After ten minutes or so, he asked if I could remount, reminding me it was important to get back on the horse immediately in order to avoid any future fear of riding. I told him I was too sore to remount from the ground, but if he'd bring the horse alongside the fence, I'd get on somehow. I walked the horse around the ring a couple of times, then told the conscientious Lieutenant I wasn't about to be afraid to ride again, and suggested we go home; I ached all over.

It was too early for the car to fetch me, so he drove me home; all the way back, he worried aloud about what the Colonel would say.

"Oh take it easy!" I interrupted impatiently, and told him there wasn't a chance that Colonel Marshall would be angry with him. It wasn't his fault—I was the one who'd catch it. I was right. Colonel Marshall was not only irritated with me but disappointed as well.

"I'll bet my hat you were carrying on some sort of foolishness and not tending to business," he scolded when he came home.

"A big horsefly stung my horse when we were galloping," I interposed.

Obviously, the Lieutenant had already reported the circumstances of my mishap, for Colonel Marshall ignored my excuse and continued the roasting. "You had the advantage of a topnotch instructor, excellent horses, and miles of riding country. Now you've gotten yourself banged up and very likely ruined a great opportunity to become a really expert rider."

Marie sat quietly, half smiling, like a spectator at a play, and I wished Lily were there to take up for me. Marie had been so solicitous earlier when I'd limped into the house. She had pulled off my boots for me, drawn a hot bath, and told me that as soon as George came in for lunch that she was sure he would take me to a doctor. After I'd dressed, she had brought me iced tea and made me lie down. But now she just sat there exactly like Colonel Marshall, leaving it up to me to defend myself the best way I could.

"Sure, I was acting up a little," I admitted. "But I wouldn't have been thrown if it hadn't been for that giant old horsefly. There's no use saying I'm sorry about the lessons or sorry I fell off, because you'd only tell me being sorry doesn't fix anything. But I'll tell you something, it sure would help me now if you'd be just a little bit sorry I'm hurt. I'm terribly sore and my right leg is absolutely *killing* me."

"You poor abandoned invalid," he mocked. "Let's go into lunch and see if a little nourishment will help you."

I assumed an air of a brave and unjustly criticized victim as I eased myself off the chaise lounge; but when I stood up, such an acute burning pain ripped up and down my right leg and side that in spite of myself, I grimaced, and tears sprang to my eyes.

Colonel Marshall came straight over to me and put his arm around my waist.

"Come along," he said gently. "I'll give you a hand, lunch can wait. We'll go to see the doctor right away and find out what's what. Maybe he can give you something to ease that pain."

"I'll telephone you're on the way," Marie said, and when I turned my head to thank her, she gave me a broad smile. Marie was quite a gal.

Nothing was the matter with me except a bruise. But it was a beaut of a bruise, black, blue, and purple, with overall blotches of a murkish, deep maroon, and it extended from my hip bone half way round my fanny, down my thigh to my knee. What bothered me most about it was not so much the pain as how dreadful I'd look in a bathing suit. Ah youth!

There was a splendid swimming pool at Benning, more like a small lake or a big pond than a pool, and nearly every day Alice Torrey and I would join a young group for swimming. Alice was the only child of Colonel and Mrs. Dan Torrey, who were very good friends of Colonel Marshall. Mrs. Torrey was a sweet, pretty, blond little lady, attractive and gracious, as well as an accomplished horsewoman. I barely remember Colonel Torrey except that he was an affable, pleasant man. I thought Alice, who was a little older than I, the most beautiful, glamorous girl I'd ever known. I think her charms were enhanced in my eyes because she was so friendly and nice to me and didn't lord it over me, even though she was engaged to the handsomest young officer on the post. She gave me a lovely dinner party, scrounged up dates for me, and showed me many little attentions over and above the requirements of courtesy.

Colonel Marshall and I, however, spent a good portion of my visit together, although we couldn't go riding. The doctor forbade me to ride after my accident, which really was too bad, because Colonel Marshall had counted on our enjoying frequent long rides. Nevertheless, after his original observation on my carelessness, he accepted the situation in good humor and thought up other diversions. He drove me all around the countryside, which I'd never seen before, and into Tennessee, because I told him I'd started a list of states I'd been in and wanted to add a new one. We went to almost every Post baseball game, which we watched in isolated grandeur from the Commandant's box; Colonel Marshall was Assistant Commandant of the post, and Acting Commandant at the time. Afternoons after work, he frequently played tennis, and would take me along as spectator. I'd have to sit there cringing with embarrassment while he played his fantastic version of the game.

If I was off with Alice or out on a date, Colonel Marshall often went out himself. He had a pleasant group of friends, and I remember one of their diversions was to go on horseback riding picnics, starting out late in the afternoon and stopping somewhere for a picnic supper. The Torreys were regular attendants on those picnic rides; Mrs. Torrey told me they were great fun, and they'd never had them until Colonel Marshall came to Benning and organized them.

If neither Colonel Marshall nor I had an evening engagement, we occasionally went into Columbus to the movies, but more often we just stayed home and talked. Sometimes Marie was present and sometimes she wasn't. Once when she was there, Colonel Marshall began a lecture on the evils of smoking—I think it was about that time he'd stopped himself—and told me he never wanted me to take it up. I'd already been smoking for some time, but sensing he would oppose it, I only smoked when I was out; or, if at the house, in the room with Marie, who smoked all the time. I continued that practice throughout my visit, and Marie, of course, never told on me. Nor, incidentally, did I yield to the temptation to remind Colonel Marshall of his own and his mother's smoking.

One evening when Marie was absent, Colonel Marshall brought up the subject of petting and asked if I had trouble with fellows making passes at me.

"Ye Gods, I'm not exactly a porcupine," I replied. "I should hope so."

"I should imagine so," he said laughingly, and cautioned me to remember that down here I was dating men, not boys. He urged me to be circumspect, not cheap.

Because of my father's and Colonel Marshall's tutelage and the experience of growing up at 2400, I was rather mature for

Colonel Marshall, 1919. This is the first picture he gave me.

Lily Marshall, *circa* 1922. Lily gave me this picture
before she and Colonel Marshall left for China, 1924.

Snapshot taken by someone at 2400 16th St. in 1919 or 1920. From left to right: me, Eleanor Pierce, Celeste. The child in front is Libby Pierce, Eleanor's younger sister.

Celeste, on the right, and me, 1920.

On one of our camping trips with Colonel Marshall and Major Lewis. I am on the left and Ann Lewis on the right.

This is a picture Lily cut out of a magazine because
it reminded her of my "bath sessions" at Fort Myer.
The handwritten comment is hers.

General Pershing sent me this picture a few days after
I introduced myself to him in the lobby, 1920.

A formal portrait in 1921. Celeste is on the right.

My father, Dr. Thomas Walker Page, *circa* 1919.

General Marshall and me.

The Sunday before Lily and Colonel Marshall left for China she took this snapshot of us, June 1924.

Brigadier General Marshall sent me this snapshot of him with Katherine from Vancouver Barracks in 1936.

My wedding: Celeste, John, me, and Murray Wilson, my brother-in-law, June 1937.

My mother, Celeste Alspaugh Page, in 1947.

This is a wonderful picture of an amused expression familiar to me. I commented on it one day and General Marshall gave me the print.

It was typical of General Marshall to dispense with time-consuming formalities. Lieutenant Colonel Frank T. McCabe lends a helping hand. *Photo by United States Army Signal Corps.*

A good picture of the "tiger smile." He was fishing off the Florida coast while on a brief vacation with Mrs. Marshall, 1944. On the back he commented, "This being your favorite pose, I thought you might like to have it, GCM." *Photo by Thomas D. McAvoy.*

My brother, Thomas Walker Page III, 1950, two years before his death.

My sister, Celeste, in 1965.

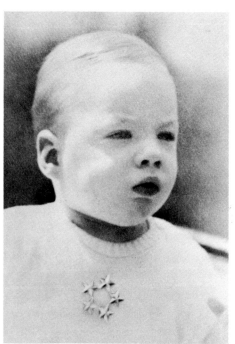

Our son, John Page Wilson, called Page, wearing General Marshall's five stars, May 1946.

General Marshall and me taken by my husband when General Marshall visited our house in Durham, N. C., 1950.

This is General Marshall's favorite picture of my children, Thomas, Celeste Rose, and Page, fall, 1953.

General Marshall sent this picture to Page for his birthday.

In Pinehurst, N. C., the day of our long visit in 1955. Tom, General Marshall, and Page.

Our son, John Page Wilson, in 1965.

Thomas Morgan Wilson, our second son, 1966.

My husband, John, in 1965.

The last picture General Marshall gave me, taken aboard ship en route to receive the Nobel Peace Prize, 1953.

Celeste Rose Wilson, fifteen years old, 1967.

My favorite picture of General Marshall, taken in
1942 or 1943. *Photo by United States Army Signal
Corps.*

sixteen, at least in respect to general information or conduct and conversation with adults. When it came to association with my peers at home, I was an average sixteen; but compared to the "older" young people at Benning, I was positively infantile. It embarrassed me, and I figured this was a good opportunity to air my problem for Colonel Marshall's advice.

"What bothers me," I complained, "is that I get along pretty well with older people or with kids my own age, but the gang down here doesn't behave like either, and it makes me feel like a darn baby. Take Alice Torrey; she's hardly any older than I am, but she knows more than twice as much as I do about how to handle boys, men I mean. Gosh, she's even engaged!"

"At your age, a year or so older makes a whale of a difference," he commented dryly, and that was all the advice I got.

I can't remember how long my visit at Benning lasted or what determined my departure. Maybe Marie's husband wanted her to come home, or perhaps Colonel Marshall had to take a trip. I do remember that by the time I left, my bruise had faded to pale tones of brown and yellow, so I must have been there about six weeks.

We motored home accompanied by a young Lieutenant's wife who caught a free ride to visit her mother, and whom I guessed had been invited as a chaperone. That must have been the only reason she was along, I thought, for she was dumb and ill-natured, whining to me in private because Colonel Marshall had asked her to share the driving. I pointed out that she only drove two one-hour stretches the whole day, and I was dying to drive myself; but unfortunately Colonel Marshall didn't have much confidence in me as a chauffeur.

When I told Colonel Marshall I thought she was a dumbbell and unpleasant, and I wished she hadn't come with us, he advised me shortly to keep my shirt on.

"Don't forget it's a very convenient arrangement for us as well as for her. You blow up over the most inconsequential matters, and I don't want you to go busting out with something rude you'll regret. You can stand her for a couple of days, and if you can't, you're dumber than she is."

The last night on the road, we were not near a town large enough to boast even a modestly decent hotel; as there were no motor courts then, we drove along after dinner until we found a respectable-looking tourist home out in the country. The Lieutenant's wife retired immediately, hinting that she had borne the lion's share of the driving and was exhausted. It was still too early for bed so Colonel Marshall and I went out on the porch and sat down in an old-fashioned swing which was the only furniture the landlady had provided for her few chance guests.

It was a beautiful, luminous summer night, and we sat quietly for a while, gazing out at the rolling moonlit pastures and listening to the crickets' shrill chirruping, punctuated now and then by an old bull frog's hoarse bass call, "Bottle o' rum, bottle o' rum."

The charm cast by the shifting patterns of moonlight and the mixed cadences of those small rural creatures would ordinarily have made conversation superfluous, but it was our last evening together and the usual sadness over parting was oppressive. I broke our silence.

"Thank you for a lovely time," I began, using my overworked childhood expression to amuse him. "Joking aside," I continued, "wasn't it marvelous? Didn't we have a grand time in spite of my accident? And no matter how you feel about 'being sorry,' I must tell you that I am truly sorry to have spoiled the riding for you, for both of us."

"I hate to let you go." Colonel Marshall murmured, "I dread returning to an empty house."

"Oh Colonel Marshall, you'll be all right," I said brightly. "You've made a lot of wonderful friends at Benning and you say your work is stimulating and interesting. Things will get better and better for you. I know they will. If nothing else, you'll make them get better, yourself."

Colonel Marshall smiled. "You're a fine girl," he said. "I appreciate your encouragement."

The next day while we were driving our last lap to Washington and the Lieutenant's wife was sleeping in the back seat, I ventured some advice I had been turning over in my mind during the night. "Colonel Marshall," I whispered, so as not to wake up our sleeping passenger, "I've been thinking. You should have a wife, you really should, and the best thing for you to do is keep your eyes open and find yourself a nice lady. You know, somebody real congenial, like Mrs. Torrey, for instance."

He smiled and patted my hand but he didn't speak.

Two years later Colonel Marshall found his "nice lady." As for his tenure at Fort Benning, his work was "stimulating and interesting" to such an extent that he instituted changes in methods of officers' instruction that proved to be so efficacious they are still in use today. In short, he did "make things get better" for himself, and in the making, better for a lot of other people too.

CHAPTER XXI

CLOSE TO SIX YEARS PASSED BEFORE I SAW COLONEL MARSHALL AGAIN. In the fall after my return from Fort Benning, I was packed off to boarding school in Boston so that the festivities surrounding my sister's debut would not interfere with my school work. The following fall I entered Smith College. At the beginning of my sophomore year at Smith—that was in 1930—Colonel Marshall wrote me that he had married a widow with three half-grown children, Katherine Tupper Brown. The news hardly surprised me. My immediate reaction was, oh good, that's great, now he'll have a home again! Naturally, I was agog with curiosity to know all about his new wife and impatient to meet her. Thinking of Lily, I took it for granted I'd love and admire anyone Colonel Marshall would choose, but foolish as it may seem, I never once considered the possibility that his choice might not like me!

The stepchildren were something else again. I was definitely unenthusiastic about them, even though I was nineteen years old and had many interests and friends remote from Colonel Marshall. Yet, for practically my whole life I thought of him as "my

186

Colonel Marshall" and it came as something of a shock that from now on I would have to share him with three unknowns.

His letter told me little about his bride except that she was a charming lady from Baltimore. It said less about her children, merely giving their names, sexes, and ages. There was Molly, the eldest, a few years younger than I, and her two younger brothers, Clifton and Allen, both in their early teens. Molly—he had a stepdaughter near my age? Damn! I barely scanned the rest of his letter which was devoted to questions about my college work and activities, concluding as usual, with expressions of good wishes for my general well-being. How typical of him, I fumed, to be so exasperatingly uncommunicative about all those strangers. When I wrote back my congratulations and wishes for their happiness, however, I did not ask for more information, for I knew he would leave it up to me to form an independent opinion after I had come to know them.

I left Smith at the end of my second year, made my debut the following season, and in the summer of 1933, wangled a job with the NRA. Meanwhile, Colonel Marshall was transferred from Fort Benning to Fort Screvin, Georgia, then to Fort Moultrie in South Carolina, and in 1933 was ordered to Chicago as Senior Instructor of the Illinois National Guard. During all that time there had been no opportunity either to see him or to meet his new family.

One morning after I'd been with the NRA for about a year, I was wrestling with a knotty problem that had come up in my work when I was interrupted by a voice as familiar to me as "the rising of the sun even unto the going down of the same."

"Hello Rosie, I've been standing here nearly five minutes and I'm delighted to see how well-developed your powers of concentration have become."

"Colonel Marshall! Hi, oh hi!" I exclaimed. Forgetting that I shared the office with four others, that I was twenty-three years old and had been enjoying the disguise of a rather glamorous blond for the past few years, I sprang out of my chair and threw my arms around the neck of this tall, dignified gentleman whose identity was unknown to my office mates. Everybody burst out laughing.

"Shut up, you dopes," I demanded. "This is my godfather and I haven't seen him for ages."

I had just finished introducing him around when my boss entered the office, walked imperiously past Colonel Marshall and me without speaking, sat down at his desk, and lowered at us. Colonel Marshall asked me in a low voice what the boss was like.

I replied out loud in code, "Mr. Clay and Miss Swift combined."

Smiling briefly, Colonel Marshall strode over to his desk and addressed him courteously, but in his inimitably authoritative manner, to which his clipped Pennsylvania accent lent an even more "I mean business" air.

"Good morning, I am Colonel George Marshall," he began.

Right away, my poor little boss shot up out of his seat and stood as nearly at attention as his frail physique and civilian disposition would allow.

"Yes sir!" he answered.

"I am in Washington for the day only," Colonel Marshall continued crisply, "and I would appreciate it very much, if at all possible, that Miss Page be allowed an extra hour or so for luncheon today." It sounded more like an order than a petition.

"Well, it's against regulations," the boss replied hesitantly, struggling to recover his lost sense of authority.

"I am sure it is," Colonel Marshall replied amiably, "otherwise I would not have made the request to her superior."

His face saved in front of his four minions, the boss immediately and with obvious relief gave his permission for the extra time.

My office was on the first floor of a building on Connecticut

Avenue, and when we came out onto the street, Colonel Marshall asked me as casually as if we'd seen each other yesterday, "Well, where would you like to have lunch?"

I suggested the Mayflower Hotel, which was close by. "That's fine with me," he agreed, and we started walking up Connecticut Avenue.

"How'd you find me? How long will you be here? Where's Katherine? Are you really truly happy? Gosh, it's wonderful to see you!" I bombarded him with a barrage of questions and comments.

"If you'll give me a chance," he said, laughing, "I'll answer you."

He told me it was easy enough to find me; he'd called Mother at the Shoreham (we had moved from 2400 to the Shoreham my freshman year at college) and she had given him my office address. He was on a quick trip and Katherine hadn't come with him. Yes, he was very happy.

"And you, Rose, how about you?"

I rushed through an abridged account of things I had not already included in our correspondence during the past few years, and returned impatiently to questioning him. He would not elaborate on his domestic life beyond a few concise remarks which sufficed to outline the picture of a comfortable, pleasant home managed by a fond and congenial wife. I withheld asking questions about Katherine with remarkable restraint for me, but I couldn't endure to maintain an equal reserve when it came to Molly. I started pumping him to find out as much as I could.

"She's not as particular about her looks as you are," he answered when I asked him about what she looked like. Then he recounted a little incident to illustrate Molly's indifference to clothes. Once, he said, Molly had received several new dresses, but instead of hurrying to try them on, she had merely opened the box, glanced at them casually, thrown them on the bed and walked out.

189

"Gosh!" I marveled.

"She's not as attentive to make-up as you seem to be," he continued, "that is, judging by your present appearance."

"Well, what's wrong with making the best of what you've got?" I asked hotly.

"I didn't say anything was wrong with it," he said, smiling, and proceeded to tell me that Molly didn't fly off the handle either, that she was a calm, sensible, reliable girl.

"She's an excellent rider too," he volunteered, laughing out loud now, and adding, "You're about as subtle as you were at eight!"

"Oh, okay, let's skip it," I replied, annoyed. I'd played the fool, and changing the subject, I asked, "How's your work coming?"

He switched over immediately, launching out enthusiastically and at some length about the C.C.C. men with whom he had been working in South Carolina. As I remember it, he expressed the opinion that the discipline, outdoor work, and sense of accomplishment served as both a mental and physical boost for those young Depression victims. The project, he stated positively, was extremely worthwhile.

At luncheon, he guided the conversation, leading me on with his attentive interest and provocative questions, so that I poured forth all my problems and hopes, and even my few small achievements. We talked every second of those few hours we spent together. Later, when our conversation had sorted itself out in my mind, I realized he had purposely used much of our time to draw me out, and I was grateful. He had advised and encouraged me in the things for which I had been starved for advice and encouragement. I had almost forgotten how skillfully and easily he was able to bolster me up and adjust my sights. Furthermore, in the event any uncertainty might have bothered me, he left me with a positive, good feeling about his own welfare. Although he referred frequently and with tenderness to Lily, I observed he could speak of her without pain, so by this, rather than by the little he told me of his present situation, I knew that his life at home was agreeable. But I was still uneasy about Molly!

It was not too long after the day Colonel Marshall and I lunched together that the Supreme Court declared the NRA unconstitutional. I wrote a brief note to Colonel Marshall saying that I'd been thrown out of a job as a result of pressure from Hamiltonian industrial leaders which had brought about a Jeffersonian strict interpretation of the Constitution. He wrote back asking for my future plans, and saying he was glad to see Roosevelt was abiding by the Supreme Court decision and not trying to impeach the Court as Jefferson had.

After I lost my job, Mother and I decided to go to California. I'd never been West, and besides, I wanted to shake off an unwelcome but persistent charlatan of a suitor. Mother wanted to go because she not only had pleasant memories of California where she had gone as a bride, but still had several close friends there from the first years of her marriage when my father had been a professor at the University of California. We went by boat through the Panama Canal, and after visiting a few weeks in Berkeley, we moved to San Francisco. The time flew by in that enchanting city, so it was November before Mother and I left to return to Washington. Instead of going by train or boat, we decided to drive. We bought a small Chevrolet coupé and motored by way of the Grand Canyon on up to Denver, Colorado, where my brother, now married and a mining engineer, was living with his wife, Susan. Tom had met his wife in Montana, where he had gone mostly for reasons of health; there he had graduated from the Montana School of Mines. He had been married "way out there," and none of our family had met Susie, so Mother and I were anxious to know her. Also, Mother was beside herself with excitement because her first grandchild was on the way.

After a pleasant visit in Denver, I suggested to Mother we had better leave; the baby wasn't expected until February, and we wanted to be home before Christmas. Brother and I sat down one evening to plot the route I should follow. Tom insisted I should take the southern route, which was safer at this season, particularly as I was doing all the driving, since Mother had given up driving once Sis and I had learned. I appreciated my brother's advice, but when we were heading out of Denver, I told Mother we were going to Chicago because it was such a good chance to meet Colonel Marshall's wife and the stepchildren.

"Fine," she agreed, "but I want to stop by Beloit, Wisconsin, and see Robbie." Mother was very fond of Celeste's ex-boyfriend who was working there.

The day after we arrived in Beloit, I reached Mrs. Marshall by telephone and she invited me for tea.

CHAPTER XXII

IT IS ABOUT A HUNDRED-MILE DRIVE FROM BELOIT TO CHICAGO, AND AS the miles spun away behind me, my excitement and nervousness mounted. Confronted at last with the actuality of meeting Katherine and the stepchildren, it was finally borne in upon me that there was a very definite possibility they might not like me. Plenty of people didn't; why should I assume they would just because Lily and Marie had? Suppose Katherine couldn't stand me—would Colonel Marshall be lost to me forever? What if Molly should upstage me? Surely by now I could control myself well enough to handle such a contingency with poise and tact. I swore to myself that no matter what happened, I wouldn't blurt out something nasty and alienate Colonel Marshall myself.

Let's look at their side, I thought. Who am I to them? I am Colonel Marshall's goddaughter whom he rarely sees anymore, and what's that compared to the family he's lived with for five years? How could they know how special our relationship had been? Or had he told them at least a little about me, maybe talked about the childhood years? The nearer I approached Chicago, the more I felt like an interloper.

By the time I found myself outside the Marshalls' apartment, I was so filled with misgivings that I stood there for several minutes unable to ring the door bell. In those few moments, I decided I'd better not call his wife by her first name unless she suggested it. It was different from being a little kid, when it had seemed to me Lily had expected me to call her by her first name. Then it flashed through my mind that when I'd met Marie, she had said simply, "I am Marie."

The recollection of how I had dreaded meeting Lily and how warmly she had received me, and how curious I was to meet Marie and how friendly she had been, made my present jitters seem absurdly self-conscious. Nuts, I said to myself, don't be such a Calamity Jane, and I rang the bell.

Mrs. Marshall opened the door and smiling pleasantly, said, "Come in Rose, it's nice to meet you at last."

"Oh thank you, Mrs. Marshall," I exclaimed. "You can't imagine how glad I am to meet you!"

We sat on a sofa and made conversation. Tea was served. For me, it was somewhat like talking to one of Mother's casual acquaintances with whom I had a mutual friend. Mrs. Marshall was the epitome of courtesy and graciousness, but I felt as if we were conversing through an invisible wall that I was totally unable to penetrate. I kept wondering where her children were, but none showed up.

I tried a sledge hammer blow at the wall. "It's so wonderful for Colonel Marshall to have a family! I know how much he must enjoy having young people around."

No success.

While we talked, I noticed that the living room was attractively and comfortably decorated with a flair for elegant simplicity; but mostly, I concentrated on Mrs. Marshall. She was neither pretty nor homely, but extremely well-groomed and chic.

Her reddish-brown hair was carefully coiffed; her dress expensive but in restrained good taste; and she had a slim, neat figure for her age, which I judged to be fiftyish.

My face was beginning to freeze into an expression my father used to call "prunes-and-prisms politeness" when Colonel Marshall came bustling in. I curbed an impulse to rush over to him, and merely stood up and greeted him as enthusiastically as I dared: "Hi, Colonel Marshall, it's good to see you! Mrs. Marshall and I have been having a nice little talk."

He glanced at us sharply, walked over and bussed Mrs. Marshall, then me. "Well, that's fine," he replied heartily. "I'm glad I could make it in time to catch the tail end of the confab."

Very soon after he joined us, I had to leave for the drive to Beloit. But before I left, Colonel Marshall invited me to return and spend a few days with them. I accepted.

Back on the highway I reviewed the afternoon, wondering if I might have said anything to put Mrs. Marshall off. Suddenly, driving along all by myself, I exclaimed out loud, "I'll be damned, if I'm not the prize fool!" All the way over, I'd built myself up as somebody Mrs. Marshall and Molly might like or detest, and the real fact was they didn't think about me one way or another. As far as they were concerned, my existence was unimportant and irrelevant to theirs. It was a tremendous let-down.

When Mother plied me with questions, I evaded the truth, elaborating instead on Mrs. Marshall's smart appearance and gracious manner, and explaining her children's absence by guessing they were out of town. I had not yet overcome a feeling of inadequacy with Mother and couldn't face telling her I wasn't even rejected, but merely tolerated by Mrs. Marshall.

When I returned for my visit, Mrs. Marshall once again ushered me in with scrupulous courtesy, and once again we sat down on the sofa. Within a very few minutes, Molly joined us.

The first things that struck me about Molly were her easy,

unaffected good manners and her cultured voice. Mrs. Marshall had told me at our first meeting that as a young girl she had had a fling as a Shakespearean actress, and obviously she had used her experience to train her daughter. Molly spoke the English language beautifully. She was well dressed; but unlike her mother, Molly wore her clothes with a casual disregard for stylishness. She was not exactly pretty, but I liked her smooth forehead framed by heavy, dark hair and accented by even, dark brows. She knows her own mind, I thought, observing her firm, wide mouth. Molly seemed a quiet girl, and I wasn't sure at the time whether her behavior was due to a natural or purposeful reserve.

We went to a restaurant for dinner that evening and as we sat waiting to be served, the atmosphere was somewhat strained; so Colonel Marshall started to brighten up the party with amusing anecdotes of his and my past experiences. He started off with the tale about our night in the hotel on our first motor trip down the Shenandoah, the one about "Mercy no, he's just a friend!"

"We've heard that one a hundred times." Mrs. Marshall interrupted.

Colonel Marshall ignored the interruption and went right on with the tale. We talked of other things for a while, and then he began another story, the one about finding my train out in the country. This time, Mrs. Marshall listened politely.

"It was a race through unknown back country to locate the train before it pulled out!" Colonel Marshall concluded, still proud of himself for having found it.

Mrs. Marshall was not entertained. With the barest, but unmistakable hint of derision, she observed, "But you were in such a mad rush to see Rose, you just couldn't wait for the train to reach the station!"

Colonel Marshall stiffened. In that cold, stern voice I had heard him use only a few times in my life, he addressed her. "Never," he commanded, "never let me hear you speak in such a manner again."

I was stunned. That does it, I thought, I'm ruined with her forever!

Colonel Marshall returned immediately to his natural manner and throughout the rest of dinner kept the conversation sprightly and pleasant, except that it embarrassed me when he kept calling Katherine, Lily.

I shared a room with Molly that night, got nowhere with her at all, and nearly froze to death because she opened the windows wide to the sub-zero Chicago night. The next morning at breakfast I was asked if I'd slept well, and replied, laughing, that I had been awfully cold, but was too sleepy and too lazy to get up and shut a window.

Molly apologized. There was nothing unusual in her words but there was something unusual in her apology—it was pleasant and it had a genuine ring. I looked at her, and observing her frank, worried little smile, I said, "Oh, that's O. K., it was my own stupidity." From that moment on I have liked and trusted Molly, and although I have not had the opportunity to know her intimately, neither have I had reason to change my mind.

Colonel Marshall arranged to have his car pick me up in the afternoon and stop by his office for him. It was the only time we had to talk together outside the bosom of his family, and it was then I found out that nobody and nothing would ever sever the bonds of our friendship.

It had been a rough time for me and he knew it. On the other hand, the fact that he had made this little private time for us was enough to tell me he knew. I had no intention of spoiling our brief talk with lamentations about my unpopularity with Mrs. Marshall. Such a course would have backfired on me in any case. Colonel Marshall most certainly would not have tolerated any vague accusations against his wife. "She doesn't like me, she makes me feel uncomfortable"—that sort of whining was repugnant even to me. No matter how long and how dear our friendship might have been, in the last analysis, the serenity of his marriage was far more important. I recognized and subscribed to this simple fact. Furthermore, I had no wish to compete for his affections either with Mrs. Marshall or, now that she had captured my allegiance, with Molly.

It was unfortunate for me that Mrs. Marshall did not like me, and I can only guess why—I don't really know. My presence might have been disquieting, for I was a kind of direct representative of Lily and a part of Colonel Marshall's life that she had not shared. Later, as her life became more integrated with Colonel Marshall's, this reason would necessarily fade, although the distaste could have remained. Very possibly, too, I just wasn't her "dish of tea"; she did not find me likable. Whatever her reasons, I should like to state unequivocally that what she thought of me was trivial in my mind compared to Colonel Marshall's well-being. I was his goddaughter and a special friend, but she was his devoted wife, and as I have said previously, their marriage was highly successful. Indirectly, all of us are indebted to Mrs. Marshall, for I know well that the comfortable home she maintained afforded Colonel Marshall the refuge he so desperately needed during the trying years of his dedication to the preservation of the life and safety of the American people.

As for my personal feelings about Mrs. Marshall, they were never very warm. But they never mattered, either, because Colonel Marshall and I remained close friends until his death.

When I picked him up that afternoon in Chicago, Colonel Marshall got into the car, took my hand and held it, saying how glad he was I had come and that he wanted to know my plans for the future. I was touched by his small demonstration of affection—holding my hand—because I understood he wanted me to feel at least secure in his welcome. I smiled in recognition of his intent, and told him that my immediate plan was to get a job after Christmas, and after that, I didn't have any plans.

"You should get married," he advised, "have a home and family."

"Oh no!" I groaned. "Et tu, Brute?" and went on to tell him it was enough to have Mother worried I'd be an old maid. I said I wasn't at all worried; I'd get married when I found the kind of guy I wanted, and I wasn't the least bit interested in getting married just to avoid spinsterhood.

"And what kind of 'guy' are you looking for?" he laughed.

"A cultured, intelligent man with high integrity, a sense of humor, and sex appeal," I replied promptly.

"What about money and good looks?" he asked. "Those are qualifications that usually appeal to young women."

"Oh, that's gravy," I answered, "not that I have any objections to either."

He talked a while about the importance of my joining the matrimony club, and gave me some astute advice on how to avoid my devil pursuer—whom I had gone West to avoid—if he continued to pester me when I returned home.

"How long now before you'll be Chief of Staff?" I asked when I got the chance.

"Well Rosie, it looks now as if I never will," he said. He laughed shortly. "Don't get your hopes up!" he warned. "If I don't make Brigadier General soon, I'll be so far behind in seniority I won't even be in the running." I was surprised and disturbed that he would admit having doubts.

"I'm not any more worried about your making Chief of Staff than I am about getting myself a husband," I scolded. "I've been sure all my life you'd be Chief of Staff, and I am sure of it now. Stop talking like that, stop thinking like that; everybody in the Army who knows anything knows you are just about the ablest officer in the country, and mark my words, the powers that be will find it out too."

He leaned over and kissed me. "Thank you for your confidence," he said simply.

"I didn't say those things just to cheer you up," I answered sharply. "It's the truth."

199

We were almost back at the apartment, and before we arrived, I slipped in one more little piece of advice.

"Colonel Marshall," I said with a smile, "you are a great officer but you're a real dope when it comes to women. Will you *please* stop calling Katherine, Lily?"

He smiled and replied that he sometimes forgot, and Katherine was not the sort of woman to hold a little thing like that against him; he was sure that she understood.

"Well," I said, "I didn't hear her calling you Clifton or Cliff, or whatever she called her first husband. I'm sure she does understand but that doesn't mean she likes it!"

That's all I remember about my Chicago visit, which was cut short when Mother telephoned that she was cold, miserable, and uncomfortable at Robbie's and suspected she was in the way besides. She asked me to come and get her "right away."

My visit had not been altogether a failure as I had feared it might. I was hurt and disappointed to have made such a poor impression on Mrs. Marshall, but I had been cured of my corroding jealousy of Molly, and Colonel Marshall had reaffirmed once and for all the mutual affection we held for each other.

The following February, he wrote me a longhand letter on his office stationery which I include here as a good example of his unchanging attitude toward my relationship with his family and with him. He simply by-passed the incompatibility between Mrs. Marshall and me; he accepted the situation and arranged matters to avoid unpleasantness. This was his way and it was sensible. He had enough serious problems in his public life not to allow the stirring up of unwanted sediment to cloud the clear waters of his sacred private life. I understood his reason and admired him for it even though it meant I saw much less of him than I ordinarily would have. More important, he kept both loyalties, to Mrs. Marshall and to me, intact and unsullied.

Incidentally, the letter mentions Mrs. Marshall's two sons whom I may have met in Chicago. If so, I have no recollection of it, probably because I was too preoccupied with Mrs. Marshall and Molly. In any event, I never knew them well, but what little I do know, I will set down in another context.

Office Senior Instructor
ILLINOIS NATIONAL GUARD
208 South LaSalle Street
Chicago, Illinois

February 14, 1936

Dear Rose,

This is not a valentine in appearance, but it carries a slight touch of the sentiments. I want to hear from you, of where you are, what you are doing, your state of contentment, and future plans.

Molly left yesterday for a month at Fort Sill, Oklahoma. Allen is doing all day at Armor Institute of Technology and 3 hours on two nights a week at a special school. His hours are, up at 6:30, home at 5:30 or 11 P.M., and to bed at 1 A.M. Pretty strenuous, but good for him. Clifton has made some good sales in the past two days and his morale is up.

Katherine and I have been frozen in pretty generally for some weeks—we have had almost a month of zero or below, now with ice and snow in layers. It warmed up yesterday, sleeted and tonight is to drop below zero again. I have frozen my ears off exercising Ponty—he likes the cold and snow. [Ponty was their Irish Setter.]

I hope, Rosie, all goes better with you and the future looks brighter. I hope, more particularly, that you have not fallen into compromises between what you know is best and what seems to be forced on you by circumstances. No more preaching!

You have my love and deep interest. God be with you 'till we meet again.

Affectionately,
GCM

201

❦ CHAPTER XXIII ❦

Colonel marshall was promoted to brigadier general in October 1936—thirty-four years after he was commissioned a Second Lieutenant. Certainly his rise through the Army's rigid seniority system had been an exceedingly slow process, but fortunately his single star had come in time to keep him eligible for further advancement. Even though he was far down the line in seniority, I wrote him that now there was no question but that he would be Chief of Staff, predicting, with more zeal than reason, that somehow the antiquated seniority rule would collapse.

The orders accompanying his promotion sent him to Vancouver Barracks, Washington, to assume command of the Fifth Infantry Brigade. That it was a fortunate assignment was very evident in his Vancouver letters, which were more cheerful than any I could remember since China ten years before.

He was a happy man! His marriage was serene, he was back with troops, which was his heart's desire, and he was once again working with C.C.C. boys, a job as interesting and stimulating to him as it was beneficial to the young men.

As for me, 1937 was an extraordinary year for our family. My father died, my sister and her husband of three years were divorced, my brother became the father of a second daughter, and I got married. A death, divorce, new baby, and a marriage all in one year were pretty major upheavals for a family.

My father's health had been deteriorating for several months, and after the first of the year, at his request, Mother, Sis, and I drove him down to the hospital at the University of Virginia where he died within a few weeks. Our grief for him was tempered by our thankfulness for his relief from suffering, and by the knowledge that he had died in the environment he had so often referred to as *mon pays*. I always suspected my father thought of himself as an exile in Washington; he loved Virginia, particularly the University and his old home, Keswick.

John Wilson and I were married in June after a relatively brief courtship. We had a quiet wedding, since my father had died only a few months before; in any event, our shaky family finances would not have permitted a splashy affair. Colonel Marshall could not make the trip East to give me away, nor could my brother, who was directing a mining operation in Montana; so my maternal uncle did the honors.

It had been easy for me to recognize in John all the qualifications I had enumerated to Colonel Marshall in Chicago, but I got a lot more than I'd bargained for. It developed that John possessed assets I hadn't even thought about: he is judicious and kindhearted, and by great luck, he's a crack mathematician! As for money and looks that I'd told Colonel Marshall were "gravy," my husband is a handsome man, but when we were married he was dirt-poor and so was I.

His father had died during John's senior year at Harvard, leaving his mother with four younger children to educate. That was 1932, in the big pinch of the Depression, so John refused to accept money from his father's estate. Instead, he borrowed from Harvard, and sent himself to the Harvard Graduate School of

Business. By the time we met, he had managed to pay off his debt to the college and was working at the Security and Exchange Commission in Washington for a miniscule salary.

My own father left practically no money at all, but Mother, anticipating this eventuality, had made a tidy little sum as an interior decorator, though not enough to provide a living income. Her wealthy brother established a small trust, sufficient to keep Mother fairly comfortable, but with nothing left over for her able-bodied grown-up children.

It upset her that I had married "poor," but I think Colonel Marshall might actually have been disappointed if I had married "rich"; he set such great store on the value of young couples struggling up together. In view of his homely philosophy, I was pleasantly surprised when our wedding present from the Marshalls turned out to be a set of beautifully designed silver dessert bowls. I'd rather expected a set of well-constructed pots and pans.

The first night Colonel Marshall dined with us in our modest little apartment, I used the bowls, and though duly calling attention to their high quality and charm, I couldn't help quipping that they were somewhat elegant for our surroundings. Colonel Marshall nailed me to my chair with a direct, sharp glance, and replied with a small, solemn smile, "It's up to you and John to see that they won't always be!"

Of course I'd told John all about my godfather who had had such a prevailing influence on my life, so soon after we were married John wrote a note to Colonel Marshall to which he received a prompt reply.

The Commanding General
Vancouver Barracks, Washington

July 27, 1937

Dear John,

I appreciated your note of July 20th, and was very glad to hear from you direct. I hope that we can get together, and that we will not have to wait a year.

My interest in Rose is very much from the heart, and I believe I am as well aware of her possibilities as her own family possibly more so. She has the makings of a wonderful wife, and while this is no time for preaching, and that would hardly be tactful, I counsel you both to cultivate tolerance for this first year. Seemingly, in modern life, tolerance and loyalty play a small part in accepted requirements for the marital relation. As a matter of fact, they rank first.

I know you will be very happy, and I hope that prosperity for you two is just around the corner.

With my love to you both,

Faithfully yours,
G. C. Marshall

It was a warm and flattering letter and I was pleased, although his heavy emphasis on tolerance unnerved me. As he said in his letter, Colonel Marshall knew me well; was he advising John to bear with me, or was he hinting to me that I should start a self-reforming project?

He and John did have to wait a year after all to "get together." Colonel Marshall returned to Washington in the early summer of 1938 to take up his new job as War Plans Chief, and in October he was made Deputy Chief of Staff—at long last he was indeed zipping to the top.

Washington summers are notoriously hot and humid, but the summer of 1938 was hellish. John and I were young and managed to make out pretty well, but Colonel Marshall had a bad time of it. He was terribly busy during the day (about which more later), with formal obligations to fulfill several nights a week; in addition, he somehow managed to squeeze house-hunting into his heavy schedule. Colonel Marshall's endearing trait of solicitous attention to women, and particularly to those who commanded his affection, naturally continued in full force with Mrs. Marshall and Molly. He wanted to have a comfortable home ready for them when they arrived from Fire Island where they were spending the summer in Mrs. Marshall's beach cottage.

I offered in good faith to take over the house-hunting, hut explained as tactfully as I could that everybody's tastes and requirements varied. It was highly possible, I warned, that Mrs. Marshall might not like my choice, but we could take a chance if he was too pressed to keep up the search. He got the message all right, and replied laughingly that he wouldn't for a minute thrust such a delicate responsibility upon me.

This little exchange took place on a July evening, the first time he dined with John and me. It was a wonderful evening, that first meeting between my husband and godfather, for those two established a rapport from the start. I knew Colonel Marshall was sizing up John by his every action and remark, and although I wasn't actually worried, still, it made me happy that he was able to bring out the best in John and that John warmed to him.

As a matter of fact, I was more nervous about the dinner itself than I was about how they would get along. I had had little experience with housekeeping and due to our tiny food budget, less experience with "company" dinners.

A lack of confidence in my cooking had kept me from inviting Colonel Marshall to dinner sooner, and the reason he dined with us that evening was because he had written to me inviting himself. He'd complained in his note that he had telephoned "no less than fifteen times and have never yet gotten an answer," and concluded, "If you can't come for luncheon, invite me for dinner some night. I am on a diet, so you won't have to cook much . . ."

Diet or not, I noticed Colonel Marshall ate everything I served him at that first dinner, from the chicken casserole straight through the strawberry ice cream (out of the wedding-present bowls), so I didn't hesitate to ask him again. He had several dinners with us that summer—he disliked dining alone as much as he disliked formal dinner parties—and consequently, those intimate little dinners provided a fine opportunity for him and John to become really acquainted.

One evening he announced it was high time we started riding again, that he'd been too busy for riding but would call me as soon as he could get off. I replied eagerly that I'd been looking forward to our first ride together after so many years, and hinted he would be surprised to see what a fine horsewoman I'd become. I had been riding almost every day since my marriage, an expensive diversion made possible through the generosity of a friend. Her horse was a king-sized sorrel hunter named New Yorker, who stood seventeen and a half hands high, had a mouth like leather, threw his head about so badly he needed a martingale, and was a great jumper—if he was in the mood. If not, I was forced to kick hell out of him and lay into him with a crop. I smile now to remember New Yorker. In spite of his faults, he was a magnificent-looking animal with a lap-dog personality.

The first day Colonel Marshall telephoned inviting me to ride, he told me to be out at the Fort Myer stables that afternoon at 5:02. I got there at 5:05, whereupon he pointed to the time and started bawling me out.

"Five-oh-two is such a dopey time," I objected, "and even allowing for your double-strict rules on punctuality, is three minutes late such an awful sin?"

He replied that if I wanted to ride with him, I'd better damn well get there when he told me to. His time was budgeted, he said curtly, and his budget did not allow for extra minutes of waiting around for me.

It was an inauspicious beginning for our reunion ride, but I apologized, promising it wouldn't happen again, and asked him please not to spoil everything by getting mad at me. I wanted him to see how well I could ride after all my practicing over the past few months.

Pretty soon, we broke into one of our well-remembered trotting sessions, and I called Colonel Marshall's attention to how quickly I had adjusted from New Yorker's lumbering gait to the polo pony's snappy pace. We were having fun; we told each other it was just like old times, and Colonel Marshall magnanimously conceded that I looked very professional. Suddenly my pony shied. New Yorker, for all his great size and strength, was a timid animal and shied at the least provocation, so I reacted automatically with the pony as I was accustomed to do with that big, tough-mouthed, sissy-baby hunter. I yanked on the reins and simultaneously leaned forward to pat the pony's neck to reassure him. New Yorker, alas, had destroyed my light touch, and the poor little pony, resenting my heavy hand, reared straight up on his hind legs and dumped me.

Colonel Marshall stopped his horse, and eyeing me plunked down like an awkward clown in a patch of tall weeds, he asked politely enough if I were hurt.

"No!" I shouted chagrined, quite aware of the ludicrous spectacle I made.

He burst into a fit of laughter and jeered, "Some great improvement since Benning!"

I began to giggle. "You're a jinx!" I cried, and sprawled back in the weeds, laughing helplessly myself.

After a few minutes, he wiped his eyes and told me to remount or we'd lose all our riding time. As we resumed our ride, I lamented that I'd let him know how confident I'd been. "Damn," I fumed, "if I'd only kept my mouth shut about how good I thought I was that dumb performance wouldn't make me feel quite so asinine!"

He replied that if it would make me feel any better, the same sort of thing had happened to him once, only much worse—it was during the Victory Parade in London after World War I.

Colonel Marshall confessed he'd believed he could handle any horse, no matter how truculent or how stubborn. Sure of his horsemanship, he offered to exchange mounts with an officer who was having difficulty with the high-spirited mount assigned him for the parade. The horse was a wild devil to start with and when the parade got underway, the cheering crowds turned him into a crazy fiend. Colonel Marshall said he was concentrating so intensely on his struggle to control the horse that he was oblivious to everything except his own draining strength and the cyclonic animal fighting against him. In short, he concluded, the horse won and threw him.

"If you were embarrassed to fall off in front of me," he commented, smiling, "imagine how I felt to land all askew on the boulevard in full view of thousands of onlookers."

"Strange you never told me that story before," I answered. "What a suitable time to tell me now—thanks a lot!"

He replied it was not one of his favorite tales, and for years he'd felt like a fool every time he thought of it. But it had all happened a long time ago, he said, laughing, and he was glad his unpleasant experience had served some useful purpose at last.

CHAPTER XXIV

MRS. MARSHALL ARRIVED IN WASHINGTON IN THE FALL, AND SHE AND Colonel Marshall settled down in a pleasant house he had rented on Wyoming Avenue, just off Connecticut. I remember Mrs. Marshall had been caught on Fire Island in the big hurricane of 1938 and Colonel Marshall had flown up to bring her back.

Mrs. Marshall's children seemed to appear in Washington, then disappear; here they were, and the next week, where were they? All three, however, were in town when John and I threw our first party, and all three came to it. We gave the party because our accumulated obligations made John so uncomfortable that I was able to persuade my sensitive husband to let me get a job so we could return the obligations. I'd had a fine job as Publicity Director for a Washington Hotel before we were married, but John had insisted that I give it up.

"I don't want my wife to work," sounds quaint, if not hilarious, these days, but John was adamant. When I appealed to Colonel Marshall to help me change John's mind, my godfather expressed full agreement with my husband. Colonel Marshall told me that to stay at home and start a family was the most worthwhile job for any woman, a sentiment he frequently repeated; in fact, he heckled me about having a baby ad infinitum.

At any rate, I compromised with John by getting a job that didn't tear me from the hearth—working at home for a friend of ours. He was a representative of a wine-importing company, and he hired me to compose and write snooty longhand letters to Washington hostesses, pointing out the social finesse of serving fine imported wines—more specifically, his company's wines. I thought I'd dreamed up some pretty persuasive notes, but when I showed a few samples to Colonel Marshall, he ungraciously said, "They make me want to throw up!"

The revenue, however, was good for the few hours a day I put in on that little job, and John and I had a terrific party, a real blast.

My "boss" made punch, insisting that it was easier to serve than cocktails or highballs, and when I hesitated, he won me over with the sensible argument that he could get the punch ingredients wholesale. He mixed the most insidious, powerful, deadly fishhouse punch ever concocted before or since. To say the party was gay is an understatement. I remember watching Molly shed her reserve and sparkle like a movie queen, and when the party broke up, I noticed she'd captured the most attractive unattached man there to take her home.

After the party, John and I and most of our guests went off together for dinner, or more accurately, late supper. Molly went home, because somebody had spilled a drink down her dress and she wanted to change before she and her beau went out to eat.

The next day I received a telephone call from Colonel Marshall, whose level, glacial tone of voice signaled that he was angrier with me than I'd ever known him to be. Briefing me as to the cause of his displeasure, he said that when he and Mrs. Marshall were returning from a dinner party the evening before, he happened to glance through a window and spot a "strange man" going up their stairs. He rushed in and grabbed the tele-phone to call the police, but in the few seconds before he was connected with the law, Molly appeared with her date stumbling after her. According to Colonel Marshall, neither Molly nor her date made much sense.

I interrupted to offer the practical suggestion that the poor guy was probably looking for the bathroom.

"They were drunk," Colonel Marshall said, outraged, "both of them!"

I played it cool. "They were?"

Oh, was he mad! "Don't pull that innocent act on me!" he cut in with biting scorn, and demanded to know what kind of abominable parties John and I gave. He said Allen and Cliff had told him it was a drunken brawl (which was pretty near the truth), and then he accused me of corrupting Molly. Finally, he asked coldly if I had lost all sense of propriety.

I was suffering from a horrendous hangover, and when he blamed me for Molly's getting plastered, all my carefully planned discretion went up in smoke. I got as mad as he was—madder. "Molly can damn well watch her own drinking!" I shouted, "and I can't help it if our party turned out so wild. It was that stupid old fishhouse punch. I didn't know how potent it was and neither did John." Choking with rage and resentment, I began to cry.

"Are you crying?" he asked evenly.

"No!" I bawled.

"What do you mean, fishhouse punch?" he inquired quietly.

I explained our friend's mysterious bacchanalian talents, and suddenly, feeling sorry for Molly, I asked him not to be too hard on her because she hadn't realized either that that sweet-tasting stuff was really brain-joggling firewater.

Colonel Marshall gave a short little laugh. "I'm glad you have a satisfactory explanation," he replied, suddenly quite amiable, although he did add a few terse remarks about the stupidity and vulgarity of drunkenness. At the end, he softened up completely.

"You don't need to drink to have a good time, because you have the sense and personality to have more fun than most. Rosie, you'll never have to rely on whiskey either to charm or be charmed."

In the face of such a rare compliment, I forgot my headache on the spot and happily forgave his accusations. I don't think it detracts too much from his generous praise to recall that since my childhood he'd been bolstering my weak ego—he had the habit. It was his way of setting me straight.

Drunkenness had always irritated and disgusted Colonel Marshall, and as I've said before, the only time I ever saw him even slightly high was on his fortieth birthday. But he was never a teetotaler. He drank moderately and was amused by, even slightly contemptuous of the militantly sanctimonious grape juice crowd.

CHAPTER XXV

Colonel Marshall became deputy chief of staff less than a year after the Munich "appeasement." Six months later, Hitler seized Czechoslovakia, and in August 1939, he and Stalin stupefied the world by signing the Soviet-German Nonagression Pact.

By April 1939, President Roosevelt passed over more than thirty senior Generals to raise Brigadier General George C. Marshall to full General, and to appoint him Chief of Staff. (What happened to the Army seniority rule? Crash!)

On September first, the same day that Hitler's highly trained, mechanized troops struck Poland for the quick kill, General Marshall assumed his duties as head of a miniature, ill-equipped American Army. Three days after he took office, Britain and France declared war on Germany. Almost immediately the United States' Declaration of Neutrality was announced to the world. Our country was being squeezed into a perilous situation just at a time when General Marshall first emerged as a public figure. Europe was crumbling rapidly under Hitler's blitzkrieg. On June 14, 1940, Paris fell to the Germans—less than a year after General Marshall began his tenure as Chief of Staff. Two months later, on the other side of the world, Japan signed a tripartite pact with Germany and her recently acquired ally, Italy. As Deputy Chief of Staff, and subsequently as Chief of Staff, General Marshall numbered among the few responsible Americans who viewed the hostile world scene with growing concern. Day after day he appeared before a stubbornly pacifist Congress to press for adequate national defense. With steadfast patience and self-restraint, he provided the anti-military legislators with comprehensive, detailed information on the imperative requirements for enlarging and modernizing our military forces.

Pacifism, however, was the American theme song, joined by a chorus *fortissimo* of isolationism that even the rising crescendo of the Battle of Britain did not entirely drown out. The shocking sequence of events in 1940, however, brought more and more citizens to the realization that the United States had better change tunes. Congress, for the most part, entered into harmony with its constituents; it passed the Selective Service Act, the first peacetime draft in our history, and began to appropriate sizeable sums for defense. Colonel Marshall was quoted in the press as saying that previously he'd "had lots of time and no money; now, lots of money and no time."

As I read his statement, my mind raced back to one fall afternoon in 1939 when we were out riding. Colonel Marshall looked so tired that day that I asked him rather sharply if he had been cheating on his rest.

It was one of the rare occasions that he openly expressed his anxiety to me. "It's been a long, difficult day," he replied wearily; and muttering, as if he'd forgotten I was there, he said aloud, "It's getting closer and closer; our time is running out."

"Oh for God's sake!" I cried in alarm. "Why is Congress so blind and deaf? What's the matter with us? Why don't we get going before it's too late?"

"Hold on!" he warned, dismissing his own anxiety with a characteristically rapid change of mood. "Our Government has been busy making life pleasanter for the likes of you while the

Nazis were concentrating on making guns and tanks and planes. Bear in mind that it's very distasteful for a democracy like ours to switch over from building for comfort to the disagreeable task of tooling up for defense. Our system may be cumbersome and slow, but once Americans are convinced that the switch must be made, we'll go ahead faster and with more efficiency than a dictator could ever achieve with any amount of pushing and driving."

He looked at me, grinning. "How could you, of all people, forget that our democratic government is the best men have yet been able to devise?"

"Excuse me, Mr. Jefferson!" I laughed.

Through such incidents which provoked Colonel Marshall into giving me advice, or just commenting off the cuff, I was able to gain some insight into his inner mind and heart. From my personal observations, I venture to say that two major factors contributing to his greatness were his capacity to "pay strict attention to business" (as he so often advised me to do); and, parallel with this practice, his total disregard for personal glory.

"A lot of hoopla and ballyhoo is no help to me," he used to tell me. "I have serious work to do, and the less limelight I get, the freer I'm left to act objectively. It is a tragic error to make decisions with an eye to making oneself popular. I don't give a hoot about popularity, it's a subordinate triviality. I haven't time for headlines anyhow, good or bad."

Colonel Marshall's modesty was a facet of his firm belief that his leadership should be dedicated to his country, which precluded any desire to create a hero image of himself. But there was something else too. "A lot of hoopla and ballyhoo" might have infringed on his already curtailed privacy, and Colonel Marshall's private life, with its affections and relaxations, was the one self-gratification he cherished all his life and valued above any amount of public acclaim. He had always protected his "time off."

Certainly throughout my childhood he had tried to train me

to guard and respect the wall between his relaxation and his duties. His training had been successful enough when I was a kid; but when he came to Washington in 1938, I was a grown woman and intensely interested in the highly charged historical events then and through the stirring years to come. But my adult interests in no way lessened Colonel Marshall's reluctance to let disturbing topics interfere with our diversion during the brief times we spent together.

He once conceded that he understood my keen interest in what was going on, and was sorry that he had to rule out talking shop. He reminded me that I knew his reasons for it, and whether or not I agreed, his reasons were more important in the long run than any academic desire of mine for discussion.

"I also know," he laughed, "that you're dying to hear some hot inside dope!"

But he continued, "Of course that's out of the question. I don't have to tell you that I would never divulge confidential information to you or anybody else. Not only that, it would be unfair to burden you with my observations on how the war is going. Too many people know about our friendship, and some of them would stop at nothing to pry information out of you. You've lived in Washington long enough to know that whatever you might unintentionally let slip, however trivial, could be misinterpreted by someone to magnify and further his own ends. It isn't that I don't trust you, but no matter how much I trust you, I also know that a trained spy or a zealous news hound could work on your loyalty to me to trick you into divulging information you might believe you were using in my behalf."

He was right and I knew it. Nevertheless, it was extremely difficult for me to keep quiet about the burning issues of the day, and at that, I didn't always succeed.

CHAPTER XXVI

One morning in the spring of 1939, shortly after Colonel Marshall was appointed Chief of Staff but before he'd assumed office, he telephoned to ask if I could meet him at the entrance of our apartment house at three o'clock sharp that afternoon.

"I need your help with something if you're free," was all he told me on the telephone.

"Sure," I agreed, "I'll be there," and I hung up wondering what I could possibly do to help him.

When he picked me up he said he was in a big hurry, but had to buy some summer clothes because he was going to Brazil.

"I have to look real snazzy," he laughed, "because I'm supposed to outdo the charming Madam Ciano, so I want you to help me pick out my wardrobe. It won't take long. I'll only need a couple of suits because I'll be in uniform a good deal of the time."

"Brazil? Madam Ciano—old stinko Mussolini's daughter? What are you talking about?" I asked in astonishment.

He explained that Hitler had invited the top Brazilian General to Germany in order to impress him with Germany's great military setup, and that Mussolini was sending Madam Ciano to add a touch of glamor to the Axis bid.

"Latin America is a vitally strategic area and I'm supposed to spread good will in Brazil for the United States," he concluded. "That's the story, so let's get on down to the Young Men's Shop. I don't have much time, I've an appointment later this afternoon."

"Colonel Marshall!" I exclaimed, "you just can't go to The Young Men's Shop! Economy is fine and all that, but you've got to have decent, well-tailored clothes for such an important trip; in fact, they shouldn't even be store-bought. At least, let's go to the best haberdashery in town. Remember? You're a big shot now!"

"Well, wherever we're going, let's get there," he replied. "I'm in a hurry."

I suggested the haberdashery John wished he could afford, and in less than an hour we bought two suits, a half dozen shirts, and several neckties.

As we were driving back to my apartment, Colonel Marshall suddenly snapped his fingers and exclaimed he'd forgotten to pick up his eyeglasses.

"Who's your optometrist?" I asked. "If he's not far and your glasses are ready, maybe we have time to run by there now and pick them up."

"Oh," he replied, "I don't have an optometrist or an oculist either. All I need is to have the printed page magnified slightly when I read; I buy all my glasses at the five-and-ten."

And he did just that. We rushed to Woolworth's where he bought four pairs of glasses in less than five minutes.

In late September of 1939, a few weeks after Colonel Marshall became Chief of Staff, the Marshalls moved from the Wyoming Avenue house to Quarters Number One at Fort Myer, the Chief of Staff's quarters, the "big house next door" that Lily and I had so accurately predicted would one day be assigned to Colonel Marshall. It would be an affectation not to admit that my mind was flooded with a thousand memories when I thought of him living at Fort Myer again. Most of all, I was bothered by aggravating pangs of regret that Lily had missed out on "George's" success, even though I realized that the resurrection of past memories was fruitless and inappropriate. The world belongs to the living, I told myself, and Lily's death is no reason to begrudge Mrs. Marshall her pride and pleasure in her husband's high station. Certainly, I was glad Colonel Marshall had not poisoned his life by ineffectually nurturing his loneliness, and, although there was a distressing coolness between Mrs. Marshall and me, it was good to know that Colonel Marshall was fond of her and took an active interest in her children's welfare. I loved Colonel Marshall and it was important to me that he should be happy, but I'm not at all sure I would have been so generous in my feelings toward Mrs. Marshall and her children if Colonel Marshall had dismissed me altogether. On the other hand, the fact that he retained his loyalty and affection both for them and for me was an indication of the character which inspired my loyalty and affection for him in the first place.

Colonel Marshall used to tell me bits and pieces about Mrs. Marshall's sons, Allen and Clifton but mostly he told me about Molly. It is a pity I never had a chance to know Molly better, but unfortunately, I can almost count on my fingers the number of times I have seen her. Perhaps my impression of her was influenced by what Colonel Marshall told me, but on the few occasions I did see Molly, I liked her without trying.

On the whole, however, I knew Molly through hearing about her from Colonel Marshall. One thing he told me I remember especially, because it not only reveals something about Molly, but also offers a good example of how Colonel Marshall filled his role as Molly's parent. Moreover, it gives additional evidence to my contention that his concern for Lily's comfort and well-being was transferred to Katherine.

Colonel Marshall arranged for Molly to take over all the housekeeping. He said that he had put her in charge because it would relieve Mrs. Marshall from the extra burden of domestic duties and at the same time would prepare Molly to run her own home more efficiently when she married. Molly, he said, was given a set sum per month "to run the show," and whatever was left over she could keep for herself.

"Allen claims Molly is starving him to death so she can add to her kitty," Colonel Marshall said, laughing.

Judging from the little he'd told me about Allen, he was the liveliest of the three children, and this sort of joke sounded like him. Actually, Molly was a very able housekeeper, according to Colonel Marshall. Her duties commanded my awe and respect, because even with adequate service, keeping house for the Chief of Staff was no small job. For instance, Colonel Marshall told me without batting an eye that Molly had to be prepared any day of the week on very short notice from his office to receive anywhere from one to a half dozen unexpected guests—and distinguished officials at that. There was no question of Molly's getting away with potluck!

John and I were rarely invited to luncheon, which is understandable in view of the fact that we could hardly have contributed significantly to national defense plans. Actually, we were seldom invited to Fort Myer at all, so I was delighted when Mrs. Marshall telephoned to ask us to share in a quiet, informal celebration of Colonel Marshall's fifty-ninth birthday. It was New Year's Eve, 1939, and I suppose that there must have been others present, but I don't remember anyone besides Colonel Marshall, Mrs. Marshall, John, and myself. At any rate, when John and I walked into the drawing room, Mrs. Marshall came forward to greet us pleasantly, but Colonel Marshall remained seated, absorbed in arranging toy soldiers and little tanks and guns on the coffee table.

He looked up at us, smiling. "I got these for my birthday," he explained, "with a note saying these soldiers and arms are probably all I'll get for defense."

We all laughed ruefully, but I wished him a happy birthday

anyway and joined him to help "deploy" his "defense forces," while Mrs. Marshall and John entered into an animated conversation. I had noticed before that Mrs. Marshall appeared to like John, and it pleased me, because it made our infrequent visits with the Marshalls a lot pleasanter. Whenever I went there alone with Colonel Marshall after riding, the atmosphere was always somewhat strained.

When John and I left the Marshalls that evening to drive on to a late party, I commented to John about how glad I was he'd made such a hit with Mrs. Marshall.

"I haven't made such a hit with her," he laughed. "Any time we go to see them, you and the General start talking to each other and ignore us. Mrs. Marshall either has to talk to me or sit out in left field by herself. Just tonight she told me, 'You and I are outsiders, you know.'"

"Nuts," I replied irritated, "it's her own doing. She could join in our conversation if she wanted to. When Colonel Marshall comes to our apartment, you and he and I, all three of us, talk up a storm. 'Outsider,' my foot, she just doesn't like me!"

"Could be," John agreed.

After that helpful observation I sat quietly, wondering if anything had been said that evening to offend her. We had only stayed a short while, because she had forewarned us that Colonel Marshall was tired and wanted to go to bed early. I couldn't think of anything particularly out of the way, except that I had noticed the old brass shell-casing ash trays, and exclaimed delightedly over them, because I hadn't seen them in years, and nothing else in the room looked familiar.

"What kind of guns did you say they came from?" I asked, laughing. This set Colonel Marshall off on telling about a few of my childhood capers. The anecdotes no doubt had bored Mrs. Marshall, but in my opinion certainly didn't call for any such drastic reaction as feeling like an "outsider." I wished John hadn't told me; it put a damper on the evening.

222

"Do you feel like an outsider?" I asked my husband plain-tively after he parked the car to go into the party.

"Hell, no, forget it!" he said, and kissed me. "Happy New Year!"

John was anything but an outsider; in fact, he was often the subject of conversation when Colonel Marshall and I went riding. Colonel Marshall demonstrated more than a polite interest in our marriage and he frequently questioned me on how things were going with us. I think he was worried because he knew that I was bucking my mother's antipathy to my husband. As I have men-tioned before, Mother was an articulate woman and she some-times made things pretty unpleasant and embarrassing for me. In the fullness of maturity, I understand that the trouble between Mother and me stemmed from a different sense of values; our whole outlook on life clashed. Not that either she or I were all right or all wrong; we were just at odds. In my youth, however, Mother's harangues were very upsetting, and Colonel Marshall's high opinion of John helped immensely to steady me. He made an all-out effort to help steer me through those early years of our marriage, not only around the extra trouble with Mother, but through all the flyaway sparks my own temperament was likely to generate. He encouraged, even urged me to unburden on him any problems I might have.

"Blow off steam to me," he'd say, "don't worry John. You'll get over whatever it is in five minutes anyway and he'll be spared a lot of misery."

One day when I mentioned that John was rather literal-minded and wasn't so hot on repartee, Colonel Marshall laughed and said that my comment carried him back to the early years of his marriage with Lily. He began to reminisce about their days at Fort Leavenworth—the Command and General Staff School for training officers.

"When we were at Leavenworth," he said, "I was an insignifi-cant, unknown young Lieutenant, identified chiefly as Lily's husband. Lily was so beautiful and so charming that without lifting a finger she drew all attention fom her unspectacular husband. Leavenworth was an important time in my career, and I used it for intensive hard work and study. I was a very serious young man, and I suspect my repartee was about as sparkling as the multiplication tables. No doubt Lily basked in her glory, yet she insisted that one day I would be famous and displace her as the center of attention. She told me repeatedly that she looked forward to taking a back seat. Well, when the time came . . ." He interrupted himself to advise me gravely, "You have a solemn responsibility. I don't believe I overemphasize when I tell you that at least fifty percent and perhaps as much as seventy-five percent of a man's success is due to an understanding and sympathetic wife. Many a brilliant man has been dragged down to failure because he was married to an inconsiderate or insensitive woman."

Colonel Marshall maintained high and exacting standards of what a wife should be. Whether he originated them himself, or whether he unconsciously absorbed them through the years of his marriage to Lily, is hard to say; it was probably some of both. For example, he was uncompromising in his desire for a pleasant atmosphere at home. But had he trained Lily to humor him, or was it because Lily, on her own, had so accustomed him to a smooth-running, happy household that he considered it unthinkable for a wife to follow any other course? Certainly, for the duration of his marriage with Lily and, I am confident, in his marriage with Katherine, he set equally lofty standards for himself as a husband. Otherwise his requirements for a wife would have been meaningless and impossible.

Someone once observed to me, "George Marshall could never love Katherine like he loved his darling Lily." The remark disgusted me even though Lily and I were devoted to each other and Mrs. Marshall and I were not compatible. I don't pretend to be so high-minded that I ordinarily spring to the defense of someone about whom I have uncomfortable feelings, but the statement reeked with malice. Nobody loves anybody "like" somebody else; the objects of a person's love evoke distinctive kinds of loving. Colonel Marshall, then, sincerely loved both his wives, and inspired in both of them the aspiration to make him happy. His vision of a wife is so perfectly exemplified in a eulogistic letter John Adams II wrote about his mother Abigail's wifely virtues, that I quote a part of it here, although Adams' extravagant sentimentality would probably have amused Colonel Marshall.

> . . . the delight of my father's heart, the sweetener of all his toils, the comforter of all his sorrows, the sharer and heightener of all his joys. It was but the last time I saw my father that he told me . . . that in all the vicissitudes of his fortunes, through all good report and evil report of the world, in all his struggles and in all his sorrows, the affectionate participation and cheering encouragement of his wife had been his never-failing support, without which he was sure he should never have lived through them. . . .

Inasmuch as Colonel Marshall's temperament was the exact opposite of that of the vain and irascible old patriot, John Adams *père,* I'm sure that Lily and Katherine had a lot easier time of it than Abigail!

I was never a member of Colonel Marshall's and Katherine's household as I had been in his and Lily's; nevertheless, after our initial poor start in Chicago, Mrs. Marshall and I got along very well—with one explosive exception.

That single exception, which John and I referred to as "the meat loaf crisis," occurred one fall afternoon when I'd returned to the Fort Myer house with Colonel Marshall after riding. There was nothing unusual about my returning with him, because he often invited me to come back with him for a quick drink and a little visit. We would go immediately to a big, second-story sun porch (Colonel Marshall told me that General MacArthur had added it to the house when he was Chief of Staff) which was the

Marshalls' favorite spot in the house. Its large windows framed a distant picture-book view of the city, and when the trees close outside were in leaf, I had the illusion of sitting in a de luxe tree house. De luxe in size, that is, for the porch was simply though attractively furnished. The main piece of furniture was a chaise lounge which was Colonel Marshall's indisputable property. It was here on the porch that Mrs. Marshall waited for us when we came in from riding.

Colonel Marshall would collapse onto the chaise lounge, highballs would appear, and we'd sit sipping our drinks and talking inconsequential chit chat. It was pleasant enough, though never free and easy as it had been with Lily. I would usually stay about twenty minutes or so, and then politely take my leave.

On the afternoon in question, when the time came for me to go, I remarked casually that I'd better run along home and get John's dinner ready. Colonel Marshall heaved a contented sigh and asked to be excused from getting up; he'd had a hard day and was too comfortable to move.

"The car's at the door," he said. "I think you can find your way out." (John had needed our Chevy that day and Colonel Marshall had sent for me.)

I replied that of course he could omit the formalities. I set down my empty glass preparatory to getting up myself, when he asked, smiling, "What are you going to cook for dinner?"

"Meat loaf," I said, laughing. "It's the one dish I'm a real pro at and John loves it." I paused, waiting for his praise, for he had congratulated me on my meat loaf when I'd served it to him one evening during the past summer.

But I heard no compliments from him; instead, Mrs. Marshall spoke up quickly. "I hope John survives it," she said. "Your meat loaf made George desperately ill when you fed it to him last summer. He had such a severe attack of ptomaine poisoning that the Sergeant telephoned me long distance at Fire Island. I rushed back to Washington in a terrible fright!"

"Why, it couldn't have been my meat loaf!" I exclaimed in genuine astonishment, and turning to Colonel Marshall, jabbered, "It must have been something else; John and I didn't get sick. Why didn't you tell me you were sick? Did *you* think it was because of my meat loaf?"

Caught in the crossfire, Colonel Marshall replied evasively, "It could have been one of a dozen things I ate that week." Intending to dismiss the subject, he concluded, "It wasn't necessary to tell you I had an upset stomach, nor was it necessary for Katherine to come back to the Washington heat. The whole business was a tempest in a teapot."

"Oh no!" Mrs. Marshall disagreed emphatically. "Indeed you were extremely ill." Then she added decisively, "And I'm quite sure it was brought on by Rose's meat loaf."

I held my temper and rose to leave. Mrs. Marshall remained seated as I stood stiffly looking down at her. Hearing myself speak, I was surprised that my voice sounded as icily courteous and haughty as my father's sometimes had when he was angry with someone. "Mrs. Marshall, I cannot believe that my meat loaf was the cause. But in any case, I am distressed to learn that Colonel Marshall was ill and that your summer vacation was interrupted."

I had seen people go brown around the edges when my father used that tone and manner; but I must have lacked the frosty touch of his withering civility, for Mrs. Marshall came back strong with a smasher of a punch line. "I'm sure it was not intentional," she purred, "it was probably just cheap meat."

Adrenalin poured through my system. With outraged dignity I replied hotly that John and I most certainly were poor. "But I'll be damned if I'd serve dog food!" I cried. "That meat was first quality from the best butcher at the P Street market." I glanced at Colonel Marshall. "I'd better go, Colonel Marshall," I said shakily, "Thank you for the drink and I enjoyed the ride." Turning abruptly, I made for the door.

Colonel Marshall rose hurriedly from the chaise lounge, took my arm, and ushered me out. I was too disconcerted to protest until we had started down the stairs, when I collected myself sufficiently to tell him not to bother to come all the way down. Half apologizing, I said I was sorry if I'd been rude, but there was a limit to what I could take.

"I'll come with you," was all he said.

When we reached the car, he dismissed the Sergeant, telling him he preferred to drive himself. It was several miles from Fort Myer to our apartment on Fifteenth Street, and we rode all the way in complete silence. I knew Colonel Marshall was waiting for me to speak first, but I was seething with indignation and didn't dare open my mouth for fear I'd make some horribly indiscreet remark about Mrs. Marshall. Finally, we pulled to a stop in front of the apartment house, and I turned toward Colonel Marshall uncertainly, not sure if he expected an all-out apology.

He looked directly at me. "Rosie?" he said, and his eyes were questioning, smiling, concerned, gentle. I hadn't seen that expression since childhood, and like a child, I burst into a storm of tears and poured out all the things I hadn't intended to say.

"I hate her, I absolutely *hate* her!" I cried. "Why would she want to insult me? Cheap meat! How dare she accuse me of serving inferior food? She baited me just to make me mad, and like a dumb Dora, I fell for it!"

Colonel Marshall put his arm around my shoulder and stroked my hair to calm me, as he used to do when I was a little girl.

"Anyhow," I raved on, "why did you even tell her about my meat loaf? Do you believe she really thought that's what made you sick? It was *not,* but even if she did really think so she chose a lousy way to tell me. It's all your fault, you shouldn't have mentioned my meat loaf!"

"Your wondrous meat loaf," he interposed calmly, "was one dish mentioned when the doctor interrogated me. There were also Lobster Thermidor and several other concoctions."

Suddenly I was filled with self-pity. Poor me, the loving, loyal, lifetime friend was despised and rejected! I began to upbraid him. "You're *my* Colonel Marshall and you had a big nerve to marry that old Katherine without asking my permission!"

Colonel Marshall removed his arm from around my shoulder and began to laugh.

"What's so funny?" I asked disconsolately.

"This is a very unusual situation for me," he chortled. "I'm flattered to have two attractive women fighting over me!"

He had jolted me into smiling. *"Touché!"* I replied, sniffling and drying my eyes. "Really, Colonel Marshall, that's the only possible thing you could have said and not taken sides."

My anger and indignation evaporated when I saw the entire performance, Mrs. Marshall's and mine, as an absurd display of feline truculence. I have no idea what Colonel Marshall said to her later, if anything, but she and I drew in our claws forever after.

Statesmen and military men have said that one of Colonel Marshall's most important contributions to the Allied victory was his uncanny ability to promote a smooth cooperation between Great Britain and the United States. I can believe it. A cat fight between two vindictive women is no less difficult to handle successfully than disagreements between two strong-willed allies.

In view of the disaffection between Mrs. Marshall and me, in addition to the social and official duties incumbent upon her as the Chief of Staff's wife, it is small wonder that she did not care to spend her free time with John and me. My opportunities to see Colonel Marshall were even further limited after 1940, because John and I moved to New York. Consequently, throughout the duration of the war and his tenures as Secretary of State and of Defense, I saw him only on the few times I visited my mother in Washington, or when he came to New York and could squeeze in a half hour or so to come to our apartment.

One of the last rides we had before I left Washington was sometime in the early fall of 1940. I remember the occasion because I forced myself to ask Colonel Marshall a big favor that afternoon.

In 1940, my brother Tom, his wife and two small daughters were living in Timmins, Canada, where his company had sent him to ferret out certain gold deposits thought to be there. Canada's declaration of war in September 1939, had brought about a profound change in the Canadian economy, and by the summer of 1940, the unfavorable tight foreign exchange made it unfeasible for Tom's company to continue its investments in Canada.

In short, Tom was out of a job. His severe hay fever rendered him ineligible for military service, and because he was anxious to be a part of our defense effort, he reasoned that his special education and experience could best be put to use in Washington. He was offered several respectable positions, but Tom was enough like our father to decline to work "just for money." He continued to search for a job in which he felt he could make a real contribution.

Sis and I worried about our brother's prospects, for he had left Washington in his teens and was not so knowledgeable as we about the complications of getting a suitable spot. My sister, Celeste, was going great guns in 1940, writing political news for aviation magazines and contributing regularly to the Washington column in *Newsweek*. Consequently, over and above her social connections, she had a wide acquaintance on the Hill and in various Government departments. When she offered to introduce Tom to Senator So-and-so or Chairman Such-and-such who might help him, he haughtily refused to go to work under the auspices of his younger sister.

"Well," I suggested hesitantly one day, "there's always Colonel Marshall. You know him yourself, and he could give you an entree to anybody you want to see."

Tom said he'd drop dead before he'd ask Colonel Marshall a favor, and that was that.

While he doggedly continued to job hunt on his own, he and

his family were living with Mother and Celeste in a house which my mother and sister had fortuitously joined forces to rent the previous year. As time went on, the strain of accumulated disappointments and the inevitable clash between different generations and between in-laws began to tell on Tom. It was a long, hot summer!

Finally, I decided to ask for Colonel Marshall's help behind my brother's back. It was a precarious gamble. Although I knew that Colonel Marshall liked Tom and was sympathetic to his predicament, I also knew that Colonel Marshall had never in his life pulled strings to advance his own career, and disdained people who sought personal favors from him. In fact, before he was appointed Chief of Staff, there had been considerable speculation on whether he or General Hugh Drum would get the appointment. The prevalent gossip was that General Drum would be the man. When I expressed concern that the political sharpshooters Drum had lined up and the publicity he was getting might eliminate my "choice," Colonel Marshall replied sharply, "You know I don't operate that way. If I can't stand on my record, I'd rather not serve. And there's another very good reason I refuse to countenance influential help. If I should become Chief of Staff, I think I'd find the position difficult enough without the added encumbrance of indebtedness to powerful men. That's too vulnerable a situation for me." He paused a moment and smiled. "My problem," he continued, "is not lining up backers, but stopping the well-wishers who want to intercede for me."

On the afternoon I had chosen to intercede for my brother, I recalled that conversation with acute discomfort, and I also remembered with distress that Colonel Marshall had told me more than once that any one who toadied up to him for personal favors was a dead duck before he started. Well, "fools rush in . . . ," and this fool was very much concerned about her brother. As it turned out, Colonel Marshall unconsciously smoothed the way for me by inquiring how Tom was making out.

"Terrible!" I moaned, and giving him a brief account of

Tom's situation, ended by telling him what my brother had said when I'd suggested coming to him.

"But I'm coming to you even if he won't," I blurted out; "I know how you feel about asking favors, but Colonel Marshall, please help Tom!"

Colonel Marshall had listened attentively, and when I finished, he smiled and stated flatly, "Tom has asked me nothing for himself. I respect his restraint and admire his dignity. I will do everything I can to give him a lift; he is intelligent, and his technical knowledge is needed. I will help him in good conscience."

"Now, stop worrying," he concluded, with a finality that I recognized as closing the subject.

The next week my brother was invited to an interview with Edward Stettinius, then Co-chairman of the National Advisory Defense Commission, who hired him on the spot as Technical Assistant in the Mines and Mineral Products Division. Later, Tom accepted an assignment with the War Production Board in the Department of Strategic Minerals. Thus Colonel Marshall made it possible for my brother to offer the kind of contribution throughout the war that he felt best qualified to make.

CHAPTER XXVII

ON CHRISTMAS DAY, 1940, MOLLY WAS MARRIED TO CAPTAIN JAMES Winn in the Chief of Staff's Quarters at Fort Myer. Molly, elegant and svelte in her exquisite wedding gown, descended the stairs on Colonel Marshall's arm looking straight ahead, with her lips set in a little, fixed half-smile. Her suggestion of a smile and her unwavering gaze were the only indications to me that she was nervous. As for Colonel Marshall, he was never nervous about anything; he looked as pleasant and composed as if he were coming downstairs to greet a few old cronies.

The wedding reception was elaborate, large, and festive, and I wondered to myself if Molly's housekeeping assignment included preparations for her wedding reception. If so, I thought, she's a genius!

Colonel Marshall told me later she had indeed planned the greater part of it, but she had relied heavily on Mrs. Marshall's expert assistance and advice.

"In fact," he laughed, "the strain and excitement of getting ready for the doings reduced Katherine to living pretty much exclusively on Bromo-Seltzers until the shebang was over!"

Molly and her husband left immediately after her wedding for Captain Winn's post in Panama, and John and I left a few days later to begin our new life in New York. I suspect Molly's absence was keenly felt by Colonel Marshall and her mother. Colonel Marshall was occupied with looking after the nation, Mrs. Marshall with looking after him, and Molly with looking after both of them, which boils down to the rather startling fact that Molly is an unsung heroine of our national defense effort from 1938 through 1940!

John started work as a tax expert with the Sperry Corporation in New York on January 1, 1941. He had been employed by Thomas A. Morgan, Chairman of the Sperry Corporation Board, and a friend of my sister's whom she had met at a cocktail party for the aviation industry, one of her "news accounts." Mr. Morgan, a brilliant, tough business executive didn't pass out jobs for friendship's sake, so I was very proud that John had succeeded in selling himself.

For Colonel Marshall and me, my departure from Washington marked the beginning of another phase in our friendship which so far had spanned twenty-two years. In the future, we were to see each other only at intervals, and never again for an extended length of time.

Toward the end of January, I received my first letter from him, which initiated our intermittent but continuing correspondence for the next fifteen years. The letter began as so many others were to begin, with an explanation that he would have written sooner but "events have developed too rapidly for me to turn to anything personal and pleasant."

It was a long, chatty letter in which Colonel Marshall included his somewhat prosaic thanks for the "delicious" Moravian Christmas cookies I had sent him and Mrs. Marshall, but sparked up his thank you with his special brand of kidding by asking where I'd bought them for "I assume you did not make them."

He wrote about his recent rides, commenting, rather poignantly I thought, that since Molly and I had left, he was riding alone and "it is a lonely business." His subsequent letters frequently referred to his lone rides, and it bothered me, because he needed the diversion of companionship that could offer him a change of pace as much as he needed physical exercise. Neither of his wives could ride, but in Lily's day, Colonel Marshall had not been the top dog, which left him free to ride with any one of a number of Army equestriennes. An invitation to ride with the Chief of Staff, however, would have involved tiresome questions of protocol and politics, aside from the fact that most of his female contemporaries had given up riding. Molly and I were the perfect answer, and we usually alternated riding with him. Occasionally, the three of us rode together.

Colonel Marshall was never one to dwell long on personal grievances. In the paragraph following his brief admission of loneliness, he launched into a happy account of Molly's enthusiasm about setting up her own house, inserting a small boast that it was fortunate she already knew how "to cook and market." Colonel Marshall always did assume full credit for having trained Molly in the housekeeping arts.

Obviously, the Marshalls had heard from Molly, but, shades of the lost fur coat, I had not yet written! Colonel Marshall needled me to write and conspicuously contrasting his own thoughtfulness with my negligence, informed me that he was sandwiching his letter to me "between pretty important affairs of the world" inasmuch as he was due in ten minutes to appear before the Foreign Relations Committee on the famous Lend-Lease Bill.

All hell broke loose as a result of Colonel Marshall's testimony for Lend-Lease. He had testified in Executive Session, and in order to dispel certain persistent reservations about the urgent need for the bill, he'd thought it advisable to give the committee specifically pertinent but restricted military information. After the meeting, some unconscionable ass of a politician leaked Colonel Marshall's secret testimony. A few days later, appearing before the House Military Affairs Committee, Colonel Marshall frigidly opened his testimony with a succinct remark that was published all over the world.

"Gentlemen, we are now playing poker with an exposed hand."

When I saw Colonel Marshall in Washington a short time afterwards, I'd commented that his poker gibe had been so widely publicized that I hoped it would shut off the possibility of another betrayal. As for the metaphor itself, I joked that for my part it was a welcome change from his favorite football talk, although it was news to me that he was a poker fan.

He countered that it was hardly necessary to be a card shark to know you can't show your cards, and added, a little piqued, that he'd needed a short, bull's-eye figure of speech. He defended his metaphor as if I'd criticized it! In considerable detail, he explained how impracticable it would have been to condense the tricky procedure of stealing a football team's plays before they could be given away, and anyhow, it was an unsuitable comparison with the politician's senseless dishonesty.

"In other words," I smiled, still teasing him, "you didn't ad-lib your famous reprimand, it was premeditated."

"Of course," he answered, unperturbed.

Following up this banter, Colonel Marshall sent me a copy of a translation from a front-page article about him which appeared in *Das Reich,* the influential German propaganda weekly. Included in the article was a stilted translation of his poker remark, "We shall now play poker while everybody looks at our cards." Also in the article was a slightly garbled version of one of Colonel Marshall's oft-repeated aphorisms—"After 3 P.M. no one has an original thought." *Das Reich* got the hour wrong; Colonel Marshall's time limit was 2 P.M.

"Nobody ever has an original idea after 2 P.M." he used to tell me long before he'd reached the quotable stage, and herein lay a bone of contention between us. I never agreed, arguing that he was confusing a particular with the universal.

"It may be so for you," I'd concede, "but not for me. I'm a night owl and so are plenty of other people. It's purely a physiological question of individual metabolism; one person may be hep in the morning and another at night."

"Physiological, my eye," he'd retort, "it's purely a question of bad habits." And so it would go. Neither of us ever convinced the other.

Returning to the *Das Reich* article, it was a revealing sample of how Nazi propaganda was contrived to mislead the German people. It gave a fairly accurate résumé of Colonel Marshall's career, while insidiously misrepresenting his character; for example, it used the deceptive epithet "Supreme War Lord" to create the absurdly inaccurate image of a power-happy military despot. Another example, ". . . He dominates the sliding scale on which the U. S. A. people have to be led to war . . . ," read as if it might have been written by an isolationist group in our own country. As a matter of fact, after the war it was discovered that the most fervent isolationists, the "America Firsters," were partly financed by Germany.

It was in one of Colonel Marshall's letters of 1941 that I learned he had nearly been forced to retire in his early years as a Lieutenant. He happened to write me about it because I'd written him I'd been having a bout with some doctors. He knew I rarely, if ever, went to a doctor, and it never occurred to me to spell out the information that I was having an investigation made to find out why I didn't have a baby. His letter was intended to hearten me in my "illness" by divulging the fact that he had been on the verge of retirement in 1911 because of a fallen arch that temporarily necessitated his using a cane. He went on to tell me he'd had another, even more serious, period previously in 1904. After two years in the Philippines, he was threatened with T. B. from exposure to winter winds at drill. "Cod liver oil," he wrote, "knocked this out and nearly took me with it!"

A few weeks after that letter, I was in Washington and Colonel Marshall started in on me for the hundredth time about the importance of my having a baby. Finally, in exasperation I asked him to lay off.

"Listen, Colonel Marshall," I said, "after being married four years and with John on his way professionally, there are only two reasons I would not have a baby: one, because we don't want a family, or two, because we can't have one."

Colonel Marshall summarily dismissed the first reason and inquired in alarm, "Is there anything seriously wrong with John?"

I burst out laughing. "Just because I've been so disgustingly healthy all my life doesn't mean I can have a baby. No, it's I, not John. Why do you suppose I went to all those doctors?"

"Oh," he said primly. "I see." There followed a few moments of silence, when abruptly, Colonel Marshall asked, "What did the doctors say?"

I told him my insides were apparently lopsided. "Probably due to all those thousands of miles you made me trot!" I joked, but assured him if I couldn't have a baby before I was too old, we would adopt a child.

Colonel Marshall appeared to be so deeply concerned and unhappy about my possible sterility that I had deliberately chosen to be flippant to conceal my own disappointment. Poor Colonel Marshall, who had always longed for a child of his own, was visibly disturbed by my news.

In March 1941, Colonel Marshall sent me a letter that he had typed himself (and pretty good typing it was) out at Fort Myer because, he explained, "Things have been too fast and pressing at the office of late to permit even the dictation of a hasty note . . ." He was still being called upon again and again to testify before Congress regarding defense measures, while at the same time he was heavily involved in directing the complicated and magnitudinous task of transforming our under-equipped, almost non-equipped, peacetime army of 174,000 men into an up-to-date fighting force which reached 1,500,000 men by July.

To give a rough idea of the obstacles he faced in steering this remarkable buildup, a few of his tasks included the establishment of induction centers for inductees, the development of camps in suitable locations regardless of the flood of petitions from local politicians and businessmen, and the all-important provision for high-caliber training.

Training was one of Colonel Marshall's biggest headaches, due in large part to the shortage of experienced officers. The inauguration of Officers' Candidate School not only offered a solution to the dilemma, but also broke tradition by discovering capable men in the ranks and affording them an opportunity to fill the leadership gap. To Colonel Marshall, the Army was composed of individual soldiers, not just divisions and regiments.

In addition to the above basic requirements (and not the least important to Colonel Marshall) was the development of his plans for setting up recreational facilities to help lift the morale of recruits. About a week before I received my March letter, Colonel Marshall had established a separate branch of the Army, the Morale Branch, which was placed directly under his supervision and control—his lifelong insistence on the importance of recreation was not confined to himself. His concern for the regular soldier was genuine. Also, he once told me he had ordered the officers on his staff to see to it that they arranged for brief times off for themselves too.

"It's a matter of common sense," he said. "Unrelieved work diminishes output, blurs perceptions. It's stupid to expect a person to keep up an exhausting pace without taking a breather now and then."

Building camps and providing for training and morale were not much use without proper equipment, and this, too, presented monumental difficulties. But the drive to reduce the formidable shortage of equipment gradually gathered momentum. Nevertheless, the national failure to accept the reality of danger earlier had held up development in all defense areas, including, for example, the Air Corps. For months, Colonel Marshall had repeatedly stressed that an effective modern Air Corps should be a primary consideration; but recognizing the pacifist-isolationist Congressional sentiment, he kept the War Department's initial request for airplane replacements within very modest limits.

"Something would be better than nothing," he told me when I urged him to hit for what was actually needed. "No, under the circumstances, it would be foolhardy to do that, impatience never pays dividends."

Meanwhile Germany was rapidly and efficiently expanding her already large and formidable airforce. Yet, in spite of General Marshall's repeated emphasis on the urgency for approving the War Department's low estimates for airplane replacements, and only two months before the Nazis entered Paris, the House Appropriations Committee would allow funds for no more than fifty-seven new planes! It was an absurdly inadequate number, far below the barest minimum the War Department had requested.

Throughout 1941, however, defense preparations moved from a crawl to a run, and Colonel Marshall was leading his team successfully through, around, and over seemingly insurmountable obstacles; yet there loomed always before him the dreadful specter of Time. Would there be enough time to ready the country before the highly probable outbreak of hostilities against it? In April, the insatiable Hitler had already begun to suck in Yugoslavia and Greece. Concurrently with these latest Nazi inroads, Colonel Marshall was further haunted by the threatened disintegration of our new Army. The 1940 Selective Service Act had authorized the retention of selectees for only one year. The year would be up in October, and it was questionable whether Congress would extend the Act. Isolationism in the winter of 1940 and 1941, though waning since the Nazi avalanche in Europe, was still strong enough to affect politicians with the vote-destroying cry, "Warmongering!"

These, then, were a few of the "fast and pressing" things that had kept Colonel Marshall from dictating his letter, and he referred to none of them. The only specific reference he made to his strenuous life was to outline a recent inspection trip on which he'd flown three thousand miles and inspected 200,000 troops from ten thirty Friday morning to five o'clock Tuesday evening. Then, on "Wednesday A.M. at ten," he wrote, "I was before a Senate committee!" He told me he'd returned to find that his work had piled up seriously, and he added a loaded sentence with no comment: "I have had to spend a good deal of time up on the Hill."

The rest of his letter deliberately switched from shop talk, turning to personal comments and questions about the welfare of my family, John, and myself. He managed to slip in a crack about my beloved Virginia and Thomas Jefferson, using a quote that he had lifted from somewhere, a snide reminder that "by the way," Jefferson had come from "'a small place in the north of the south.'"

He mentioned for the first time a simple diversion of his and Mrs. Marshall's which was to become something of a habit with them throughout the crowded years ahead. Whenever they could manage it, they would take off for the small, clean movie theatre in Buckingham Village, a new housing development near Fort Myer that had mushroomed overnight. Sometimes they would go on Thursdays—national cooks' night off—to have a simple, early dinner before the show in the little restaurant next door to the movies. Colonel Marshall could not always avoid official evening appointments, but in order to conserve his strength for the demands made upon him, he shunned social events and, most particularly, Washington's famed dinner parties.

"They bore me stiff," he complained, "and worse than that, too many guests buttonhole me for favors. Those kind of dinner parties are unnecessarily exhausting."

Consequently, he went to bed early and was at work in his office by seven or seven thirty in the morning, when he could concentrate without interruption. No wonder his deadline for original ideas was 2 P.M.! Colonel Marshall never maintained, however, that the different cognitive process involved in carrying out original ideas, his or anybody else's, shut off at 2 P.M. On the contrary, most of official Washington, and especially the War Department, was working long after hours.

Colonel Marshall wrote me in July that during that summer, while the daylight hours lasted longer, he could sometimes get off in time to go canoeing with Mrs. Marshall down the Potomac in the cool of the evening. On weekends, he would join her as often as possible at "Dodona Manor," a small estate Mrs. Marshall had bought sometime in the spring of 1940. It was near Washington, in Leesburg, Virginia.

Colonel Marshall had described Dodona Manor to me one day, and the setup sounded delightful.

"It must be simply lovely—wonderful!" I enthused. "And in Virginia—the country around Leesburg is so pretty, and absolutely superb for riding."

"Oh, you'll love it!" he smiled.

I probably would have, but I was never invited there.

The summer of 1941 was awful for the Chief of Staff. In May, his rising concern over the Nipponese aggression had prompted him to recall General Douglas MacArthur from retirement as Military Advisor to the Philippine Government, and prevail upon President Roosevelt to appoint him Commander of all the United States forces in the East. In late May, the President declared an "unlimited national emergency"; in June, Germany launched her massive invasion of Russia in flagrant violation of their Non-aggression Pact; and by July, Japan had gained control of French Indo-China.

On July first, the Chief of Staff released for publication his first Biennial Report to the Secretary of War. The report was not only a readable, concise account of military defense preparations so far, but also clearly stated his reasons for recommending an extension of the period of service for draftees and Reserve officers. His proposals for the extension, General Marshall wrote, had "but one purpose, the security of the American people. . . ." Although his report stirred up a hornet's nest of debate, neither the report nor the German invasion of Russia precipitated a mighty chorus of "yeas" for the Selective Service Extension Act. It squeaked through the House on August 18, three and one half months before Pearl Harbor, by the fantastic majority of one vote!

In August, General Marshall and President Roosevelt vanished from the public eye to attend the ultra-secret meeting with Prime Minister Churchill in the North Atlantic. There, the Atlantic Charter was born, redeclaring Roosevelt's "Four Freedoms" and adding four more points hopefully dedicated to a better future for the postwar world.

The Atlantic Charter meeting has a personal significance for me. Colonel Marshall sent me one of the four-star insignia he had worn at the historic event. He had suggested before I left Washington that it would be appropriate to have a set of silver stars made for me in view of my dogged confidence through the years that he would be Chief of Staff. He sent me the four stars for my birthday, pinned to an amusing but touching little note he dashed off in longhand.

After some pleasant remarks about the importance of my birthday, he wrote, "but I must confess I have recalled its significance somewhat intermittently with the result that I have failed to have made for you a proper silver pin. . . ."

I cherished the stars he had worn as a memento from my godfather, from Colonel Marshall, not from the remote Chief of Staff in the headlines. I received his insignia a little less than three months before the infamous Japanese assault on Pearl Harbor. After that black December 7, my godfather became more and more of a public figure, with the result that for me, Colonel Marshall temporarily lost his identity in the General Marshall I read about in the newspapers.

❧ CHAPTER XXVIII ❧

NEITHER COLONEL MARSHALL'S CHRISTMAS LETTER NOR ANOTHER letter in January 1942 so much as mentioned Pearl Harbor! It was frustrating, even aggravating that he didn't write a single word about the Japanese attack. His sole acknowledgment that a war was in progress was to tell me in his Christmas letter that the War Department was running all day Saturdays and Sundays.

In February, however, I was in Washington, and while we were out riding, Colonel Marshall voluntarily told me how he had spent the several hours leading up to the attack and, surprisingly, made a few observations of his own. He opened the subject by joking mildly that as it was obvious I "was bustin'" to hear something about Pearl Harbor, and as he could see and appreciate the strain I was under to keep from asking questions, he would reward me by going over a few of the details. Frankly, I thought that I had behaved with admirable restraint, and anything he might have told me that afternoon would have been a help. Like everybody else in the nation, besides suffering outrage and shock, I was downright scared.

Colonel Marshall told me little that was not appropriate for public knowledge, but hearing the story from him made a deep impression on me. He plunged into his account, speaking rapidly in concise, pithy sentences, engrossed in that magical concentration of his that had always evoked my absolute attention.

"I went to bed early Saturday night," he began. "I was very tired. It had been a strenuous week. I slept through the night, and when I woke up, I was thankful that no news had come in that was sufficiently urgent to call me to the office in the middle of the night." On Sunday morning he went riding, and when he returned home, he received a telephone call asking him to come to the War Department but not, in Colonel Marshall's words, urging him to get there "on the double." (He did not tell me who telephoned him.) Colonel Marshall said that in any case he showered and dressed hurriedly, reached his office at approximately ten minutes past eleven, and sat down at once to read the vital intelligence waiting for him. It was then that he learned of the near certainty of a sudden Japanese attack somewhere in the Pacific.

"Immediately after I finished reading the information," he continued, "I quickly drafted an alert to all Pacific Commands."

He gave the alert to a waiting officer (unnamed) with instructions to send it out at once. Something went awry with the Army communications system, and incredibly, his warning was transmitted over commercial wire. But no one informed Colonel Marshall of this unaccountable irregularity.

"You will find this hard to believe," he said, "but a Western Union boy was riding his bike to deliver my alert to General Short [Commandant at Hawaii] when the Jap bombs hit."

Colonel Marshall emphasized the irony of the whole hapless sequence, not by raising his voice, but by decelerating the usually rapid pace of his speech. Quietly but distinctly accentuating each word, he said, "I already had news of the attack and was talking to General Short on the telephone before my message reached him."

"That much was a tragedy of mishaps and errors," he conceded. "Nevertheless . . ." He paused, reined in his horse, and looked directly at me, his eyes boring a hole through my head while I sat in my saddle, rigid and motionless before that mesmeric glare. When he spoke again, his voice was even and controlled, and by the unemotional coldness of his tone, I knew that he was very angry. "Nevertheless, it is inconceivable to me how the attack could have been such a complete, such a total surprise. Previous alerts had been sent. They did not follow orders. They were careless and overconfident—a fatal mistake."

Again, he called no names, and I wondered if his "they" referred to both the Army and Navy commands in Hawaii or only to General Short and his staff. I did not ask. I didn't dare interrupt him.

"As for the Philippines," he continued in that iron tone of voice, "I will tell you that four hours passed from the time news of the Pearl Harbor attack reached our Philippine headquarters until the Japanese struck the Manila airfield. Four hours, and our aircraft were still on the ground in the open—perfect targets. I had sweated blood to get planes to the Philippines. It is inexplicable."

Colonel Marshall was silent a moment as he started up his horse, and pushing him into a trot, said a little impatiently, "Come along, keep up." But when I rode up beside him he smiled at me and spoke with such calm confidence and determination that I was ashamed that I'd ever been afraid. "Remember only this," he said. "The important consideration now is to look ahead, and God willing, gain the initiative as soon as possible and get along with the business of winning the war."

With that, he reverted to his easy, pleasant voice, and shutting off any questions or comments I might have had, said gaily, "That's enough war talk for a young lady and her godfather out to enjoy a very small part of a pretty afternoon."

"Gain the initiative as soon as possible. . . ."—at the very moment he spoke those words on that February afternoon in

246

1942, the United States was teetering precariously before the gates of Hell and destruction while disaster followed disaster in rapid succession. Bataan fell on April 9, Corregidor on May 6. "We have done our best," General Wainwright wrote the Chief of Staff just before his surrender, "and though beaten, we are still unashamed. . . ." The day after our surrender of the Philippines, the Japanese struck the American fleet in the battle of the Coral Sea. Our strong resistance in the Coral Sea, together with our decisive victory in June in the fierce battle of Midway, restored the balance of power in the Pacific. Our finger was in the dike.

By the end of 1942, we had "gained the initiative" in the Pacific, but V-J Day was a long way off. The Japanese retained their firm grip on vast territories in the Far East and on islands stretching halfway across the Pacific, including the Aleutian Islands which directly threatened Alaska and our Pacific Northwest.

While a war is going on, public attention is naturally focused on whatever battles are in progress, but because of intrinsic complications and essential military secrecy, few are conscious of the planning, strategy, and control necessary for the successful outcome of a single battle. The intelligence and fortitude required for the direction and control of the magnitudinous needs of global war stagger the imagination. It was on these vital aspects of warfare that General Marshall's genius was brought to bear. Innumerable high tributes have been paid him in this connection, one of the most apt of which was from the eminent historian, Samuel Eliot Morison, who wrote that General Marshall was a leader who "combined the patient wisdom of Washington with the strategic savvy of Lee." One outstanding example of the truth of Morison's statement was General Marshall's idea to establish the combined British and American Chiefs of Staff—my team-minded godfather! The combined Chiefs, of whom General Marshall was the acknowledged leader, reporting to the heads of their respective states, were the co-coaches who conceived the

247

"plays" on the basis of such variants as "when and where"; size and strength of the enemy; uses, types, and amount of equipment; deployment of forces; and many other pertinent factors. The Generals and Admirals in the field, the quarterbacks, made on-the-spot decisions and called the "plays" for the huge Allied teams of ground, naval, and air forces, thus coordinating their movements all over the globe.

Concurrently with our struggle to "gain the initiative" in the Pacific, United States forces and matériel were crossing the Atlantic—swarms of German U-boats notwithstanding—in such large numbers that by June, the Chief of Staff established an American Headquarters in England and selected General Dwight D. Eisenhower for the command. By July, President Roosevelt, Prime Minister Churchill, and the Combined Chiefs arrived at a final decision to launch an expedition into northwest Africa. General Eisenhower was designated Commander of the Allied forces.

The British-American invasion of North Africa, begun on November 7, 1942, was the greatest display of successful teamwork in the history of warfare and a forerunner of future Allied cooperation throughout World War II.

✿ CHAPTER XXIX ✿

NEEDLESS TO SAY, THE DEMANDS ON COLONEL MARSHALL GREW heavier and more diverse in proportion to expanding United States participation in the war; his letters were few and far between. Soon after I returned to New York from my Washington visit in February 1942, I had a little note from him enclosing the handwritten rhymes he'd composed when I was a child, beginning, "A little girl I strive to please . . ." In March he sent me a poem, "High Flight," by the young American Pilot Officer John Gillespie Magee, Jr., who had enlisted in the Royal Canadian Air Force and was killed in action in December 1941. The poem was mailed in an envelope addressed in Colonel Marshall's handwriting, but there was no additional message from him—only a single mimeographed sheet containing the poem, a brief biography of Magee, and Archibald MacLeish's comment that "High Flight" ranked with Rupert Brooke's "The Soldier" and John McCrae's "In Flander's Fields." It was a joyous, sensitive little poem filled with exquisite imagery reminiscent of Saint-Exupéry's prose, and I'm sure Colonel Marshall liked it or he wouldn't have bothered to send it to me.

After the poem arrived, there was a gap in our correspondence until early December, when I received a letter which opened, "I had not heard from you for so long that I called Celeste at the Mayflower . . ." and closed, "Send me a note and tell me what is happening to you. I think it is four or five months since I heard of you . . ."

He hadn't heard from me for several reasons. First, during those four or five months my sense of closeness to him had waned for the first and only time in my life, not so much because I neither saw nor heard from him, as because I continued to read about General Marshall this, and the Chief of Staff that, in the news. It seemed almost presumptuous to write to such a remote, harassed patriot.

Another reason I hadn't written was that I had been working like a dog six days a week from the dark of morning until the dark of evening. I had become a member of the "Industrial Front." My husband didn't object to my job, because this time I had not gotten a job merely for "something to do" or to supplement his salary.

I was a factory worker, laboring incognito in one of the Sperry Corporation factories. I was incognito insofar as I chose not to reveal my personal connections with the management, because I preferred to work uninhibited in an environment where executives were highly unpopular—referred to as "them rich guys in the office," "them birds upstairs," who shuffled papers around, talked big talk, and didn't know the meaning of a hard day's work. John had advanced by this time to become Assistant Secretary-Treasurer of the Sperrygyroscope Company, another nearby subsidiary of the Sperry Corporation, and I couldn't have tolerated personal attacks against my husband. In any case, it seemed to me that I detected a note of envy underlying the contempt for company officials, so talking about my husband's position would have made me appear to be a show-off. If letting on about John's job would have seemed boastful, naturally I didn't sound off about my illustrious godfather. Furthermore, the disclosure of my brother-in-law's identity would have been grossly tactless—laid me open to charges of trying to throw my weight around. The friendship between my sister and Tom Morgan had ripened into romance and they had been married shortly after Pearl Harbor, so that, as Chairman of the Board, my brother-in-law was the biggest "bird" in the flock!

I never gave up on my defense of "dirty" executives, but my painstaking explanations to my co-workers about the weighty responsibilities, complicated decisions, and other difficulties borne by management met with derision at best, and downright anger at worst. Nevertheless, I was generally well tolerated, mostly because I was considered a well-meaning, though misguided greenhorn with too much schooling and a funny Southern accent.

In short, Tom Morgan had converted all the Sperry factories to full-fledged war production, and John, who had been a polio victim and whose slight limp barred him from military service, was pouring his guts out working at Sperrygyroscope Company. As for my part in the war effort, such was my antipathy to sewing circles and committee meetings that I had decided to attend one of the Sperry Factory Trainee Schools to learn how to operate complicated machinery and read a micrometer. After my "graduation," I was assigned to the Assembly Department where in time I was shifted to putting together clock mechanisms which skilled mechanics incorporated into gargantuan cubic units bristling inside and out with big and little saw-toothed wheels, nuts and bolts, vari-colored electric wires, metal plates, and God knows what else. My "clocks," used to time the automatic firing control of big Navy guns, required exacting and delicate work, but I had an excellent and very patient supervisor-instructor who was a watchmaker by trade.

My hours were ostensibly from 8:30 A.M. until 6:30 P.M., but like everybody else, "upstairs" and "downstairs," I frequently worked overtime. Added to commuting time, this meant that John and I often had dinner as late as ten o'clock.

The Sunday after I received Colonel Marshall's request for

news, I wrote him a long letter about what was "happening to" John and me. For one thing, I was learning a lot more at the factory than how to assemble timing units, and I included some of my new knowledge in the letter. In his reply, Colonel Marshall dismissed the good and useful things I'd absorbed as requiring no comment other than that he was "greatly interested" in my experiences. Instead, he took me to task for certain unfavorable observations I'd made about the curious persuasions of some of the factory personnel. What had shocked me most, aside from the probably quite average percentage of goldbricking, was that so many of my co-workers expressed the most singularly bizarre opinions not only about management, but also about our conduct of the war, our Allies, the United States political and military leadership, about anything or anybody outside the limited orbit of their daily lives. I wrote Colonel Marshall that their convictions seemed to me to have sprung from preposterous myths which apparently had been sanctified by blind repetition, and thus rendered indisputable. I couldn't figure out, I told him, whether their ignorance was innocent or willful, but either way, I was honestly concerned that it might endanger the overall war effort.

Colonel Marshall wrote:

> . . . I do hope that you are not initiating the procedure so aggressively that you will ruin your health. Aside from the difference in physical stamina, you and Allen proceed in much the same manner. He wishes to reform the world, politically and otherwise, in the first twenty minutes of his career, and I can see that you are headed for a similar reorganization of the conduct of labor. Be careful that your natural energy, and your impatience with sluggish brains, and your intense desire to get on with the war, do not defeat you in the long pull.
>
> I am very glad that you are occupied in this way and I should like to have a look-in on you and your watchmaker. . . .

When I finished his letter, I smiled to myself and thought, that's my same Colonel Marshall all right, still warning me not to set my own booby traps! Once and for all, he emerged clear and distinct from that distant national figure I was encountering and would encounter again and again in the reports and opinions of other people.

Another "Colonel Marshall" touch in his letter, a trait of his I had almost forgotten, was his regard for the limitations of the "weaker sex" as evidenced in his reference to the difference in physical stamina between Allen and me. I was immediately reminded of Lily languishing against her little lacy pillows, and of how she used to tell me that if George seemed overprotective, it was due to his unusually chivalrous attitude toward women. Feminine softness had certainly been one of Lily's beguiling wiles, for aside from her very real heart problem, she had consciously fitted herself into Colonel Marshall's knightly concept of fragile womanhood. But I, who had always had the physical stamina of an Amazon, was amused and flattered to be included in his archaic notions.

Soon after the first of the year, however, I had occasion to wonder if maybe, just maybe, Colonel Marshall had the right idea. Late one Saturday afternoon when I'd knocked off work, I was startled to feel the floor undulating beneath me. To keep from falling, I automatically thrust out my arm, whacked it on a small jeweler's lathe nearby, and broke my elbow. The doctor said it was remarkable I hadn't fainted, because I was in a state of complete exhaustion—but of course an accident like that could have happened to a man as well as to me, couldn't it?

At any rate, I wrote Colonel Marshall a breezy account of the mishap, emphasizing the disappointing result of having to temporarily withdraw from the war effort, but omitting to mention that John and the doctor had forbidden me to return to the factory— crow is a very distasteful dish.

Colonel Marshall was attending the Casablanca Conference when my letter reached his office. He was absent from the city "on an inspection trip," his secretary informed me. On his return, he sent me a sympathetic little reply—"a hurried note," he said, "in my first hour at the office"—telling me that *he* was well, although he'd covered a good many miles and had had some trying experiences.

Trying they must have been, a rigorous physical and mental exertion; and of the two, the mental strain was certainly more exhausting.

"Oh, Min!" Colonel Marshall had exclaimed happily one night long ago. "What a delight to go to bed when I'm tired from a day of outdoor exercise. It's a real pleasure to be tired in my bones and not in my head."

Lily had come back with a silly little joke: "If you had only been born a bonehead, you'd be delighted all the time." That trifling exchange was brought to mind when I reread Colonel Marshall's notation about his long flight to Africa and his "trying experiences." I suspect now that he was more tired than he admitted or perhaps realized at the time.

To be sure, in January 1943, the prospects for our side were not so black as before: The Russian resistance at Stalingrad and Field Marshall Montgomery's smashing defeat of Rommel's armies at Al Alamein in late 1942 had saved the United States from disaster. Fortunately, British and Russian courage and parenthetically, German miscalculations, had granted us the crucial additional time we needed to pick up speed on our military and industrial mobilization. Consequently, when Roosevelt, Churchill, and the Combined Chiefs of Staff met at Casablanca, the possibility of an Allied victory had for the first time become a probability though by no means a certainty. The success of the next steps toward victory depended heavily upon the wisdom of the military plans laid at Casablanca. The next steps agreed upon at that memorable conference were to assault Sicily as soon as the Allies had mopped up North Africa, and to amass forces in England as quickly as possible for the invasion of Normandy. The latter, General Marshall called "the most tremendous logistical undertaking in military history . . ." Both decisions followed the basic Allied strategy to beat Germany first before attempting an all-out offensive against Japan.

Another forward step taken at Casablanca was that the British Chief of Staff, Field Marshall Sir Alan Brooke, and the United States Chief of Staff, General Marshall, directed their Air Force Commanders to launch a joint air assault on Germany. This important directive presaged orders which called for continuous American and British heavy bombing of industrial centers in Germany and Occupied France throughout 1943—some team!

It was not until March that Colonel Marshall found time to needle me about my accident, putting his point across, as always, without resorting to pomposity or derision. I quote from this letter as I have from his other letters, because it reveals a little bit more about General Marshall.

> . . . My battle has always been to keep going and conserve my energies in every possible way. You apparently had great hard luck but I wonder if you did not overplay your hand at the start. However, that is a natural reaction of youthful ardent enthusiasms as compared to sluggish elderly philosophies such as mine. . . .

The following month I went to Washington to attend the dedication of the Jefferson Memorial, and fortunately, Colonel Marshall was able to arrange to go horseback riding with me; but neither one of us mentioned either the war or my accident. The whole ride was taken up with one of our most absorbing Jefferson-Hamilton arguments. The Washington meeting was one of several we had during the spring and summer of 1943. I didn't have a war job during that period, and although I didn't go to Washington again in 1943, I was able to be at home when Colonel Marshall showed up occasionally in New York.

If he expected to be in New York and could arrange to sandwich in a visit with me, I would receive a long distance call from his office that always followed the same pattern. I would be told what day General Marshall would be in New York (sometimes the call would come on the morning of the same day), the hour he would come to our apartment (4:22 P.M., 5:11, or whatever curious time he'd set), and then asked if I would be at home. My invariably affirmative reply would be followed by a warning repeated on every call: "Do not mention to *anyone* that the General will be at your apartment."

When Colonel Marshall was due to arrive after the first such call, I waited for him downstairs in our small lobby so that I could show him the way to our apartment. I didn't wait out on the street because, female that I am, I didn't want my hair to blow all to pieces; so I watched for him through the glass entrance door. I had just glanced at my watch and was thinking he'd show up within two minutes when an unmarked black sedan, driven by an Army chauffeur, pulled up to the curb. Immediately after the car stopped, Colonel Marshall jumped out without waiting for the chauffeur to open the door, and walked quickly into the apartment house.

"Hi!" I said. "Lucky the entrance is deserted."

He gave me a quick kiss and made straight for the automatic elevator without speaking. On the way up, I surmised by his taut expression that he was still wound up from whatever conference he had just been to; so I began chattering that the fellow at his office had been so emphatic about my keeping silent that I hadn't even dared tell John he was coming. Colonel Marshall's face relaxed into a smile, and he kidded me that maybe he'd better recruit me for Army Intelligence if I was all that cautious. He dismissed the idea of security precautions, explaining that he didn't want word to get out that he would be there because his presence might draw a few curious onlookers and would certainly draw the press.

"Then I'd be hooked," he concluded, "and I only have a half hour."

When we entered our apartment, Colonel Marshall asked right off to see all of it, a tour that lasted five minutes, but which I had anticipated and spent a couple of hours preparing for. After he made a few polite compliments on my neat housekeeping, I offered him a drink, and again, as I had anticipated, he accepted.

I knew he liked Scotch, and was thankful that John and I had a bottle of Haig and Haig with enough left in it for one drink, which I also knew would be all he'd take. Since it was next to impossible to buy Scotch during the war, Tom Morgan, after I'd told him and Sis that Colonel Marshall might visit again, generously gave me one of his last bottles of Scotch so that I wouldn't have to resort to rum.

While my godfather was sipping the dregs of our Scotch on his first New York visit he told me a rare story about a misadventure he'd had on his trip to England with Harry Hopkins in the spring of 1942. Colonel Marshall said that the English had stretched their imaginations as well as their rations to help make them comfortable during their conferences there, and although he and Hopkins were deeply appreciative and touched, nevertheless they'd damn near starved to death.

"I never want to see another plover's egg again," he laughed, "let alone eat one. People here have no conception of the privations suffered by the English."

(For those youngsters who don't remember Mr. Hopkins, he was the President's Special Adviser, an able man, but frail and sickly.) In order to spare Mr. Hopkins as much as possible, Colonel Marshall continued, it had been arranged that he and Hopkins be billeted in a small, private country estate where it was thought that their surroundings would be more comfortable and quieter.

"The house was unbelievable," Colonel Marshall told me, laughing and shaking his head, amazed all over again as he thought about it. "Sitting here in your neat, attractive little apartment, you can't imagine the hopeless disarray of that house."

He went on to say that as they walked into the entrance hall, they were confronted by a large pile of old newspapers and empty

257

boxes stacked helter-skelter in a corner. Colonel Marshall said that he thought perhaps they had been mistakenly led in through a side door, but no. When they entered the drawing room, he observed that it, too, was extremely messy, and its rather handsome furnishings were thickly layered over with dust. They were greeted by the pleasant, though stiffly formal, lady of the house, who seemed perfectly oblivious to the dirt and disorder around her.

"She was very much of a lady," Colonel Marshall said, "and I can only guess that her able-bodied servants were off at the war or working in the factories, and it had never occurred to her to put her hand to a bit of scrubbing. Certainly, no sprucing up had been attempted for her expected guests except, thank God, clean sheets on the beds."

His hostess, he continued, showed them to their rooms, announced the dinner hour, and with a grand and graceful gesture, designated the location of the bathroom at the far end of the corridor. Colonel Marshall said that he opened his door, stumbled over a big wrinkle in the carpet, brushed off a chair with his handkerchief, and sat down, dumfounded.

It was already dark when they had arrived, he continued. It had been an exhausting day, and furthermore, he hadn't had a chance to go to the bathroom for hours. After a few minutes in his room, he decided he'd better hike down the corridor to what he assumed was the only bathroom in the house.

"I opened the bathroom door somewhat hurriedly," he laughed, "and to my astonishment, the bathtub was occupied by a little girl about ten or twelve years old! There was nothing for it but to beat a hasty retreat back to my room."

He waited ten or fifteen minutes, he went on, and returned to the bathroom, this time listening at the door before he opened it, and to his dismay, he heard the little girl still splashing about in the tub. The situation had now become critical, so he went back to his room, turned out the light and opened the window. The only trouble was, in the dark he didn't notice the sentry below his window, and judging from the sentry's outcry, Colonel Marshall made a direct hit.

"Oh, Colonel Marshall, how awful!" I exclaimed. "How awful for both of you!" I added, thinking at once of the incongruity of the mishap with Colonel Marshall's innate dignity, and of the shameful, however unintentional, damage to the soldier's aplomb.

"Most embarrassing thing that ever happened to me," Colonel Marshall said. "There was nothing I could do to make amends, and I can only hope the poor fellow never found out it was I. I'll tell you one thing, Rosie, that's one error I will never admit publicly."

On one of Colonel Marshall's subsequent visits, I remember a more sober topic we touched on when I called his attention to Churchill's well-known predilection for late-night conferences. I had trimphantly used the illustrious Prime Minister to prove that Colonel Marshall was mistaken in his tenet that nobody had an original idea after 2 P.M. Colonel Marshall retorted that Churchill's late hours were a pain in the neck, and for him it boiled down to the simple fact that the British leader had fallen into habits as bad as mine. Indeed, he told me Churchill's preference for late hours worked a great hardship on him, for he had to be up early the next morning to contend with matters demanding his uninterrupted concentration, whereas Churchill stayed in bed until after ten o'clock. Colonel Marshall added that he was not alone in deploring the off-beat schedule, that it was a grievous inconvenience to many others, British and American.

"Don't you like Churchill?" I asked.

"Yes, I do like him," Colonel Marshall answered.

"Is he as able as he's said to be?"

"Yes."

There was a short silence. I had skated on thin ice by asking for his opinion about a renowned war leader. Colonel Marshall sat there smiling, and absently using the tip of his forefinger, casually stirred his ice around in Tom Morgan's Scotch. He was definitely amused at keeping me in suspense, and also, quite probably, he was deciding what and how much he would tell me.

After a minute or so, he spoke. "He is brilliant, a charmer, and witty. He is also stubborn as a mule and has a formidable temper. Fortunately, I am able to get along with him; but more fortunate than our good relationship, he is undoubtedly a gifted leader."

Colonel Marshall may have withheld specifics, but this was no bland statement to put me off. It was a broad assertion of what he actually thought of Churchill; my godfather was not given to making cover-up statements to me. He either told me what he believed or said nothing.

Colonel Marshall found himself heavily involved in one of Churchill's post-midnight conferences when the British leader came to the White House in May, about a week after General Omar Bradley's capture of Bizerte and Montgomery's capture of Tunis had ended the North African campaign. That May 1943 conference, called Trident, Colonel Marshall maintained may have been one of the most historic military conclaves of the war. Here it was decided that Italy was to be knocked out of the war; also, plans concerning the invasion of Normandy were firmly agreed upon with D-day tentatively set for the following spring. Yet the President, Prime Minister, and Combined Chiefs of Staff did not deviate from the basic Allied strategy to keep Germany as the primary target.

Japan was thoroughly discussed at the Trident Conference. It was agreed to continue hard pressure on the Japanese, regardless of the appalling requirements for the Italian campaign and mighty build-up for the Normandy offensive. Plans were formulated to increase the flow of matériel into China via the air route over the Himalayan "hump"; to work toward ending that beleaguered nation's isolation from the Allies by beginning operations to reestablish land communications, and to start a Burma Campaign in the fall of 1943 when the monsoon season was over.

After Trident, Churchill, Field Marshall Sir Alan Brooke, and General Marshall flew to Algiers to confer with General Eisenhower, who had been appointed in February as Commander in Chief of the Allied Forces in North Africa. It was a year of numerous conferences; bluntly, 1943 was the year when the wisdom of overall military planning by the top echelon meant the difference between future victory and defeat. General Marshall returned from Africa in June, and in August, Roosevelt, Churchill, and the Combined Chiefs reconvened in Quebec to survey "the whole field of world operations."

Meanwhile, American and British forces attacked Sicily early in July. The island's collapse after only forty days of fighting kayoed the Italian political system and Mussolini threw in the sponge. After weeks of tedious negotiation with the new Italian Government, General Eisenhower, acting under General Marshall's directive to gain as great a military advantage as he could manage, was finally able to arrange an acceptable armistice. The same day the armistice was signed, September 3, Allied forces landed on the Italian mainland; thus began the slow, tortuous struggle to wrest the "boot" from the hard-fighting Germans.

In July, General Marshall's second Biennial Report (July 1, 1941 to June 30, 1943) to the Secretary of War was released to the press and published in its entirety by many newspapers here and in England. The Report summarized every important aspect of our Army during those two years, from an accurate account of the Army's growth, development, and organization, through specifics on logistics, strategy, and Allied teamwork, to a full explanation of battles and operations all over the globe. As with his first Report, the second was organized for maximum clarity and written in a direct, simple style free from esoteric military terms; for it was General Marshall's hope that the information in his Report would serve to disseminate a better and broader understanding of the conduct of the war.

His first Biennial Report had stirred up a whirlwind debate; this one drew extravagant praise from all over the country. It was dubbed "Marshall's Masterpiece," and hailed as a war report which had no precedent as a valuable historical and military document.

I liked it too! As far as I was concerned, the diverse and complicated aspects of the global war were like pieces of a vast jigsaw puzzle. It was difficult for me to assemble all the pieces, much less make them fit, particularly since effective news coverage obscured the overall picture with a deluge of important bulletins and flaming communiqués. Colonel Marshall's Report gave me a whole war picture for the past two years, and provided clues for putting together the next year's pieces. I wrote to him how proud I was that his report had had such a splendid reception, saying that I was one member of the public whose understanding had been enormously increased; and I asked him please to send me a bound copy of his famous "masterpiece." I finally got my copy the last week of September, complete with maps, notes, charts, and a tongue-in-cheek dedication from Colonel Marshall: "To Rose: With affectionate regards and without obligation to read this."

I didn't have a chance to discuss the report with him, because a few days after he sent my copy, I accepted a temporary position as Personnel Director for a new factory organized to produce thermostatically controlled suits for aviators. The war had created a dearth of Personnel Directors, so a lawyer friend of John's and mine who was involved in the company's organization had bamboozled me into taking the job at least long enough to hire operators to run the machines, and to help set up a nucleus of other necessary personnel. When I reminded our friend that my knowledge about personnel work was not merely limited, it was nonexistent, he argued that I'd worked in a factory and worked in an office so I must have picked up something. To supplement the "something," John brought me a batch of Personnel Manuals from Sperrygyro. After a week of poring over them, I became a Personnel Director, and kept on learning how to be one all the while I was pretending to be one. I worked my head off and had a lion's share of lucky breaks, so that six months later when a professional was finally located, I'd somehow gotten the show on the road—but I was decidedly relieved to get out before I'd made a fatal mistake.

After such a facile escape, it was easy to minimize my good luck, and I began to feel rather cocky. My ego soared to giddy heights when I received a letter from the Chairman of the Board overflowing with praises for my "efficiency," "valuable contribution to the war effort," and so on. The Chairman of the Board happened to be the friend who had hired me in the first place, but in order to eliminate suspicion of bias in my favor, I did not divulge this connection when I forwarded his letter to Colonel Marshall. I wanted to impress my godfather with my brilliant success and to emphasize how great I was, but I attempted to disguise my conceit with suitably "modest" comments—something to the effect that I hoped he would be pleased.

Nobody gets away with tooting his own horn to Colonel Marshall! I still squirm when I remember his reply. His letter was not unfriendly, except for a conspicuous lack of interest in my job. He wrote pleasantly of other things, but his acknowledgment of my "superiority" was a brief, cooly courteous statement that the letter of commendation "must be very satisfactory to you." Exit glory!

Actually, Colonel Marshall was not totally indifferent to the praise he received himself, for though he was immune to flattery, he did appreciate commendation if he thought he'd earned it. The difference between him and me, or, in justice, between him and 99 percent of the people, is that he was neither swayed nor bedazzled by it.

Certainly, he'd been deluged with praises during the summer and fall of 1943. The acclaim he was given for his Biennial Report was followed by more tributes when President Roosevelt announced in late August that General Marshall would stay on as Chief of Staff even though his four-year term of office had expired. The nation reacted with approval and relief that General Marshall would continue to direct the Army's vast global operations in this worst of all wars. The press emphasized his surpassing military ability and meritorious character; but there was something else that went beyond the recognition of a great leader and which Colonel Marshall told me later had touched him deeply—it was the national atmosphere of confidence in him and the widespread expressions of gratitude for his superior performance of the prodigious duties laid upon him.

At about this same time, hot speculations were beginning to percolate concerning who the President would appoint to command the expeditionary forces for the coming invasion of Western Europe. General Marshall was ardently supported in some quarters, while in others it was argued that no one was capable of taking his place as the grand master of planning and strategy. I was reminded of the public debate before he was appointed Chief of Staff, and prayed that the current furor wouldn't destroy his chances for a job I knew he would want most of all. The country's impatience to learn who World War II's "General Pershing" would be nearly boiled over as the year approached its end, but President Roosevelt refused to be rushed into making a serious and difficult decision. He had not yet made the announcement when the Cairo and Teheran Conferences convened in late November.

The Cairo Conference was chiefly concerned militarily with the war in the Pacific, and marked Chiang Kai-shek's first personal appearance at a top Allied conference. When the Chinese leader arrived in Egypt on November 22, we had already made significant gains in the Pacific. We had won the bloody battle of Guadalcanal, retaken the Aleutians, and begun a major offensive against Japan. United States forces had landed on Bougainville Island in the Solomons, and Allied troops were attacking the coast of New Guinea. Meanwhile, American engineers were struggling to cut the Ledo-Burma Road (renamed Stilwell Road) through the jungles and over the mountains from India to China.

Finding a way to end China's isolation from her Allies was the top priority problem at the Cairo Conference, but the critical shortage of landing craft all over the world ruled out the possibility of an amphibious attack on Burma. Such an attack would have meant the unthinkable abandonment of the projected confrontation with Germany in Western Europe, so plans were laid for the Herculean task of sending in troops and supplies by land and airlift over the "hump." The whole Burma Campaign was unique in that it was sustained throughout by air supply. Indeed, according to a public statement by General Marshall, all the "Asiatic operations were carried out at the end of the most precarious supply line in history."

After Cairo, the Combined Chiefs went to Persia to be present for a part of the Teheran Conference, where, incidentally, President Roosevelt and Stalin met face to face for the first time. A tentative date for the invasion of Western Europe was decided upon, but as the military discussions at Teheran were brief— generally about American-British-Russian cooperation against the Axis for the coming year—General Marshall was free to leave before the heads of state had finished their political sparring. He returned home by way of the Pacific Theatre, a long and precarious hop for 1943, but he arrived safely back in America just in time for Christmas. Meanwhile, on the day before Christmas, President Roosevelt announced to the world that General Dwight D. Eisenhower would be the Supreme Commander of all Allied forces in the European Theatre.

Immediately upon hearing the news, I was overcome with

unhappiness. Poor Colonel Marshall, poor Colonel Marshall, I thought, what a terrible disappointment for him! It was the second time I had suffered his disappointment, and as resentment built up against the powers that had denied him his due, I experienced again the dismay and rage of the little girl who'd stood weeping before Major Marshall in the lobby of *2400*. Put aside your childish emotions, I told myself, and withhold judgment until you know what's what.

CHAPTER XXX

A FEW DAYS AFTER CHRISTMAS, COLONEL MARSHALL SENT HIS NEW Year's greetings to John and me along with his thanks for some plants I'd ordered for the Dodona gardens. His letter made no mention of Eisenhower's appointment or any other hot news, of which there was plenty, much of it directly affecting him.

When I read the letter to John, I laughed at what a stickler my godfather was for thank-you notes, vividly remembering the effort he'd spent in goading a procrastinating kid to write hers.

"I didn't really expect him to say anything about all that's going on," I told John. "Just the same, it's fantastic when you think he's been back in Washington less than a week, but come hell and high water, he had to get off his bread-and-butter letter for a couple of lousy rose bushes. I can hear him now," I mused, and imitating Colonel Marshall's rapid-fire speech and you-listen-to-me tone, I recited to my husband, "If someone takes the interest and trouble to send you a present or do you a favor, you see to it that you take the time to express your appreciation. You should write immediately, the same day, but never under any circumstances let me hear of you waiting longer than a week.'"

I thought Colonel Marshall's circumstances that Christmas week of 1943 might have allowed him to relax his rule a little, particularly since he admitted in his letter that it was difficult to get "rested up after my travels" because of "the accumulated work I found awaiting me. . . ." And besides his work, he wrote that he'd received several thousand Christmas cards. He tactfully omitted enumerating his presents, and I can't begin to guess how many of those he had to acknowledge, but I'm sure he acknowledged all of them promptly. Courtesy was one of Colonel Marshall's irrevocable rules for personal conduct, and though courtesy may be an attribute of lesser worth than such mighty virtues as integrity and charity, its practice often requires a disproportionate amount of self-discipline.

I used to think self-discipline came easier to Colonel Marshall than to most people, but I don't believe that now. Certainly the demands he made upon himself were bolstered by his faith and leavened by his humor, and of course he was highly intelligent, but a lot of people who have faith, humor, and brains are short on self-discipline. What they lack is a comparable quota of his moral courage. Colonel Marshall just wrestled harder with his angel, which didn't make self-discipline any easier for him—quite the contrary.

I know that he was deeply disappointed not to have been appointed the Supreme Allied Commander, yet it was his self-discipline that most probably kept the appointment from him. By the same token, self-discipline resolutely subdued his disappointment lest any vestige of it hinder the discharge of his duties as Chief of Staff—"to get along with the business of winning the war."

President Roosevelt won approval from most quarters (excluding my little corner) on the wisdom of his choice for Supreme Allied Commander. General Eisenhower's conduct of his Mediterranean Command had deservedly won him a favorite spot in the public eye, particularly after the successes of the North African and Sicilian campaigns.

On the other hand, the President was praised for *not* appointing General Marshall Supreme Commander—for keeping him on as the Army's top boss. The news media, Congress, the Cabinet, the Services (Army and Navy) all reflected the confidence accorded the Chief of Staff throughout the nation. Certainly, General Marshall was not then, or ever, the object of public idolatry. His genius was always respected, often revered, by his colleagues and associates as well as by his "boss," President Roosevelt, and by Prime Minister Churchill. But his antipathy to razzle-dazzle publicity excluded the possibility of inspiring the populace to wild adulation. By the end of 1943, however, a realization of his unobtrusive greatness had penetrated throughout the fiber of the American citizenry.

During December 1943 and January 1944, Americans were profuse in their tributes to General Marshall. To cite only one example, he was *Time* Magazine's "Man of the Year" for 1943; but many other editorials and essays in various newspapers and magazines emphasized one or more of General Marshall's contributions to the nation's safety. He was hailed for his genius as a global strategist. Attention was focused on his remarkable achievement in steering the development of the largest, most efficient Army in history and deploying it on six continents across two hemispheres. Due to two of his outstanding successes, he was called our greatest military statesman since George Washington. First, he had established a smooth-working relationship not only with both the Joint and Combined Chiefs of Staff, but also, *mirabile dictu,* with the Navy! Secondly, through his solid integrity, high ability, and endless patience he had achieved the impossible—captured an unprecedented respect and confidence of both parties in Congress.

("Oh, Colonel Marshall, you can do anything!")

As for my personal reaction to the President's appointment, I was sure Colonel Marshall would have made as superior a Supreme Commander as he had Chief of Staff. Furthermore, there was no doubt in my mind that he would have wanted to lead the great offensive he had had a major part in planning. I was heart-sick for him. I tried to calm myself with the old cliché that I was "grown up now" and could not allow my loyalty and affection for Colonel Marshall to blind me to the central issues. I realized that General Eisenhower had unquestionably proved his suit-ability for the high command. I reasoned, also, that if Colonel Marshall was such an able Chief of Staff, it would be difficult to replace him just when the country was poised for a great offen-sive. I was applying the right remedy to myself, all right, but the only effect it had was to help me keep my mouth shut. Inside, I was unhappy, mad, and frankly, beastly jealous of General Eisen-hower's plum.

In early February of 1944, I spent a weekend in Washington. When Colonel Marshall and I went riding, I could barely wait until we were out of earshot of the groom before I asked him point-blank, "Why is General Eisenhower the Supreme Com-mander?"

"Because the President appointed him and I recommended him," Colonel Marshall shot back with equal directness.

"Why?" I asked, and infuriatingly, my eyes filled with tears.

Colonel Marshall glanced at me and smiled. "I think I'd have been hurt if you had grown too sophisticated to shed a few tears for me," he said. "Of course I wanted the command, but don't worry on my account. I think I could have had it if I'd been willing to make a play for it."

"What happened?" I burst out. "I mean, can you tell me?"

It was no great secret, he said, and if it would make me feel any better, he'd tell me; but I was not to talk about it, "Because it's nobody's business and this sort of thing is grist for the gossip mills."

At the Quebec Conference the past August, Colonel Marshall told me, Prime Minister Churchill had recommended that the Supreme Allied Commander be an American and that he, Mar-shall, should have the command. President Roosevelt had expressed full agreement with Churchill at Quebec, but it was too soon last summer to make the announcement.

As time went on, Colonel Marshall continued, the President began to have reservations about releasing him from his duties as Chief of Staff. Finally, one evening when they were in Cairo, Roosevelt had sent word asking Colonel Marshall to come to see him.

"The President told me he wanted to know how I felt about the matter," Colonel Marshall said, "and then asked me whether I preferred to remain as Chief of Staff or to command the Allied offensive."

"Oh no!" I interrupted. "He passed the buck, that's not fair!"

Colonel Marshall ordered me to stop butting in. I apologized hastily.

"Anyhow, tell me what you said to the President," I urged.

Colonel Marshall answered that he'd told the President the only thing he could, and right away we automatically fell into one of our little acts, with me, as usual, playing the stooge.

Colonel Marshall leveled a steely blue, unwavering gaze straight into my eyes. "Mr. President," he said in a voice that unconsciously echoed the calm dignity of an avowed soldier, "I cannot evaluate my own services. You are my Commander-in-Chief and I will serve in whatever capacity you believe I can be most useful."

"You put me in a very difficult position, George," I ad-libbed, taking a puff on my cigarette and blowing out a stream of smoke.

Colonel Marshall burst out laughing and broke up the act.

"Sometimes, Colonel Marshall, I wish you weren't so damnably upright," I complained.

"You do, huh?"

"No, not really. It's only that I know you'd have wanted to take a more active part in the big doings coming up in Europe."

Colonel Marshall repeated that he had wanted the command very much, but that what he wanted was irrelevant to where he was needed. With a wry smile, he told me Roosevelt didn't seem to think he would feel as secure about the country if another officer took over as Chief of Staff during the war.

"So you recommended General Eisenhower for the job you wanted?"

"Yes."

In his book *A Soldier's Story* (Holt, Rinehart and Winston, Inc., 1951), General Omar Bradley had this to say in regard to General Marshall and the Supreme Command:

> . . . If ever a man deserved the appointment, that man was General Marshall. Yet in the Army hierarchy of command the appointment of General Marshall as Supreme Commander would have entailed a stepdown from his post as Army Chief of Staff. But stepdown or no, had General Marshall left Washington to go to Europe, no one—not even Eisenhower—could have taken his place.
>
> In the Army we often scoff at the myth of the indispensable man, for we have always maintained that Arlington Cemetery is filled with indispensable men. General Marshall, however, was an exception, for if ever a man was indispensable in a time of national crisis, he was that man. . . .

After Colonel Marshall told me what had happened about the Supreme Command, we rode along in silence for a while. I was racking my brain trying to think how I could express my admiration for his selflessness in sacrificing his personal aspirations. I wanted to come up with something pithy and ungarnished, because I was confident that lavish praise would be meaningless to him, would actually irritate him. Nothing I thought up hit the nail on the head, so I decided to crib from Jefferson and tell him that I was proud to know at least one man holding a public trust who truly considered himself public property. I thought that would go over well, especially since using Jefferson would amuse him; but I lost my chance to get it off, because Colonel Marshall suddenly said gaily, "You will be interested to know that I pulled a trick on the President."

"Whatever did you do?" I laughed.

"It was my long trip home from Cairo," he said. "The President didn't know I was going until I was on my way and it was too late to stop me."

He went on to tell me he'd thought it essential that he visit the Pacific theatre to get first-hand knowledge of how things were going there. He knew the President would have disapproved of his risking such a long flight, so he had taken off while Roosevelt was conferring at Teheran.

"Oh, MacArthur!" I quipped. "How is that splendid, handsome, heroic God's-gift-to-the-world?"

"Sarcasm is puerile," Colonel Marshall commented drily. "As for *General* MacArthur," he continued, "he's got a bad case of localitis and with more justification than some."

"What's localitis?" I asked, "and some who?"

Colonel Marshall explained that each General in his particular theatre of the war quite naturally became totally engrossed in his own operation, but unfortunately, to the exclusion of projected or current campaigns in other parts of the globe. Consequently, each one clamored for more and more men and supplies.

"That's what I call localitis," he said, "a prevalent disease throughout the Army and almost impossible to cure. You see, Rose, it's my responsibility to allocate resources according to immediate emergencies, overall plans—any number of circumstances determine who gets what and how much. General MacArthur is badly bitten by the localitis bug because of heavy demands right now for troops and matériel elsewhere."

"I'll bet a million he's sore we aren't concentrating everything we've got on Japan," I suggested.

"You can bet anything you like," Colonel Marshall replied shortly, "but not with me."

During 1944, all the field commanders' "localitis" must have grown from severe to critical, for in that year the war reached a furious pitch all over the world. In the Southwest Pacific, General

273

MacArthur's Allied forces, aided by the Seventh Fleet under Admirals Kinkaid and Barbey (nicknamed "MacArthur's navy"), captured all of New Guinea.

Meanwhile, in the Central Pacific, Admirals Nimitz and Halsey were playing a deadly game of leapfrog—from key island to key island. One after another, the Marshalls, Carolines, and the Marianas fell under the assaults of massive amphibious forces and naval and air bombardment. By the middle of September, Admiral Halsey's Third Fleet had captured the Pelau Islands, the last Japanese bases in the open Pacific.

Halsey then sent a message to Nimitz recommending that our forces strike Leyte in the central Philippines as soon as possible. A copy of his message went to the combined Chiefs of Staff who were attending their second meeting in Quebec. General Marshall insisted that General MacArthur should be allowed to express his views on the stepped-up schedule before Admirals Nimitz and Halsey received their instructions to go ahead. General Marshall wired MacArthur, who replied within a few hours that he was prepared to shift his plans to land on Leyte October 20 instead of December 20.

With no reservations, General Marshall immediately gave MacArthur the green light, and in his final Biennial Report (July 1943 to June 1945) he credited MacArthur's switch in plans as "a remarkable administrative achievement."

On October 19, a vast armada of combat and assault vessels carrying matériel and over 100,000 soldiers entered Leyte Gulf— thereby easing General MacArthur's "localitis," but by no means curing it. The next day, two Sixth Army Corps went ashore, followed a few hours later by General MacArthur. Looking every inch the conquering hero, erect in sharply creased khakis, shirt collar open, and worn battle cap accentuating his handsome features, MacArthur strode down his landing-barge ramp and resolutely waded ashore through the waves—several times. The repetitions were called for to allow news photographers to shoot the best possible pictures of this dramatic and historic event. Unfortunately, not all the cameras were set in time to catch the first wade, and on the second one, so the story goes, the General stepped into a hole and momentarily disappeared from view. His cap bobbed crazily to the surface, but it took a stronger force than Neptune to daunt General MacArthur. He snatched his famous battered headgear from the sea god's mischievous grasp, went back to his ship, changed to fresh khakis, and once again splashed purposefully toward the beach. Every camera ground and clicked and this time successfully captured the memorable scene for posterity.

"People of the Philippines," General MacArthur proclaimed as soon as he had reached the shore to stay, "I have returned . . . Rally to me."

He had returned indeed, and rally they did.

. Before MacArthur pushed on to victory, he ordered his forces to establish their beach areas and await the outcome of the momentous naval batle which began on October 23. The Battle of Leyte Gulf was the last great naval battle of the Pacific. The thunderous encounter lasted for five days, until our Navy had crushed the backbone of the Japanese fleet and knocked it out of the running for the rest of the war. It was a thrilling victory!

CHAPTER XXXI

MORE THAN ONCE, IN VARIOUS WAYS, COLONEL MARSHALL TOLD ME
he believed that concentrating on the defeat of Germany before
we conquered Japan would be the fastest route to victory. Not
that he discussed strategy with me, but from time to time he
would blow off steam, knowing full well I would never disclose
anything he said which might be remotely construed as verging
on the confidential. Frankly, even if I'd had a mind to, I wouldn't
have dared repeat one sentence of our *entre nous* conversations—
whew!

For example, one day he was lamenting the heavy toll war
was taking on the nation's youth, and from there branched out
into a little sermon on the dichotomy of the political and military
aspects of conducting war. He then began to work himself up
about the hardships of war generally. He seemed so tense and in
such low spirits that I tried to ease him by commenting half-
jokingly that it was too bad for him he wasn't tough like "Old
Blood and Guts" (General George S. Patton, Jr.).

"No kidding, Colonel Marshall," I said, "for a man who's
committed himself to an Army career, you sure do hate war!"

276

"Of course I do," he answered. "All my energies are directed toward ending the war in the shortest possible time. If you didn't know that already, you're not very bright." He looked squarely at me, and said, with such absolute conviction that I could never forget it, "and the sooner we beat Germany, the sooner the war will end! The shorter the time, the less lives lost; that's very simple logic. You must pray for that, Rose," he concluded abruptly, "pray that we can get it over with fast. Each single day added to the war adds hundreds of graves to the cemeteries."

In December 1943, there was extra need for such prayers, because a segment of the American people themselves menaced the nation with a useless prolongation of the war. The railroad workers voted to strike for higher wages and the steel-workers threatened to do the same.

It would be unfair not to recognize that on the whole, American labor performed miracles for war production, or we wouldn't have won the war; but "sluggish brains" unquestionably gave birth to the bastard idea of strikes during wartime.

In the end, the railroad strike failed to come off because President Roosevelt ordered the Government to seize the railroads. The Administration had adamantly declined to hand over an invaluable advantage to the enemy because a gang of avaricious men in key jobs wanted to stuff their pockets. It was unthinkable that the transportation of troops and matériel be allowed to halt for as much as one day; campaigns all over the world would have been crippled. But unfortunately, the very threat of strikes had already caused immeasurable harm to our forthcoming European offensive.

It was a wretched homecoming for General Marshall, fresh from the fighting fronts of the Pacific and faced with deep involvement in the execution of overall plans for the great Allied invasion. He was outraged by the laborers' callous unconcern for the welfare of their nation and particularly for their compatriots fighting overseas. He could not tolerate the peoples' ignorance of the tragic damage which had resulted directly from arrant self-interest. He struck out against it. Unwilling to involve the War Department in labor controversies, he used the most suitable avenue open to him. General Marshall called in a few selected correspondents, and giving them a graphic background briefing, laid it on the line. As I have mentioned before, my godfather was a poor orator when he was required to use a prepared text, but when he spoke spontaneously he was a compelling speaker.

When I had seen Colonel Marshall in February, the labor blow-up was about over and I had avoided bringing up an unpleasant subject. Consequently, it was about a year after that "exclusive" press conference before he told me what he had said. Characteristically, he reenacted the scene, and I'm reasonably sure his version for me was as close to being verbatim as he chose to make it. Colonel Marshall's memory did not play tricks. As I sat listening to him in my New York apartment, his wrath had had time to lose its cutting edge; nevertheless, I could easily picture the unforgettable impact he must have made on those newsmen.

He told them right off that months of careful, vital work had been destroyed. The Allies, he explained, had been striving to induce an early defection of Germany's Balkan satellites who, fearful of reprisals, were reluctant to abandon Hitler unless they were sure he would lose. Now, just as our victories and propaganda had brought us to the verge of success, the railroad brotherhoods and steel-workers had chosen to agitate for more money.

"Not much chance of the satellites breaking away," Colonel Marshall observed bitterly to me (the correspondents), "when they learn the United States Government has been forced to take over the railroads and a steel strike may be in the offing."

He then elaborated on the boost the strike furor had undoubtedly given to Nazi morale—"Provided the enemy with a greater incentive than Hitler, himself, could have wished for."

By this time, Colonel Marshall's eyes were flashing blue sparks. He fired off his closing staccato sentences, precisely aiming each distinct word to hit and hit hard. "Here is the brutal truth. The threatened strikes might literally have cost the nation hundreds of thousands of lives!"

As he reached the climax of his account, his distress mounted and I hastened to break the spell. "I know, Colonel Marshall!" I exclaimed. "I read about the dreadful cost of lives. It was horrible, still is. But you forgot to tell me one thing you said."

"What's that?"

"You told them it was 'The damndest crime ever committed against America!'"

He smiled. "It is indelicate of my goddaughter to call attention to one of my rare lapses into cussin'."

Actually, I had already read most of what he told me. When the story first broke, it had been duly attributed to "a responsible source," but the anonymity didn't last long. The St. Petersburg, Florida *Times* (which had not been represented at Colonel Marshall's briefing) boldly printed the news that the "responsible source" was none other than the Chief of Staff himself. The War Department neither confirmed nor denied whether General Marshall had given out the story, while Steve Early, the White House Press Secretary, announced that "'the responsible source' and the President were thinking along the same lines."

In any case, there was no gray reaction to the release; it was sharply black or white. Labor leaders railed against it, one source referring to General Marshall's information as "filthy propaganda." The rest of the country condemned wartime strikes in utterances varying from raw anger to eloquent protest.

But the steel strike was called off.

The year 1944, as it may be remembered, was a Presidential election year. Along with the usual political noises that precede the hullabaloo of Party conventions, a sizeable group of wishful thinkers was trying to drum up action on "General Marshall for President." His unsolicited drummers began to beat louder and harder after Colonel Marshall's blast against wartime strikes, which, though never officially confirmed, was generally accepted as coming from him. The insertion of political implications in his denunciation of the strikes was patently absurd. Colonel Marshall's whole concern was with the war and, contingent thereon, the calamitous effects of the strikes.

His backers, dissatisfied with Roosevelt and not favorably disposed toward the two Republican prospects, Wendell Willkie and Thomas E. Dewey, could not have had the faintest idea of the true character of their own candidate. Colonel Marshall did not like politics and did not want to be President.

Once I'd complained to him about not being able to vote because I lived in the District of Columbia.

"Well," he'd replied, "I was raised an Episcopalian and a Democrat. I chose to be an Army officer, and because I try to be a good one I go to church and have never voted in my life."

In explanation, he told me he believed an Army officer should remain strictly aloof from politics, that he should serve his country impartially regardless of which party was in power.

It was laughable to imagine that Colonel Marshall would throw aside his responsibilities as Chief of Staff to run for a political office. It was unthinkable that he would desert his Commander-in-Chief to campaign against him during the most critical period of the war.

"What're you going to do about the 'Marshall for President' talk?" I asked him on one of our brief get-togethers.

"Kill it dead!" he replied.

"That's very inconsiderate of you," I complained. "Just think how nice it would be if I could run in and out of the White House."

"I'm sure you'd enjoy that," he laughed, "but it's one pleasure I will have to deny you."

"But Colonel Marshall!" I objected, putting on sweet little dumbbell airs.

"Don't but me no buts!" he countered.

I switched to a grandiloquent pose, and quoting some of the

rhetoric that was currently circulating, I began to orate, "You don't seem to understand, General, you are the man who will preserve our God-given heritage. You have courage, character—"

"That's enough!" he interrupted. "You can spare me the guff."

"You know, Rose," he said seriously, "all other considerations aside, I would make a very poor President."

"Nuts!" I disagreed. "You can do anything you want to. I'll amend that—you can do anything you think you ought to."

"Will you ever learn not to exaggerate?" he admonished, showing a flash of irritation before he returned to the subject. "I repeat," he said earnestly, "I would make a very poor President even if I were not an Army man. A first-rate President requires a long apprenticeship in politics, and a political career never had the slightest appeal to me. I could not make the kind of compromises in politics that are considered necessary but are so often apt to force detours around inconvenient truths. I couldn't tolerate the inevitable personal obligations involved; all the paraphernalia that accompanies making a President is distasteful to me."

"Yes," I agreed, "that's for sure!"

He continued on another tack. "You were too young to take it in at the time, but there was a movement after the last war to draft General Pershing for President. I personally intervened to stop it and General Pershing was very angry with me." He paused and smiled. "He eventually came round to agreeing I was right," he concluded with satisfaction.

One strong "Marshall for President" supporter was a gentleman who happened to belong to the same country club that John and I did. One weekend he passed around a couple of mimeographed sheets touting Colonel Marshall for our next President. Entitled "America Needs a Man," the first sheet set forth fifteen points in short sentences, all starting with "A man who . . . ," and stating the kind of man this fellow thought America needed.

The second sheet was given over to praises for General Marshall, all slanted to fit him into the fifteen points of the first, and ending with, "For he is the type of A-man who should be the next President of these United States."

It was a sticky appeal, chock-full of gooey political clichés— "America First," "free enterprise," "no coddling of pressure groups," and so on—but omitting less tasty sentiments such as concern for the little man or compassion for the underdog. It puzzled and disturbed me that anyone's imaginative ideas about Colonel Marshall could have been so far afield.

I mailed the stuff to Colonel Marshall with a penciled note at the bottom saying, ". . . this is a statement handed me by a friend—according to you, he's way off base . . ." Colonel Marshall returned it to me with a single comment: "This is a pain in the neck."

Not long afterwards, the press carried General Marshall's unequivocal answer to the possibility of his candidacy for President.

"I will not accept if nominated and will not serve if elected."

CHAPTER XXXII

IN JANUARY OF 1944, GENERAL EISENHOWER ARRIVED IN ENGLAND TO assume Supreme Command of the Allied Expeditionary Forces. His successor as Supreme Commander in the Mediterranean Area, General Sir Henry Maitland Wilson, was charged with continuing the Italian campaign until the Allies succeeded in prying loose the Germans' tenacious grip on Italy. It was a bitter campaign, described by General Sir Henry Wilson as a "slow painful advance through difficult terrain against a determined and resourceful enemy. . . ."

On January 22, ten days before United States forces established their beachhead on the Kwajalein atoll in the Pacific, Allied forces in the Mediterranean landed on the beaches near Anzio, twenty-five miles south of Rome.

The hard-pressed Anzio forces were joined in early June by Allied forces who, after long, hard fighting, had finally captured the heavily fortified German stronghold atop Mt. Cassino. Rome fell to the Allies two days before Normandy D-day.

Ahead lay weeks more of "slow painful advance" over the

high Appenines to the north. Behind were thousands of dead and more thousands of wounded who had paid the high price for the capture of the first Axis capital. Among the dead was Mrs. Marshall's youngest child, Second Lieutenant Allen Tupper Brown, killed May 29.

Two days before Allen was killed, I'd had a letter from Colonel Marshall telling me he would be "very glad to dine with you Wednesday night, but Mrs. Marshall will probably not be able to as she is looking after her grandchild."

I knew that Mrs. Marshall had three grandchildren, because Colonel Marshall kept me pretty well up to date on the Brown grandchildren. Allen was married, had a son, and was overseas. Cliff was unmarried and also overseas. Molly had two little children, a son, Jimmy, and a daughter, Kitty, named for Mrs. Marshall. Her husband was overseas too. Colonel Marshall never told me in which theatres any of them were.

When I read about Allen's death so soon after Colonel Marshall's letter, I wondered sadly if the grandchild Mrs. Marshall was "looking after" could have been the one who had lost his young father.

I knew Allen Brown very slightly, but he had impressed me as an aggressive, wide-awake boy. I was desperately sorry for Mrs. Marshall and wrote directly to her expressing my heartfelt sympathy. Colonel Marshall replied with a form letter which I suspect, with the probable exception of Mrs. Marshall's close friends, was sent to the hundreds of people who must have written the Marshalls about Allen. In a few masterly words, the note implied that the particular sentiments of the sympathizer had made a special impression on the Marshalls.

> Mrs. Marshall and I appreciate very much your note of sympathy. Thank you for writing as you did.

The note was signed "G. C. Marshall," which tipped me off that it was a form letter, for Colonel Marshall usually signed his personal letters to me "GCM." Underneath his formal signature he had scribbled in longhand, "Sorry not to see you Wednesday." We had missed our dinner date! Colonel Marshall's consideration for other people, no matter how pressed or disturbed he was himself, never ceased to amaze me. I am sure he was saddened by Allen's death; but besides that, his note was dated June 6, 1944—D-day!

As the vast build-up for Operation Overlord, code name for the Normandy invasion, continued to grow in England, the Allied air assaults on Germany expanded and grew in intensity. America had come a long way since 1940 when Congress had answered General Marshall's plea for modern aircraft with an allotment of fifty-seven new planes!

The Army Air Force (there was no separate Air Force until September 1947) was commanded by General Henry ("Hap") Arnold, a member of the Joint and Combined Chiefs of Staff. General Arnold wrote in his book *Global Mission,* "Marshall was the most potent force behind the development of the Air Force. . . . It is hard to think how there could have been an American Air Force without him." (Harper & Row, 1949)

Three weeks before D-day, General Eisenhower reported to General Marshall, "There is no question at all as to the readiness of the troops. They are well trained, fit, and impatient to get the job started and completed."

Over 3,000,000 Allied soldiers, 1,533,000 of them Americans, were raring to go, but the same old problem plagued the Combined Chiefs: not enough landing craft. June was also the month of United States amphibious landings on the Marianas in the Pacific. A compromise had to be made.

General Marshall re-scheduled the landings in Southern France for a later date so that landing craft used for the Channel crossings could be hastily transferred for re-use in the Mediterranean. On June 6, D-day, the weather was murky and the sea rough, but rather than wait for several weeks, General Eisenhower made the difficult and courageous decision to set in motion the greatest offensive in history, or, as General Marshall wrote later, "an operation so complicated that it almost defies description."

American, British, and Canadian forces hit the Normandy beaches along a fifty-mile front. There followed the Battle of Normandy, the brilliant American breakthrough at St. Lô, and the amazing Battle of France—the liberation of Paris by August 25, and the spectacular American race across the rest of the country. By November, the Allies had expelled all Axis troops from France.

On December 16, to quote from General Marshall's written report, "The German armies of the west, commanded by Field Marshall von Runsted and acting on direct orders of Hitler, made their last desperate attempt to stave off disaster."

That was the fearsome "Battle of the Bulge." But two days after Christmas, the Allies switched from defense to offense, and by the end of January 1945, the bulge was flattened. Dead ahead lay the Siegfried Line.

American G.I.'s fought valorously, but soldiers do not fight as well as the Americans did without superior leadership. The American Field Commanders in World War II, in both hemispheres, were remarkably talented men. We had leaders of such high caliber in the right places because General Marshall recognized their special abilities and selected them for their commands. He was familiar with the performance and ability of more Army officers than anyone else in the Army. This is a prime example of how he put his phenomenal memory to use. He chose for command men on whom he could depend to perform under their own initiative. Regarding his selections, Colonel Marshall told me that aside from the necessary prerequisite of personal bravery, one of his criteria was the kind of high military ability that included the capacity for handling serious and complicated issues as they arose in the field. Another was the fortitude to take orders or allocations issued for the benefit of our widely disbursed "team," regardless of temporarily adverse effects on one's own operation.

History has borne witness to the success of his first criterion. As to the second, "localitis" was a prevalent disease throughout the war, but it was never a fatal one.

It seems absurd to compare Colonel Marshall's efforts to teach a child and to guide a young girl with his method of selecting the great leaders of our military campaigns. Nevertheless, there is a sharp analogy. The self-reliance, independent thinking, and discipline he tried to instill in me are the exact same qualities (on a higher plane) that he required of the men who led our troops to victory!

I know Colonel Marshall received daily reports on our progress and reverses in every theatre of the war, and I know he traveled hundreds of thousands of miles to make inspection trips to various fronts so that he could keep in as direct touch as possible. I do not know what specific orders he might have given, but I knew Colonel Marshall. It is safe to assume that he kept his orders, if any, to a minimum, that he observed and listened more than he spoke, and that any orders he gave were brief, perspicacious, and as cooperative as possible. I am sure, too, that he spread confidence and encouragement wherever he went—"Charity never faileth. . . ."

I have intentionally made few direct references to Colonel Marshall's religious commitment. The record of his life suffices to illustrate his faithful adherence to Christian principles. He was, moreover, as unostentatious in his attempt to fulfill these principles as he was in the conduct of his high offices. On Easter Day, 1944, however, the Chief of Staff was asked to offer a prayer at the sunrise service attended by thousands of worshipers in the Arlington amphitheatre. He sent me a copy of his prayer which I recognized at once as his own composition. It was a brief, simple, earnest petition from a modest and compassionate man.

> Almighty God:
>
> *May those* who have given their lives in the service of this nation rest in Thy care.

May those who are wounded in body find spiritual comfort under Thy guidance in the knowledge that through their sacrifice a great cause has been served.

May those who offer their lives in support of that cause, by land and sea and air, find strength in Thy divine guidance.

May those of us who serve this nation in its great purpose to secure freedom for all peoples be sustained by Thy blessing.

Give us strength, oh Lord, that we may be pure in heart and in purpose to the end that there may be peace on earth and good will among men.

May we be mindful this Easter morning "still stands Thine ancient sacrifice, an humble and a contrite heart."

CHAPTER XXXIII

AMERICANS DO NOT LIKE TO FEEL THAT ANYONE MIGHT BE SUPERIOR to them either in fact or appearance. In keeping with the notion that "there ain't nobody bet'rn us," a dissatisfied hue and cry arose because the topmost British officers outranked the topmost American officers. Finally, on the recommendation of the Secretary of War, Stimson, and the Secretary of the Navy, Forrestal, the House passed a bill creating a new five-star rank for the four highest officers in each service. The new rank, "General of the Army," together with the new five-star insignia were awarded to Generals Marshall and Arnold, members of the Joint and Combined Chiefs of Staff, and to Generals Eisenhower and MacArthur. In the Navy, the rank "Admiral of the Fleet" and five stars went to Admirals William D. Leahy and Ernest J. King, also members of the Joint and Combined Chiefs, and to Admirals Chester W. Nimitz and William F. Halsey. As Chief of Staff, General Marshall was the first Army officer elevated to the higher rank in order that he would technically have seniority over the others.

When I saw him a few months later, I made a big to-do about his being the first five-star General in the United States. He replied laconically that yes, he supposed he was, but he couldn't see that this " 'tremendous honor,' as you call it, will change the course of history." He was much too occupied with the war, he said, to bother with superfluities. He did tell me though, that before the bill was passed, a Congressman had asked him informally how he felt about the proposed equal rank with the British. Colonel Marshall replied outright that he thought it entirely unnecessary. He told the Congressman that no officer worth his salt needed the added prestige of equal rank to make worthwhile contributions. What he did need was to know his stuff and have the wherewithal to back it up. Colonel Marshall chuckled and added that all his reactions to the higher rank had been negative; he had flatly refused to be called "Marshal Marshall!"

I knew Colonel Marshall would tell me what he thought about his stars when I had a chance to ask him, so I would have been a jackass to expect he'd mention them in his December letter. I enjoyed getting all Colonel Marshall's letters and reading the bits of personal news they contained, but I'd long since given up gleaning them for any other kind of news.

The Battle of the Bulge had just reached the turning point (although I didn't know it at the time) when Colonel Marshall wrote me his usual combination Merry Christmas/Happy New Year/thank-you letter. Poor Colonel Marshall! He wrote, "This Christmas season for me has been a busy one as you can imagine and I do not foresee any let-up, certainly for some time to come." I was further depressed to learn from his letter that Mrs. Marshall had had pneumonia. I knew from way back that Colonel Marshall would continue to worry about his wife until she fully recovered, so I, in turn, worried about him, but unnecessarily. In the very next sentence he told me good news. He had sent Mrs. Marshall to Pinehurst, North Carolina, for a three-week recuperative vacation, and she had become so entranced with the resort that she had bought a charming furnished cottage.

". . . So it is probable," he wrote, "that she and Molly will spend some time there this winter as the climate is very agreeable and healthful."

That's great, I thought; with Dodona closed for the winter, Colonel Marshall will have a refreshing haven away from Washington. Even when he can't get away for a whole weekend, I reasoned, he should at least be able to fly down there for Sundays.

I was quite naturally concerned with the terrible strain Colonel Marshall was under; and if he didn't "foresee any let-up for some time to come," I had no idea in December 1945 but that the war might continue for another couple of years. The Battle of the Bulge had shaken me as it had all of us at home, and I was also unhappy about the seemingly endless Italian campaign.

While the Allies had fought and won the Battle of France and were in the process of flattening the Bulge, we had been beating against the "Gothic Line" on the Italian front for nearly three months. It appeared that we were stymied behind those rigid German fortifications before the Po Valley. But in the spring, the Allies broke through the Nazi defense, entered the Po Valley, and from then on moved swiftly northward.

"The Italian triumph is a striking demonstration of the solidarity of the United Nations," General Marshall wrote. "Fighting under the Fifteenth Army Group, at some time during the campaign, were Americans, British, Canadians, French, New Zealanders, South Africans, Poles, Indians, Brazilians, Italians, Greeks, Moroccans, Algerians, Arabs, Goums, Senegalese, and a brigade of Jewish soldiers."

The final plans for the defeat of Germany was a top item on the agenda for the Yalta conference in the Crimea which was scheduled to convene on February 4. Before going to Yalta, the Combined Chiefs held a military conference at Malta to hash out the plan they would present to the heads of state. Before General Marshall arrived at the Combined Chiefs' conference, he arranged a secret meeting near Marseille between himself and

General Eisenhower. It was a significant meeting in view of the subsequent controversy at Malta.

At the Malta conference, the British strongly disagreed with the American plan for the military campaign to defeat Germany. They argued tenaciously for the British plan and insisted that General Eisenhower should be ordered to throw all possible weight behind Field Marshal Montgomery. General Marshall, fresh from his consultation with Ike, held out against the British plan and refused to countenance the issuance of instructions to General Eisenhower. The American plan was accepted, and how it worked!

It took the Allies only three months to defeat Nazi Germany. On the seventh of May 1945, in General Eisenhower's headquarters, General Alfred Jodl signed the unconditional surrender of the German forces.

By then, Hitler had already committed suicide. Dead, too, was his Latin would-be counterpart, Mussolini, shot by his own people. Also dead was America's exhausted President Franklin Delano Roosevelt, who collapsed of a massive stroke on the twelfth of April.

The last words President Roosevelt wrote were, "The only limit to our realization of tomorrow will be our doubts of today. Let us move forward with strong and active faith."

The war was won in Europe. General Marshall could now turn his full attention to ending the war with Japan. He knew that vast problems and much sorrow lay ahead. But the Colonel Marshall I knew surely faced his future responsibilities without "doubts," and was supported by his "strong and active faith."

☙ CHAPTER XXXIV ☙

CHURCHILL ONCE WROTE THAT GENERAL MARSHALL WAS THE "TRUE organizer of victory." Colonel Marshall wanted to be the true organizer of peace, or at least, the true organizer of every effective measure possible to protect the United States from aggression. He had no illusions about human nature's historical propensity for war. "If man does find the solution for peace," he wrote in his last Biennial Report, "it will be the most revolutionary reversal of his record we have ever known."

Colonel Marshall believed that adequate protection for the nation rested on a wise and strong diplomacy backed by a sound security policy, principles he took seriously and worked hard to implement.

"We have tried since the birth of our nation to promote our love of peace by a display of weakness," he warned. ". . . Weakness presents too great a temptation to the strong, particularly to the bully who schemes for wealth and power . . ."

Long before V-E Day, Colonel Marshall was pushing plans for postwar defense. He strove to prevent a recurrence of the nation's unpreparedness which had so nearly permitted the extinction of freedom in the first terrible months of the war. Yet, though he had prevailed and succeeded in building the greatest Army of our history, he strongly opposed a large standing professional Army. He advocated a citizen's Army created by universal military *training,* as distinct from the universal military *service* intrinsic in a professional Army.

Early in the spring of 1945 he came to see me in New York and spent almost the whole visit explaining the importance of a citizen Army. It was also the one visit when he'd caught me totally unprepared. I'd been out all day, and as I got off the elevator at our apartment house in the late afternoon, I heard the phone ringing and ran down the hall to answer it. It was General Marshall's aide, calling to say he had been unable to reach me and that the General would be at my apartment at such-and-such a time. He was due to arrive in less than fifteen minutes. I rushed around the living room, picking up odds and ends, throwing everything helter-skelter into the untidy bedroom I'd left early in the morning. I had just completed a whirlwind clean-up and a hasty swipe at my nose with a powder puff when I heard Colonel Marshall's tappity-tap-tap code knock on the door.

When I let him in he gave me a quick kiss and asked, "May I use your telephone?" He said he had to make two important calls, one to Bishop Spellman and one to Bernie Baruch.

"Oh my God!" I exclaimed, "the phone's in the bedroom." I opened the bedroom door, spluttering apologies for the mess. Colonel Marshall looked in, turned and glared his disapproval at me for a miserable moment, and without a word stalked in and firmly shut the door behind him. I slunk into the living room, cursing my luck that he'd shown up on a day I had left the apartment in a hurry. When he came out, he didn't mention the shambles, so I assumed he'd given me the old "stew in your own juice" treatment. Besides, he was obviously still keyed up over his telephone conversations, which had probably related to the citizen Army, because that's what he started right off talking about.

He asked if I'd read anything about Universal Military Training, and without waiting for my answer, observed curtly that people who criticized military training as undemocratic didn't know what they were talking about. If we wanted to live in a democracy, he said, we couldn't expect to enjoy it on faith, we had to protect and maintain it. Colonel Marshall's devotion to democracy had led him inadvertently to paraphrase Jefferson's theme song: democracy entails responsibilities, and freedom, restrictions. Also, as he pointed out to me, his advocation of a citizen Army was not original. He had cribbed the idea from George Washington. I'm sure he was burned up by complaints that Universal Military Training would infringe on a man's individual freedom. Although he didn't say so, I assumed he believed that such objections exposed a shocking indifference to self-discipline and duty.

I wasn't very clear on exactly what a citizen Army was, so I hedged by observing that another objection seemed to be that a big standing Army was equated in people's minds with a totalitarian state, and they didn't understand the difference between the professional Army and a citizen Army.

He caught on to that ploy right away. "Do you understand the difference?" he asked.

"Not really," I confessed.

Very patiently, he explained to me that Universal Military Training and the maintenance of a large standing Regular Army was entirely different. Of course, he said, we would need a small professional Army, but with only as many soldiers and officers as the country needed for specific purposes, including training the inducted citizens. A citizen Army, however, would be comprised of young men who had completed their training period under the pros and who would then be placed on a reserve status. In other words, in case of an emergency, we would have a substantial pool of trained, reserve, citizen soldiers and officers who could be called into service with a minimum loss of time. The important factor, he continued, would be that unlike our past wars, we

295

would not be forced to send raw recruits into combat, or as in this war [World War II], to suffer the perilous delay of setting up training facilities and then training the men.

He added that because science and technology had revolutionized warfare, a future crisis would permit no time for delay. Speed in mobilization would decide the issue. Also because of science and technology, military training would become more complicated over the years. Modern weapons would be needed for sound training, and consequently, weaponry and training would have to keep pace with the times.

Colonel Marshall emphasized and reemphasized that we would be unforgivably negligent to chance facing a possible future crisis in the same state of unpreparedness that we found ourselves in at the beginning of this war. He said he believed that should all diplomatic efforts fail to avoid the dangers of a crisis, the existence of large numbers of highly trained citizen soldiers plus a reservoir of sufficient equipment, all available for rapid mobilization, would go a long way toward discouraging an aggressor nation's ambitions to attack.

"I want you to understand, Rose," he concluded, "that a citizen Army is a peacetime Army; its purpose is to avoid war, not to provoke it."

He did not go into details about actual plans for the set-up and operation of Universal Military Training, nor did he mention his foresighted establishment of a postwar planning committee, headed by the retired General John D. Palmer, which was hard at work while the war was still in progress. I found that out later on my own.

When Colonel Marshall left that afternoon, he looked at his watch, exclaimed, "Good Lord!" jumped up, and apologized for using up all our time talking shop. Pausing briefly outside my front door, he smiled down at me, his eyes alight with a mischievous glint. "By the way," he said, "that was a very pretty pink nightgown I stepped on in the middle of the floor!"

I laughed and replied thanks, I thought so too, and he turned and walked briskly to the elevator.

I stood outside the door watching him. "Wait!" I called on an impulse. "Wait a minute!" and hurried down the hall to catch him before the elevator came.

I had intended to blurt out, "Guess what? I'm pregnant!" but in a split second I decided against it; the baby wasn't due for a long time yet.

Instead, I asked, "Any idea when I'll see you again?"

"No, Rosie," he answered as he entered the elevator, "it's impossible to say."

After V-E Day, I wrote him an ecstatic letter in which I expressed my joy that at least half the war was over, congratulated him on his splendid broadcast following V-E Day, and broke the news that I was going to have a baby in August.

He wrote back that he was delighted and surprised "as you probably are," that I was going to have a family and added, ". . . I feel certain that it will make a great change in your life for happiness and contentment . . ." He told me to be sure John wired him at the proper time although "I might be out of the country but that will make no difference." It was a hurried note focused on my coming baby. He brushed off my complimentary remarks about his broadcast with a brief, uninterested thanks.

I thought his broadcast was important. He paid high tribute to the men who had fought and worked to win the war against Germany. Then he solemnly warned the country that there could be no relaxation on the home front, for we still had a hard, bitter fight ahead. His simply worded speech did not ring with oratorical fervor. It was the unmistakable note of calm sincerity that distinguished his message.

The United States took one deep breath of victory, exhaled, and buckled down to defeat Japan.

The war in the Pacific raged on until August. Iwo Jima fell in March. By mid-May, General MacArthur liberated the Philippines; Okinawa was captured in June. The ground fighting in Okinawa was bloody and savage, and the Navy took a wicked battering from the Japanese kamikaze attacks, suicidal Japanese pilots crash landing their bomb-laden planes on American ships.

In the Far East, by the end of January 1945, the U.S. XIVth Air Force was flying 46,000 tons of supplies a month into China. Also by the end of January, American army engineers completed the fabulous Stilwell Road from India to the Burma-China frontier. In May, Rangoon fell to British and Indian troops. The Burma campaign was ended.

During July, our bombing attacks subjected Japan to punishment as devastating, or more so, than the mighty aerial assaults on Germany. The Japanese, though reeling under almost continual bombardment, were egged on by their militaristic leader clique to defend their homeland regardless of the possibility that their suicidal resistance might end in national extinction. In Japan, an army of two million men was prepared and resolved to withstand an American invasion for which General Marshall had long since formulated the strategy. His plan had the full support of Admiral King and General "Hap" Arnold, and all three agreed it would probably take a minimum of eighteen months to conquer Japan.

The Joint Chiefs of Staff had dismissed the creation of a Supreme Commander in the Pacific as impracticable due to the apparently incurable jealousies existent between General MacArthur and the Navy. General Marshall overlooked this mutual dislike, which had plagued both him and Admiral King, because we needed MacArthur's superior military leadership for the Japanese invasion. On April 6, he appointed General MacArthur Commander of the United States Armies in the Pacific. That General Marshall should by-pass MacArthur's feud with the Navy is a great tribute to the latter's military talents, for General Marshall took a firm stand on the importance of pursuing smooth cooperation between the Services—teamwork! As for his own relationship with the Navy, certainly he inspired the confidence and respect of Admiral of the Fleet King, who took occasion to commend him publicly as a superior Chief of Staff, and added, ". . . in all matters where we have been in contact I have found him at all times sympathetic to the Navy point of view. He is an officer of the highest ability and a great American. This country and the Allies may consider themselves fortunate to have him in the position he has so ably filled . . . I am happy to count him as a firm friend. In his professional capacity he has no peer. . . ."*

Admiral Nimitz, who had directed a series of spectacular naval victories, was placed in command of the Pacific Naval Forces.

While MacArthur and Nimitz were priming their respective forces for the Japanese invasion, the Combined Chiefs, President Truman, Prime Minister Churchill (later replaced by Atlee who had defeated Britain's indomitable war leader in the July 26 elections), and Stalin met for the last big wartime conference at Potsdam, Germany. The conferences opened on July 17. On July 16, the first atom bomb exploded over the New Mexico desert. The awful responsibility of whether or not to use the terrifying and terrible new weapon rested squarely on President Truman as Commander in Chief of the United States Armed Forces. At Potsdam, with the approval of the Joint Chiefs of Staff, he made the fateful decision to end the war. The concerted opinion was that dropping the atom bomb on Japan would save a half million American lives, since it was estimated that that number would be lost if the United States opted to invade the Japanese homeland. Whatever the moral implications of using the bomb, and there are plenty, eighteen months or more of hideously bitter fighting would not only have caused the death and mutilation of thousands upon thousands of Americans, but would have tripled Japanese casualties as well. The brutal fact is that prior to Pots-

* Lincoln Barnett, "General Marshall," *Life,* Jan. 3, 1944.

dam, United States bombings had killed nearly 150,000 *more* Japanese than those who died from the atom bombs, wounded 200,000 *more* than those injured by the atom bombs, and destroyed close to 2,500,000 homes.

"Each single day added to the war adds hundreds of graves to the cemeteries," Colonel Marshall said to me when I had teased him about being an unwarlike general.

At 9:15 A.M., August 6, the atom bomb fell on Hiroshima; on August 9, a second bomb hit Nagasaki—after United States aircraft had sprayed warning leaflets over the city. Thus the agonies of World War II concluded in holocaust.

On August 10, Japan sued for peace and on August 14, President Truman announced Japan's surrender.

CHAPTER XXXV

AT SEVEN-THIRTY TUESDAY MORNING, AUGUST 7, COLONEL MARSHALL stole a few moments to write me the following letter in longhand.

> Dear Rose:
>
> I have been thinking about you as August approached and wondering how you are getting along. At the same time I have been moving about so continually that I failed to write as I should have done.
>
> Please send me a card telling me about yourself.
>
> I have been quite well, though very busy. My time at Potsdam was completely occupied by business, but I did get in two short trips to the Bavarian Alp region, one to Hitler's hide out village and another to a fishing lodge with Gen. Bradley. Went over via Newfoundland and returned via Bermuda.
>
> The family is at Leesburg where I struggled with an over-grown garden this weekend. With my love,
>
> Affectionately, G.C.M.

On August 16, 1945, John Page Wilson was born into a shocked, exhausted, panting, warless world. Two days later, I was resting in my hospital bed, radiantly happy and still bemused by the unmistakable evidence—doctors' predictions notwithstanding —that at last John and I had a son. Suddenly my telephone rang, breaking up my woman's-magazine reveries. "Mrs. Wilson?" a voice said. "General Marshall is calling." After the usual preliminaries—"Congratulations on your first son. How are you? How much did the baby weigh?"—Colonel Marshall paused; but before I could start bragging, he asked abruptly, "Tell me, Rose, what do you think now about Universal Military Training?"

I was stunned. "Colonel Marshall!" I cried. "What a helluva question!"

"Well?" he replied, and in the background I thought I heard laughter.

"Are you at your office?"

"Yes."

"Oh nuts!" I laughed, "tell whoever's there anything you want to, but yes, I'm still for it, I have to be. Gosh, Colonel Marshall, there's nothing like making a new mamma face reality right off the bat."

"You are?" he replied, ignoring my last comment. "That's splendid news."

He said he hoped he could see the baby soon, although he didn't know when that would be, and hung up.

He saw the baby when he came to New York at the end of October to deliver a speech on Universal Military Training before the *Herald Tribune* Youth Forum. That's when I learned what his game had been when he'd telephoned me at the hospital.

He said he had intended to call me that day anyhow, but hadn't planned on doing it quite the way he had.

"As a matter of fact," he told me, with a cat-that-swallowed-the-canary smile, "telephoning when I did was one of my best spontaneous ideas."

He explained that an important meeting of high officials had been going on in his office, and each man had very strong and very different opinions about the subject under discussion. The atmosphere had grown from warm to heated, and as he'd watched tempers rise, he decided something had to be done to break the impasse. He'd ostentatiously looked at his watch and announced, "Gentlemen, I'm afraid I will have to interrupt you briefly."

He placed his call to me, and while he waited for it to go through he explained he was telephoning his goddaughter who had just become the mother of her first child, a little boy.

"Just stay where you are," he'd urged them, "I won't be a moment."

"They were as shocked and surprised as you were," he said, "and it amused them that I was so cruelly tactless as to ask a brand-new mother about military training. But I succeeded in jolting them out of their bad humor!"

Everybody returned to their normal senses, he concluded, and the meeting turned into a very satisfactory one. Of course, I wanted to know who was at the meeting and what they'd been angry about; but as expected, he refused to tell me.

Colonel Marshall stayed a longer time than usual that afternoon, so long in fact, that I began to get nervous. My infant son had the appetite of a hippopotamus, and as Colonel Marshall had been due to arrive a half hour or so before the baby started yelling for food, I had stuffed him with Pablum to keep him happy. Colonel Marshall stayed well beyond feeding time and Pablum or no Pablum, Page tuned up and began what I knew would be an unbroken howl until he was fed.

"What's the matter with him?" Colonel Marshall asked anxiously. "He seemed such a good baby. Are you sure you haven't left a pin sticking in him?"

"No," I quipped, "he's probably worried about military training."

"Oh, you're a great wit," Colonel Marshall replied derisively.

"Actually, he's hungry. I'd better heat up a bottle," I amended. Colonel Marshall followed me into the kitchen where we shouted nonsensical jokes at each other while the bottle warmed and Page squalled.

"You don't seem to have much trouble with his appetite," Colonel Marshall observed.

"I do too," I disagreed, "I can't fill him up."

"Will he drink that whole full bottle?"

"Sure, more if I'd give it to him."

"Poor John, his son is going to eat him out of house and home!"

While Page was contentedly guzzling his milk, I said, "Colonel Marshall, John and I thought maybe you would be Page's godfather. Will you? Will you please, Colonel Marshall?"

"Of course," he said. "Had you even considered asking someone else?"

"No, we hadn't," I laughed, "and thanks a lot; that's great! Just think, Colonel Marshall, you're the only person I ever heard of who'll have a 'grand-godchild.'" We made tentative plans for the baby's baptism to take place sometime soon after Colonel Marshall retired. I remember that I suggested bringing him down to Washington and having the ceremony in the Bethlehem Chapel of the Cathedral where I had been confirmed.

What a light-hearted afternoon we spent. The time flew by as we conjured up halcyon dreams about the future. From wild speculations on what a great man Page would be, we progressed to delightful prophesies about the pleasant life Colonel Marshall would lead after his retirement. He would go to Dodona, have a leisurely tea every afternoon with Mrs. Marshall, ride mornings, and work in his vegetable garden. We were naming all the vegetables he would plant when I remembered his little zinnia patch he'd tended so lovingly in the old days at Fort Myer.

"And what about flowers?" I interrupted. "You know, zinnias and such."

"Flowers are Katherine's department," he answered. "While I'm grubbing in the potato patch, she'll be tending her beautiful flower garden."

"That figures," I said. "Well, you be sure to raise some big, old, beefsteak 'tomahtoes' like they used to have at Keswick."

"I'll raise 'tomaytoes' like they used to grow in Pennsylvania," he teased.

And so it went, all gay talk. I hadn't seen him as happy and relaxed for a long, long time; I hated to see him leave.

A mutual friend who had been present at his speech on military training that evening reported to me that he had asked General Marshall if he had seen Rose's baby.

"Oh, yes!" Colonel Marshall replied, "this afternoon, and I stayed until the last burp."

That he had, and longer. After he had gone, I laughed to myself, thinking that the Chief of Staff was as impatient as any G.I. to get home. Incongruously, I wondered how he would go about computing his own points.

The Point System was the method used for demobilization. General Marshall had come to New York to make a speech about Universal Military Training at the same time that he was deeply engrossed in the demobilization of the Army! It was a stupendous job, for the Army had grown under his leadership from 174,000 to 8,333,000, including about 150,000 women. The Point System had been worked out so that individual soldiers could be demobilized just as individual soldiers had been drafted. Each soldier's points were based on such things as his length of service, how much time he had spent overseas, how hard his fighting had been, certain decorations, whether he had a wife and children, and various other specifics. Determination of the basis for the points had been guided by a consensus of the G.I.'s themselves. Due to General Marshall's ever-present concern for enlisted men, he had ordered a wide survey to determine their opinions on what they believed to be the fairest allocation. Less than a month after V-J Day, more than fifteen thousand men per day were being processed, discharged, and sent home. In view of the inevitable emotional tensions, however, there was considerable griping, impatience, and misunderstanding about how the system worked.

"Bring the boys home! Bring the boys home!" "The United States had had a bellyful of war. Universal Military Training?" Defense for a future war? Go jump in the lake!"

In November, President Truman finally allowed General Marshall to lay down his duties as Chief of Staff. On November 26, in a public ceremony at the Pentagon, the President awarded him an Oak Leaf Cluster to add to his Distinguished Service Cross. His citation began, "In a war unparalleled in magnitude and horror, millions of Americans gave their country outstanding service. General of the Army George C. Marshall gave it victory . . ." and concluded, ". . . He takes his place at the head of the great commanders of history."

Colonel Marshall had served his country for nearly forty-four years. At last the time was at hand when he could indulge in personal interests and pleasures. The time was at hand, but it did not come. Less than two weeks after his retirement, General Marshall left for Chungking. He had reluctantly but dutifully acquiesced to President Truman's request that he become his Special Representative to China. General Marshall was assigned to unravel, if he could, the disturbing Chinese tangle that was becoming more and more snarled with alarming rapidity.

Before my godfather left, he somehow found time to make a thoughtful gesture that he knew would delight my heart. He ordered a silver set of five stars for me, "because now that you are a mother, you have earned a promotion."

CHAPTER XXXVI

HOSTILITIES BETWEEN CHIANG KAI-SHEK AND MAO TSE-TUNG HAD hamstrung a united Chinese war effort against Japan, in spite of strenuous efforts by Chiang's two successive American Chiefs of Staff. After V-J Day, the Nationalists and Communists were released from the more or less restraining bonds of a common enemy and the smouldering hostility between them flared up and began to spread.

The United States ambassador, Patrick J. Hurley, had thrown himself exuberantly into the task of settling their differences and returned home in the fall of 1945 brimming with optimistic predictions that the troublesome hostilities were about to be resolved. Chiang and Mao, he believed, had buried the hatchet. So they had, but it was a shallow grave. Soon after Hurley's return to the States, fighting broke out again, and it appeared as if China was fast moving toward a civil war.

On November 24, President Truman turned to General Marshall for help. Two weeks later, he sent General Marshall to China to "endeavor to persuade the Chinese [Nationalist Central] Government to call a national conference of representatives of major political elements to bring about a unification of China, and concurrently, to effect a cessation of hostilities, particularly in north China."*

Colonel Marshall's mission to China was a failure. He did not succeed in choking off the civil war. In view of my affection and admiration for him, one would expect me to write an apologia for his failure. On the other hand, it is important to bear in mind how painstakingly he tried to impress upon me the importance of subjugating personal feelings to an objective appraisal of any person whose actions one is attempting to evaluate. In this respect, he set a perfect example. Those who were in a position to know have repeatedly stated publicly that General Marshall never permitted his judgment to be influenced by his compatability or incompatibility with a personality. He chose the man he considered best for the job whether he liked him or not. Our continuing Jefferson-Hamilton discussions illustrate an attempt on his part to teach me to make similar judgments. Consequently, I will make a special effort to explain General Marshall's frustrations in China as objectively and as briefly as I am able. The causes that foredoomed his attempts to carry out President Truman's mission are extremely complex and lengthy. Some of them I read about in various written accounts. Others, Colonel Marshall told me. In any case, it would be impractical to air all of them here.

Why did General Marshall fail in China? Here, I am reminded of Jefferson's comment that a person "is less remote from the truth if he believes nothing than he who believes what is wrong." There is a good deal of wrong belief about Colonel Marshall's mission to China. Some of it stems from irresponsible emotionalism; some from genuine misconceptions; and most from

* Harry S Truman, *Years of Trial and Hope,* Signet Book, The New American Library, p. 87.

insufficient knowledge about the historical Sino–United States relationship, about China per se, about the nature of the Kuomintang under Chiang Kai-shek, and about Communism under Mao Tse-tung in those days.

As for our wartime China policies, they can be simplified to: support Chiang Kai-shek's Nationalist Government politically against Mao Tse-tung's Chinese communists, and militarily against Japan.

Why did Roosevelt's military advisors, including General Marshall, urge on him the importance of Russian participation with us in the war against Japan? Why did Churchill agree?

In assessing the decision, it is difficult to remember that at the time of the Yalta Conference, the cold war was a phenomenon yet unheard of. Furthermore, the Allies had not yet crossed the Rhine, MacArthur's liberation of the Philippines was still in the future, and there was no assurance that the atom bomb would be feasible. Finally, over and above these considerations, Roosevelt and Churchill, right or wrong, were extremely apprehensive that Hitler and Stalin might sign a separate peace treaty.

The Joint Chiefs of Staff hoped that the Red Army would help us to end the war sooner and thus (again the prime concern) save American lives.

The value of a Russian alliance with us in the Japanese war was taken for granted by most of the military top echelon. The tactical reason for favoring it was clearly expounded by General MacArthur in a conversation with Secretary of the Navy Forrestal. According to an entry in Forrestal's diary dated February 19, 1945, MacArthur told the Secretary we could count on little help from the Chinese for our invasion of Japan, and in his opinion, we should persuade Russia to launch a forcible campaign in Manchukuo (Japanese name for Manchuria) with a minimum of sixty Red Divisions. Such a campaign by the Russians, MacArthur pointed out, would free the United States to reserve its strength for the Japanese mainland.

So much for the ideology boys' loud charges that General Marshall's recommendation for the "surrender" of Manchuria to the Soviets was a contributing factor toward the Communist take-over of China. But General Marshall bore the brunt of the heaviest attacks on the military. During and after Colonel Marshall's China mission, Americans were bewildered that China could possibly be "lost to us."

Politically Chiang Kai-shek's Nationalist government was militarist. He reverted to the old ways of his authoritarian political heritage, and his government became as corrupt and insensitive to the needs of the masses as that of the Manchus.

Mao Tse-tung used both Japanese aggression and Chiang's mistakes to hoodwink the people into believing that his concern for their welfare was genuine. He wooed the peasants by assigning them patches of land taken from large estates, bided his time before instituting collectivism, and shrewdly watched his political control expand. Mao's "agrarian reform" had great appeal to the huge numbers of ignorant, rural Chinese who have always loved the soil.

In spite of Chiang Kai-shek's poor leadership and corrupt government, the reasons we supported his Government throughout the war and immediately afterward are apparent. While the war was in progress, we could not abandon China to the Japanese, either for her sake or ours. During the war, we poured in one and a half billion dollars in aid, gave Chiang an American Chief of Staff, and raised China to great-power status. After the war, we were hardly inclined to switch allegiance to the Communists and sit by impassively while they overran territories that the Japanese had occupied.

In November 1945, three months after V-J Day, Chiang's Nationalist troops began to move into formerly Japanese-held areas. For their part, the Communists began to move into Manchuria, contrary to the agreement set up by United States Ambassador Hurley just before he returned to this country. At this point, President Truman sent General Marshall on his hopeless mission to China.

Characteristically, before he left for China, General Marshall told the President that he believed the ultimate responsibility for resolving their political differences lay with the Chinese, and that the United States should not impose American will upon China. President Truman expressed his unqualified agreement with these principles.

During his first few days in China, General Marshall listened to both sides but said little himself. He told me later, "I made it clear from the start that I intended to remain impartial." After acquainting himself with the grievances and demands of the Nationalists and Communists, he was convinced that no political settlement could be made without a permanent end to hostilities.

General Marshall succeeded, with great effort and tact, in arranging a cease-fire between the two parties as early as January 1946. After the truce was established, he made various suggestions to maintain the peace. One accepted suggestion was the establishment of truce teams to act as impartial authorities in the field. Each team was composed of one Nationalist General, one Communist General, and an American Colonel. The teams were enthusiastically received by both sides—temporarily.

General Marshall also flew three thousand miles through northern China to explain the purposes of the truce in person to the commanders in the field.

He even suggested a plan for the consolidation of the Chinese armed forces and offered to assist both parties to carry it out. According to General Marshall's report to the President, the Communists appeared to be more favorable to the proposed consolidation than the Nationalists. The Communists, he observed, were more sure that they had a stronger political hold on the people and were willing to take their chances in a political showdown. The Nationalists, having failed to establish a rapport with the masses, were fearful of relinquishing what they supposed to be their military supremacy.

In April, General Marshall came home for consultations with President Truman and to try to establish a loan for China. He arranged a loan of $500,000,000, but it was never granted. Before the negotiations with the Chinese ambassador here were completed, back in China, Chiang Kai-shek broke the truce by delivering a vehement back-to-arms speech.

General Marshall returned to China on April 18. Endless negotiations ensued. Before either party would agree to stop fighting, the Communists asked for unreasonable concessions from the Nationalists, and, in turn, the Nationalists made unrealistic demands upon the Communists. General Marshall's truce teams succeeded in stopping the fighting in a few provinces, but for the most part, both sides ignored the teams.

General Marshall, with superhuman effort, arranged a second truce in June. This one was limited to fifteen days, but he hoped that some basis for an agreement to the cessation of hostilities could be reached in that time.

A complication within complications was the boasting of Chiang's incompetent Generals that they could wipe out the Communists in battle, and they succeeded in convincing Chiang that his armies were invincible. Patiently, Colonel Marshall explained to the Generalissimo that the Nationalists could not defeat the Communist forces, particularly since the Russians would most likely come in to help the Reds. There was no way to defeat Mao and the Russians, General Marshall told Chiang, unless the Americans intervened on a large scale to help him, and to this the United States would never consent. President Truman had stated flatly that he would not commit American troops to fight Chiang's battles. Even more important than the President's declaration was the sentiment of the American people, "Bring the boys home!" A full year had not yet passed since the termination of the bloodiest war in history; not for all the tea in China would Americans have agreed to entering another war and running the almost certain risk of large-scale involvement with the Russians.

Nevertheless, the highly publicized American political sentiment for Chiang Kai-shek contributed to the breakdown of the second truce. The Communists refused to believe that General Marshall was acting in good faith as an impartial mediator, and openly accused America of duplicity.

The fighting resumed forthwith, each party blaming the other for starting it. Neither Chiang Kai-shek nor Mao Tse-tung chose to operate within a framework of honesty. They were either incapable of recognizing General Marshall's integrity and impartiality, or they discounted these qualities as unimportant. The Chinese leaders were governed by deep distrust of each other, and they were motivated by their respective appetites for self-aggrandizement. Neither Chiang Kai-shek nor Mao Tse-tung would listen to the moderates within their parties who hoped for a viable political settlement. And neither Chinese leader would agree to the establishment of a truce long enough to permit reasonable political discussions. Civil war was now inevitable.

As I reflect on those arduous months Colonel Marshall spent in China, and as I recall my reaction when I first heard about his assignment, it strikes me that this was the third episode of his career I had bewailed and resented. Poor Colonel Marshall! No rest, no break at all after the dreadful strain of the war. Poor Colonel Marshall, indeed! What did I expect—that he would rest on his laurels, tell the President his ex-Chief of Staff had given enough for his country? In Colonel Marshall's book, there was no such thing as giving "enough" for his country or for humanity. Refuse to serve when and where he was needed? Never!

Yet, I think his acceptance of the China assignment was the hardest self-disciplinary act of his life. His first letter to me from China, written a few weeks after he had arrived, shocked me, not because he was unhappy and homesick, but because he admitted it. His letters during the war had frequently mentioned how busy he was, or how lonely his horseback rides were, or how weary he was from his extensive travels to various fronts. I had worried then about the pressure of the terrible responsibilities he bore; but his observations of this sort had been made off-handedly, more as reasons for not writing sooner.

His January letter from China was the first and only letter to me wherein Colonel Marshall allowed himself to confess that he was downright miserable. He wrote that he had left home with a minimum of preparation. Not only was his time short, but most of his days had been taken up by Congressional hearings. During his lunch hours, he had had to rush over to the White House or the State Department. Since his arrival in China, he had been "intensely busy" every hour from nine to five, sometimes until midnight, and it looked as if the grinding pace would keep up for some time to come.

> I long for personal freedom and my own home and simple pleasures. My shooting trips were all arranged for the winter along with horseback rides on the lovely Pinehurst trails and a month in Florida at a luxurious cottage that had been placed at my disposal. But, here I am.

There he was, because he chose to be. The pity was that he had to make the choice.

He finished his letter with a gracious little apology about the "godfather delays," but said that if I still wanted him to serve as Page's godfather, he would be honored to do it.

Colonel Marshall came back to Washington in April to seek the loan for China, and we planned to have Page baptized while he was here; but our plans fell through again because he did not have one spare minute. He had flown up to Mr. Stimson's place on Long Island one Saturday afternoon, met Mrs. Marshall in New York that evening, had a business meeting Sunday morning, and flown back to Washington immediately afterwards. He wrote me the above itinerary from Washington the next morning, two days before he left again for China, saying that he was sorry he hadn't even had time to telephone me, and adding, ". . . I have only a moment to dictate this note now but will write you more in detail later. . . ."

When he returned to China after that quick trip home, his letters were more cheerful although he continued to wish for a release from his unceasing labors, as evidenced in the quotation earlier in the book about picnicking down the Shenandoah Valley. I think the main reason his spirits picked up on his second "shift" was because Mrs. Marshall went back with him in April.

At any rate, his letters were newsy—not about the negotiations —and descriptive. One letter from him written in August throws a sidelight on his activities in China. It seems that the summer during which the Nationalists and Communists were carrying on their divisive debate was an extremely hot and humid one. Colonel Marshall wrote that he was shuttling between Kuling, where the Generalissimo was established for the summer, and Nanking, where the United States Embassy was located. Also, the principal Nationalist officials remained in Nanking during the summer and the Communist negotiators were quartered there. Usually, he stayed three days at Kuling and then returned to Nanking for four or five days.

His frequent trips to Kuling were tiring but interesting. The first lap was by air, an hour-and-three-quarters flight along the Yangtze. Next, Colonel Marshall transferred to a Japanese gun-boat which took him down and across the river to Ku-Kiang, which he wrote, was a center for fine porcelain and china. From Ku-Kiang he drove about thirty minutes by car to the foot of a mountain. There he embarked on the last lap of his trip, by chair, with eight bearers to carry him 3,500 feet up the mountain. The bearers trotted up a fantastic mountain path of stone steps and ominous curves to the village of Kuling. Colonel Marshall omitted to tell me how long that took!

Mrs. Marshall, or Katherine, as he always called her if his letters were in longhand (as was this one), was not subjected to his peculiar commuting schedule. She had a delightful lodge at Kuling "in the cool of magnificent scenery . . . and as Nanking is frightfully hot, I am vastly relieved to have her out of it."

Colonel Marshall stayed on in China through the fall and early winter of 1946 because the President had requested that he remain as an observer. During that time, Chiang asked General Marshall to accept the position of adviser to his Government, but General Marshall declined. He did not believe that an American adviser to Chiang's Government would serve any good purpose, because of strong anti-American sentiment rife among the extremist elements of the Kuomintang party. In spite of Chiang's invitation, General Marshall was not able to dissuade the Generalissimo from his decision to occupy northern China and Manchuria. With this rejection of his military advice, General Marshall formally requested the President to recall him. Since Chiang had chosen to ignore his repeated warnings that a battle confrontation with the Communists would be disastrous, General Marshall felt that he could be of no possible use at all.

Colonel Marshall did not come home with the expectation of enjoying the comforts and pleasures of Leesburg and Pinehurst, but with the knowledge that he must assume yet another and heavier burden. Discord had developed between the Administration and the Secretary of State, so that President Truman had accepted the ailing Secretary James F. Byrnes' resignation. On January 7, 1947, the President announced that General George C. Marshall was the country's new Secretary of State. When the announcement was made, Colonel Marshall was still somewhere far out over the Pacific ocean.

CHAPTER XXXVII

WHILE COLONEL MARSHALL WAS BEATING HIS HEAD AGAINST THE wall of Chinese politics, the United States was experiencing the throes of postwar reconversion. In January 1946, homesickness for the "organizer of victory" was of no consequence to the citizenry, but homesick G.I.'s were something else again. They were returning in droves. "It was no demobilization," Colonel Marshall commented later, "it was a rout."

The precipitate demobilization was only one aspect of the sick-of-war passion that gripped the country. Another was an insatiable desire for consumer goods. Everybody wanted everything. Prices skyrocketed. Domestic problems arose, abated, and arose again while our future Secretary of State struggled wih the rise and fall of his efforts for peace on the other side of the world.

In regard to the positon of the United States in the postwar world, we and Russia had emerged as the two greatest world powers. In the newly founded United Nations, democratic and communist ideologies publicly crashed head-on. The seeds of American hatred and distrust of the Soviet Union began to germinate. As the year wore on, the seeds sprang up, fertilized by Stalin's duplicity and Russian intransigence. By the time Colonel Marshall was sworn in as Secretary of State in January 1947, the terms "iron curtain" and "cold war" and what they stood for were familiar to every American citizen more than five years old.

The reaction of an anxious nation to Colonel Marshall's appointment as Secretary of State was almost unanimously favorable. Here was a man with guts—a doer whom one could trust! His reputation for patriotism, integrity, impartiality, and high ability had won the confidence of the American people, if not their adulation. I remember smiling when I read one press report which referred to his "aloof greatness." The point is that General Marshall's record spoke for itself. "If I can't stand on my record, I'd rather not serve," he had told me seven years before when he refused to "campaign" for the appointment as Chief of Staff.

Of course, Colonel Marshall's public statements, the testimony of his colleagues, the respect of Congress, and many other factors contributed to the public confidence he aroused; but thousands of Americans also had read his brilliant final Biennial Report at the conclusion of the war. This report had made an even greater impact than his others. One high official had gone so far as to tell the press that General Marshall's Report not only should be required reading for all Americans, but should be included in the curriculum of all our public schools!

The only honest objections were by people who, though paying tribute to General Marshall's morality and talents, expressed concern that a military man should assume the highest appointive civil post in the Government. These dissenters had only to read a few of General Marshall's public statements to allay their fears. For example, after he returned from China, he said, "Though I speak as a soldier, I must here also deplore the dominating influence of the military. Their dominance accentuates the weakness of the civil government."

Happily, Colonel Marshall did not have to rush directly home from his struggle with the turmoils of China to contend with the turmoils of Europe. First, he had a wonderful, though brief, vacation in Hawaii. He sent me a longhand letter from there, replying to a letter of mine and telling me about the "lovely time" he was having.

My letter had informed him that once again I had confounded the medical profession and was expecting a baby in April. He replied that he was "astonished" and "delighted," and that I had guaranteed my future happiness. Colonel Marshall, because of his own disappointment at his childless state, attached tremendous importance to my having children, and I sometimes wonder what he would have advised in the light of the present terrifying world population explosion. In one of his letters from China he had written that my little son Page was "a magnificent confirmation of my repeated recommendation for your future happiness. All you need to do now is to save him from being ruined by spoiling as an only son by having another baby! They used to have five or ten as a matter of routine!" If it hadn't been for his exclamation points, I'd have thought Colonel Marshall was getting balmy.

After his characteristic comments on the advent of my second baby, he said that he was "taking it easy," loafing on the beach most of the day in the shade of bordering palm trees in the morning and on the sand in the afternoon. Colonel Marshall was no more a sun worshipper than Lily had been. He certainly didn't have her creamy, transparent skin, but he did have the easy-to-burn complexion that went with his sandy hair.

He and Katherine, he wrote, had a lovely, roomy cottage in a grove of palms facing the ocean; and Mrs. Marshall's amah (the Chinese maid she'd brought along) was an enthusiastic cook, so they were enjoying delicious food. He said his orderly was a good cook, too, and that they had a Cadillac and chauffeur at their disposal. I burst out laughing when I read about the car and chauffeur; it was the epitome of luxury to Colonel Marshall! In

319

all his years as an important world figure, I don't think Colonel Marshall ever got over a kind of childlike surprise and pleasure that he was in a position to enjoy certain creature comforts above the average.

"Taking it easy" for Colonel Marshall had a different connotation than it did for the likes of me. He reported that his lolling on the beach was interrupted by a minimum of thirty messages a day, some of them two and three hundred words long. "One from Winston Churchill just arrived," he wrote. The letter went on to say that he hoped to stay a week or ten days—he was never in a position to enjoy above-average lengthy vacations—depending upon whether or not the President sent for him to hurry back to Washington. He added that his plane was all ready to go with his "goods and chattels aboard." If possible, he said, he would like to spend a day in Hollywood with his former aide, Colonel Frank McCarthy, who had accepted a position as Eric Johnston's assistant. "You met McCarthy with me at the Waldorf," he reminded me.

It was a wandering, chatty letter, and as I read it I could visualize him propped up in a beach chair, writing away between intervals of gazing out at the sea or dropping off for a little snooze. As he had all his life, Colonel Marshall was taking full advantage of his brief respite from work and worry to build his energies for the ordeals that lay ahead.

About two weeks after Secretary Marshall was established in the State Department, the United States Ambassador to Greece, Lincoln MacVeagh, reported that strong rumors were circulating that the British would soon withdraw their troops from Greece. Such a move bore ominous prospects. After the war, King Paul, with his charming young Queen Frederika, had returned to Greece to establish a constitutional monarchy resting on a strong anti-communist base. For some time, Communist partisans had been heckling the Government politically, and armed Communist guerillas were causing serious trouble. So far, the explosive situation had been kept under control by the presence of British troops. Finally, the British ambassador informed Secretary Marshall that due to financial difficulties in the aftermath of the war, Britain would be forced to discontinue aid to Greece. On March 30, the British withdrew all economic and military support. Immediately a vicious civil war broke out. Communist guerillas were reinforced militarily and economically by Communists from Bulgaria, Albania, Rumania, and Yugoslavia—all urged on and supplied by their avaricious master, Stalin.

Even as Greece was torn by Communist-inspired civil war, Stalin was making threatening gestures toward Turkey, demanding a share in the control of the Dardenelles.

Danger to the whole free world was evident. ". . . Like the Battle of the Bulge," Secretary Marshall described it. The President, Secretary Marshall, and Under Secretary Acheson hastily conferred and thoroughly reviewed the reports submitted to them by United States experts. Secretary Marshall stated bluntly that we must act fast or lose by default, and adding that poverty and hunger were communism's strongest allies. He urged that the United States send aid to Greece and Turkey as soon as possible. Out of the Greek-Turkish crisis, the Truman Doctrine emerged.

When the President delivered his important foreign-policy speech before a joint session of Congress, Secretary Marshall was in Moscow attending the Council of Foreign Ministers which was meeting to consider peace terms for Germany and Austria. The President's now famous speech vividly explained the imminent, frightening danger that Soviet designs on Greece and Turkey posed for the free world at large and the United States in particular. After asking for economic and military aid for the two beleaguered nations, he enunciated what was to be called the Truman Doctrine. President Truman said, "I believe that it must be the policy of the United States to support free peoples who are resisting subjugation by armed minorities or by outside pressures." Truman scared the hell out of Congress, which forthwith appropriated millions for Greece and Turkey. In short, Greece was saved, and Turkey was helped to the point of becoming a bastion of freedom in the Near East.

Many people have drawn an analogy between China's position and that of Greece, arguing that similar strong backing from the Government would have saved China. Greece, however, was a mite compared to the Chinese monolith. It is highly questionable that in 1946 Congress would have consented to giving military aid to China, for reasons already given. Even so, during the Chinese civil war, we poured two billion dollars worth of arms and munitions down the Kuomintang rat hole.

Well, Secretary Marshall had been home from China for less than two months when he took off to join in the Big Four Conference in Moscow. The discouraging, fruitless conference lasted seven weeks. While Colonel Marshall was in Russia, my second son, Thomas Morgan Wilson, was born on April 10, 1947. Colonel Marshall sent me a letter from Moscow, written April 14, instructing me to have John send him a note when the baby was born, and to be sure to address it care of the State Department so they could put it in the diplomatic pouch.

"I have thought of you frequently this month," he wrote, "and I do hope all is going well with you." If it had been anyone but Colonel Marshall, I would have doubted the veracity of that statement, because I had read reports of the endless round of negotiations going on in Moscow. Colonel Marshall wrote:

> I have been here now for five very busy weeks. As this is my seventh year of almost continuous conferences, I shall welcome a change.
>
> There has been very little of social trimmings to this gathering. I have gone to one dinner and reception given by Mr. Molotov. Also one evening of the ballet given by him. Then there have been a formal dinner at the British Embassy, several informal meals there, and a formal dinner at the French Embassy. I gave a dinner for the principal conferees Friday night and last night

a reception and dance for the American contingent here, some 250, which broke up at one o'clock this morning. That completes the agenda, I believe, of the social aspects.

I am most comfortably established at the American Embassy, but aside from walks about the city, have done no sightseeing and most days I have only gone out to attend meetings.

With my love,

Affectionately,

G.C.M.

American, British, and French efforts to arrive at satisfactory peace terms for Austria and Germany were thwarted by Soviet objections to the fundamental principles of freedom for all of Germany, and Russian insistence that Germany be forced to pay ten billion dollars in reparations. In a statement at the Big Four Conference, Secretary Marshall opened his address by saying:

> The Berlin conference instructed the Allied Control Authority "to prepare for the eventual reconstruction of German political life on a democratic basis, and for the eventual peaceful cooperation in international life by Germany." . . . I realize that the word "democracy" is given many interpretations. To the American government and citizens it has a basic meaning. We believe that human beings have certain inalienable rights— that is, rights that may not be given and taken away. . . .

His brief address was published unabridged in the New York papers, and I smiled when I read "inalienable rights," and laughed out loud at Colonel Marshall's succinct definition of them. What had amused me was the contrast between his short, apt phrase and the torrents of rhetoric on the same subject which usually flow from the speaker's podium. In commenting to me later on the Russians' reaction to his speech, Colonel Marshall said, "It would at least have been a novelty if they'd laughed at me like you say you did—"

"I didn't laugh *at* you," I interrupted. "I told you it was on account of—"

323

"Rather than filling the air with their routine charges of 'imperialism' and 'warmongering,' " he continued, cutting me off and ignoring my denial.

Colonel Marshall got back from Russia on April 26, and with the prompt attention he customarily gave to both personal and public affairs, he wrote me at once about my new baby. It was a dictated letter, telling me he had just received the news and saying, "I have just arrived at the office this morning and have only a moment for this letter." He then gave me a glimpse of his home circumstances. Mrs. Marshall, it appeared, had brought her Chinese amah back to the States, and they had left her at Pinehurst to clean the house when they closed up to return to Washington. They were established in a house in Washington on plush Foxhall Road for two or three weeks, which, Colonel Marshall wrote, "will be very convenient for me" until Dodona Manor would be in shape for the summer.

On the fifth day of June 1947, at Harvard University, Colonel Marshall delivered his renowned speech introducing the concept of the Marshall Plan. Characteristically, he had condensed untold hours of labor into a brief, concise, explicit address which turned the course of history—and took barely ten minutes to deliver!

The background for his speech had been supplied by the Policy Planning Staff Secretary Marshall had created in the State Department. One of his first acts after becoming Secretary of State had been to streamline the department, as he had streamlined the Army while Chief of Staff; now, as Secretary of State, he secured the services of the best brains in the country for the job at hand. The man who headed the Policy Planning Staff and who contributed largely to the Marshall Plan concept was George F. Kennan, the outstanding experienced diplomat thoroughly familiar with all the tricks in the Soviet bag. Peons of praise for the Marshall Plan have been and still are expressed all over the free world. Unquestionably, it prevented the encroachment of communism into the free nations, gave hope to the people of the

West and restored their national dignity. To me, everything I had ever known about Colonel Marshall, everything he had ever taught me, the very essence of his character as I knew it, were reflected in the words he spoke on that sunny June morning.

Jeffersonian idealism and Hamiltonian realism met in the Marshall Plan speech: humanistic concern for "the long suffering peoples" and pragmatic concern for the need to rectify "the dislocation of the entire fabric of European economy . . ." As for the importance Colonel Marshall had always placed on self-reliance, "The initiative, I think, must come from Europe . . ." The speech also reflected his repeated admonitions to curb runaway emotions with factual knowledge: "an essential part of any successful action on the part of the United States is an understanding on the part of the American people of the character of the problem and the remedies applied. Political passion should have no part . . ."

On June 4, the eve of the Marshall Plan speech, Colonel Marshall wrote me the following letter:

THE SECRETARY OF STATE

Washington

June 4, 1947

Dear Rose,

I do not recall whether or not I acknowledged your letter of May 19 about the christening exercises for Page.

I feel very apologetic that I have been responsible for the long delay in administering this rite. As I will probably be in New York in September and October in connection with a meeting of the Assembly of the United Nations, I should think that we should not have any difficulty in finding a convenient time for all of us.

It will interest you to learn that we moved to 2400 16th Street yesterday having taken a temporary lease on Mrs. Whitaker's [Mother's good friend] apartment she having gone to Europe. It was necessary for me to have somewhere to spend the night in case I finished up too late to commute to Leesburg. I doubt if I use the apartment more than two or three nights a week and Katherine will only use it when she is in town for an evening engagement.

We are leaving in about an hour for Boston where I am to receive a degree from Harvard initiated a year ago but finally to be resolved tomorrow.

With my love,

Affectionately,
G.C.M.

Twenty-six years had passed since those days at *2400*. The whole world had changed, and we stood on the threshold of a new era. In that quarter of a century, Colonel Marshall had risen to become one of America's most illustrious sons, but he hadn't changed, not basically.

It was happy news for me that Colonel Marshall would be coming up to the U.N. Assembly meeting, because John and I were about to move to Kings Point, Long Island, only a few miles from Lake Success, the first site of the U.N. offices. During the war, John had had to commute in reverse; we lived in Manhattan and he worked on Long Island. His office had been in the huge Sperry Gyroscope Building, leased by the Sperry Corporation from the Defense Plant Corporation which had built it. After the war, Sperry sublet half of the two-million square foot building to the United Nations for their temporary headquarters. In fact, the signatories at the little ceremony transferring the space to the United Nations were Trygvye Lie, Secretary General of the U.N., and John Wilson, who had become Treasurer of the Sperry Gyroscope Company.

"Sperry Gyro" continued to operate in the remaining half of the building at Lake Success, and since the postwar housing situation had eased somewhat, John and I were anxious to move our two babies out of the city and locate our home somewhere near his office. We paid an absurdly high price for a charming little house which faced the meadows of a deserted farm across a seldom-traveled road. The house was set back on a plot of about a half acre, pleasantly landscaped with lovely trees, shrubs, and flower beds. Our little home was extremely picturesque, though it sometimes gave me the feeling it had been put together with glue and phonograph needles. Nevertheless, I had lived in apartments since I was seven years old, so it seemd gloriously spacious to me; I loved it and couldn't wait to show it off to Colonel Marshall.

When Colonel Marshall's letter indicated he would be able to attend Page's baptism sometime in September or October, John and I decided to have the two boys baptized the same day; my brother-in-law Tom Morgan, had consented to serve as godfather for his namesake, Thomas.

Colonel Marshall did manage to sandwich in a visit to our house between his appearances at the U.N., but there was not time for a baptism. It still staggers me to remember how hard he worked for so many years.

The U.N. Assembly opened in September. In August, Colonel Marshall had attended a conference in Rio de Janeiro which was geared for the discussion of mutual defense, but which the Latin Americans had attempted to switch to a discussion of their economic difficulties. Colonel Marshall, however, always adept at sticking to the subject at hand, succeeded in getting the conference back on the defense track. He returned to Washington after having arranged an agreement whereby no nation would remain neutral in case of an attack on another. The twenty-one Latin American nations further agreed that each country could decide individually whether to participate militarily or in other ways, such as an economic blockade or the breaking off of diplomatic relations.

After Rio, Secretary Marshall came to New York to present a new idea to the U.N. Assembly. His speech called attention to the fact that "one permanent member of the Security Council" had paralyzed efforts of the United Nations to deal with the situations before it. He proposed that the U.N. create a "Little Assembly" composed of delegates from the fifty-five nations (the entire U.N. membership at that time) to sit in continuous session for at least the next year, on issues blocking efforts for peace. After the usual vituperative attacks from the Soviet delegates, Secretary Marshall's proposal was adopted by the General Assembly on November 13.

When Colonel Marshall telephoned me in September that he was coming to see me for a flying visit, I went into a frenzy of activity to spruce up our "property" so that it would appear its very best for his first impression.

John had mowed the grass the Saturday before Colonel Marshall was due, but when he left for work the day of Colonel Marshall's visit, he suggested I hand-trim the flagstone walk. It was a backbreaking job of which I had been happily ignorant during my city life, so that when Colonel Marshall arrived, I could hardly straighten up.

My godfather appeared to enjoy inspecting the house and "grounds," and was genuinely enthusiastic about our pretty country surroundings so close to New York. As for the kids, two-year-old Page behaved very well, and baby Thomas slept throughout the visit.

Colonel Marshall talked mostly about the house and children and about how pleased he was with John's advancing career. He worried a good deal that I couldn't find a maid, and said I looked too thin, but that he was happy we had such a pleasant home. We went out to have a drink on a big, open back porch, and when I eased into my chair, Colonel Marshall asked rather anxiously if I'd hurt my back. After I'd explained about trimming the walk, he laughed and said it would take me a while to get used to the rigors of country life, but it was good for John and me and good for the babies.

The porch looked out over our fenced-in back yard, beyond which stretched the wooded property of an old estate. It was a pleasant setting, and Colonel Marshall and I sat together, relaxed and comfortable. Page was playing in the yard. Colonel Marshall was watching him with amusement when Page, whose appetite never adhered to schedule, abruptly interrupted his project of trying to dig an escape tunnel under the fence. He came running up asking for his supper.

"Will you fix me a little something to eat, too?" Colonel Marshall asked. "I have to go to a tiresome banquet tonight and I never eat banquet food if I can get out of it."

He wished he could wait and have a proper dinner with us when John came home, he lamented, but he was committed to the banquet. I drew Page's high chair up to the kitchen table, where he and the Secretary of State ate their scrambled eggs, cheese toast, and fruit, which I had prepared in a mad rush so that Colonel Marshall could return to New York and change for the banquet.

"Colonel Marshall," I warned as we walked to his car, "don't let those Russians get you down!"

"Thanks," he laughed, "I'll remember your good advice." He kissed me good-bye and drove off. It was probably a Government car and chauffeur, but was it a Cadillac, I wondered later? I hadn't noticed!

When he left that day, I figured that Page would probably be ready for preparatory school before Colonel Marshall would be free long enough to participate in a baptismal rite. It seemed to prey on his mind that Page's baptism had been put off for two years, so I wrote and suggested I get a stand-in for him. Colonel Marshall replied that he would not for the world delay a christening, and as he couldn't promise a definite period, "I suppose it is best for you to go ahead as you suggest." His letter also said, "Today I am leaving for Chicago and Thursday I must leave for London."

He made a speech in Chicago blasting the Russians for their distortion of American efforts to restore Europe. After that, he

329

left for a Council of Foreign Ministers meeting in London, to make another try at arranging a peace treaty for Germany and Austria. In London, since all attempts failed to break what Colonel Marshall called "the tragic stalemate," he suggested that this session of the Council adjourn. When he returned home in December, he delivered a nation-wide radio address to explain that the meeting had failed because the Russians had refused to disclose vital information necessary to formulate a peace treaty, and had prohibited meaningful discussions by their outrageous accusations and lack of cooperation.

On April 3, 1948, Congress passed the Foreign Assistance Act creating the European Recovery Program, the technical name for the Marshall Plan. President Truman appointed Paul G. Hoffman, a Republican, as Administrator of the Program for which Congress had authorized funds amounting to nearly $5,500,000,-000 for the first year's operations.

Republican Senator Vandenberg persuaded the Taft Republican isolationists to vote for the Marshall Plan, which, he said, "seeks peace and stability for free men in a free world"—by economic rather than military means. His arguments were practical and forceful, but what probably catapulted the Program through Congress was the blatant Soviet seizure of Czechoslovakia at the very time the Congressional debate was going on.

In March, before the Marshall Plan had been implemented, Secretary Marshall appeared before Congress to plead for more immediate aid to Greece and Turkey. At the end of the month, he departed for Bogotá. This was the Ninth International American Conference with an agenda devoted to the discussion of the South American nations' economic plight. It was a difficult conference for the father of the Marshall Plan. He explained to twenty-one disappointed Latin American countries that they must understand that the present overwhelming responsibilities of the United States prohibited loans to them, and he pointed out that they would benefit by a peaceful, reconstructed Europe as much as would the United States.

While Colonel Marshall was in Bogotá, the Wilson boys were baptized on Thomas' first birthday, April 10. Colonel Leonard Henry, better known as "Deadeye" Henry, stood up for Colonel Marshall. Inasmuch as "Deadeye" was a great friend of John's, Tom Morgan's, Sis's, and mine, and an Army officer to boot, we all agreed he would be a fine choice. I had previously written to Colonel Marshall about "Deadeye," praising our friend's attributes, but explaining that I wasn't sure whether he'd acquired his nickname during his West Point days because of his splendid marksmanship or because of his reputation as an irresistible ladies' man.

When he returned from Bogotá, Colonel Marshall wrote that he hoped the ceremony went off well and teased me about Colonel Henry. In an effort to convince Colonel Marshall what a fine fellow his stand-in was, I'd gone overboard with some rather far-fetched recommendations. Colonel Marshall wrote that Carter, his Special Assistant and apparently another friend of Colonel Henry's, had commented that if "Deadeye"'s former West Point classmates ever learned of my flowery comments about him, "Deadeye" would be a "Dead Duck."

Incidentally, Colonel Marshall also told me he'd suffered no ill effects from living at 8,900 feet at Bogotá, "which presents some difficulties to most people."

In July, I received a very amusing letter from Colonel Marshall. I had written him complaining about what an inexperienced dope I was when it came to gardening. My letter had reached him in the hospital where he was having a checkup, he explained, so that the doctors would have a full medical history on him, and in case he ever got sick, would know what he *didn't* have.

He told me that my gardening difficulties were nothing com-

331

pared to his. He had followed an old Indian custom of burying fish heads under the corn he'd planted, and "every cat in Leesburg descended on me one weekend and practically dug up the foundations of the house getting at the fish heads." "On second thought," he added, "the corn was sent to me by Henry Wallace, so perhaps the cats were after that."

August 1948 was the hottest month of the hundreds of hot months I have lived through. In my capacity as cook, nurse, gardener, and laundress, most of the goings on in the outside world barely registered on my addled brain, engrossed as I was in getting one task done so that I could begin another. Colonel Marshall sent me a letter at the end of the month asking why I hadn't written and how I had survived the heat wave. "I had intended to ask Webb of the Budget if he had seen you recently. . . ." he wrote; but he hadn't had a chance. He was referring to James E. Webb, who had formerly been with Sperry Gyroscope. He is the same James Webb who became the head of the National Aeronautic and Space Administration (NASA), a man of unusual ability and a loyal friend.

I paid as little attention to the Dewey-Truman campaign that summer as Colonel Marshall probably did, not that I was imitating his aloofness from politics, but because it was a dull campaign.

But the Berlin Blockade that the USSR set up in June, and the resultant tensions that built up during the summer, electrified even my atrophied brains. The blockade attempted to shut off Berlin from the Allied-occupied zones of West Germany and grab all of Berlin for exclusive Soviet occupation. It was a retaliation against the Marshall Plan which had killed Stalin's ambitions to suck Europe into the communist orbit. Unable to endure the economic progress and representative government established in West Germany, Stalin resorted to his drastic measure.

Two official statements and one Presidential order illustrate United States action on the Berlin blockade. Secretary Marshall stated, "We will proceed to invoke every possible resource of negotiation and diplomatic procedure but we will not be coerced or intimidated in any way." General Lucius D. Clay, Commander of the American occupation forces in Europe, announced, "We will continue to fly our airplanes [carrying supplies into Berlin] no matter what happens in the air corridors." Lastly, President Truman directed that the airlift be put on a full-scale basis and that every plane available to the United States European Command be pressed into service.

In the fall, Colonel Marshall went to Paris for a United Nations Assembly meeting. The grave issue of the Berlin blockade had by then been referred to the U.N., but Soviet obstructionism rendered negotiation impossible. At the President's direction, Secretary Marshall left Paris to go to Greece in order to help straighten out complications about the United States loans which had arisen there. He returned to the United States around the end of October, and the news pictures I saw of him shocked me. He looked tired and ill. In December, he entered Walter Reed to undergo an operation for the removal of one kidney.

Because of the spectacular success of the Marshall Plan, few people realize today, or for that matter were aware at the time, of the magnitude of the other burdens Colonel Marshall carried during his tenure as Secretary of State. I have skimmed over only a few of them in order to emphasize his selflessness and devotion to his country. After the strenuous six years of his war leadership, followed by his exhausting year in China, Colonel Marshall, as Secretary of State, plunged into innumerable critical conferences and traveled thousands upon thousands of miles. No wonder he looked tired and ill! For the past nine years he had performed his grueling duties under the constant pressure of knowing that the results of his judgments did not entail merely his personal reputation, but meant the difference between the life and death of freedom in the world.

On January 29, 1949, Secretary of State Marshall and Under

Secretary of State Robert Lovett (who had so efficiently carried out the responsibilities of office when Colonel Marshall was abroad) both resigned from the State Department. Colonel Marshall was succeeded by Dean Acheson, and Mr. Lovett, by Jimmy Webb.

I was unhappy that Colonel Marshall had had to undergo an operation, but he appeared to have come through it very well and besides, oh joy, at last, at last, he could "go home"!

❧ CHAPTER XXXVIII ❧

IN THE SPRING OF 1949, JUST WHEN THE WILSONS HAD BECOME acclimated to the King's Point house, John was selected to be the president and general manager of Wright Machinery Company, a subsidiary of Sperry's in Durham, North Carolina. His new position was a big change for us and I knew Colonel Marshall would be pleased; he'd been rooting for John ever since we were married. On the occasion of one of my husband's previous promotions, Colonel Marshall had written, ". . . John will go from one success to another because in big business firms they have an immense regard for stability and dependability as well as good common sense, all qualities which he seems to have well developed." Then, half in fun, half in earnest, Colonel Marshall added, "He should make a good sea anchor for you, but I doubt if you would recognize such service."

I telephoned Colonel Marshall about John's new job, and right off, he fired at least a half dozen questions at me, none of which I could answer to his satisfaction.

"What does the factory make?"

"Packaging machinery."

"Anything else?"

"I think so."

"What?"

"Some sort of stuff for Sperry."

"The main product is packaging machinery?"

"As far as I know."

"What sort of packaging machinery?"

"Well, I'm not sure but I think it's machinery to make machinery that packs things mechanically."

"Big things or little things?"

"I don't know!"

"Well, before you go down there," Colonel Marshall replied calmly, "you'd better learn more about the caboodle than you know now."

"Good Lord, Colonel Marshall, of course I will, but I only found out yesterday John was going." I was piqued and a little hurt. "I only called up to tell you John had a fine new job and we're going to move down South."

Colonel Marshall laughed. "I got that much, and for your information, I am delighted for both of you. Tell John I congratulate him."

"Thanks!" I said, feeling better.

Colonel Marshall told me to hang up now and not waste John's money talking too long over long distance. He added, "but I'm glad you called to give me the good news."

Supplementing our telephone conversation, he sent me a little note of advice.

> . . . I think it is a step up that has been given John and I feel quite confident in his ability to carry it off in fine shape. You will have something to do as the wife of the President. I counsel tolerance, humility, and recognition that the world cannot be changed in twenty minutes. I write this having in mind your reform movements when you had that war-time job. You have all sorts of charm, so turn it on full force.

Tolerance, humility, and patience were Colonel Marshall's own trademarks, and as for his complimentary remark, he'd always sugared his admonitions to me.

After his little sermon, he wrote that we should be seeing more of each other since Pinehurst and Durham were so much closer than Washington and Long Island. Neither of us suspected that many years would pass before we would actually be "seeing more of each other."

Colonel Marshall stayed in Leesburg in the summer of 1949 until the end of July, although he frequently commuted to Washington. A letter from him in July told me he had just come back to Leesburg from the boiling heat of Washington and a tiresome day of long interviews and preparations for Congressional hearings on the "Atlantic Rearmament Act." He was referring, I presume, to the Congressional hearings on the appropriation of funds for military assistance under the North Atlantic Pact. He threw in a random sentence that he'd had lunch with Dulles at the Metropolitan Club on the same subject.

His longhand letters were always more informal and chatty. He sent me another newsy letter that July to tell me about his immediate future. First, he wrote that he and Katherine were going to fly up to Racquette Lake in the Adirondacks where they had been loaned a cottage for the summer. The "cottage" was the former J. P. Morgan's camp, but Colonel Marshall wrote, "they swear it is a simple establishment." In the last sentence of his letter, he informed me casually that he would probably be appointed president of the American Red Cross on September 15.

Although John had gone to North Carolina in May, the children and I spent the summer on Long Island until I could sell the house there and John could buy one in Durham. About the middle of August, I finally sold the house at a considerable loss. Meanwhile, John had bought another one at a great bargain, and we joined him in Durham on the first of September. The house John had bought was in the Tudor style of architecture, which neither of us particularly liked, but we were enchanted with the layout inside; the rooms were large and there were plenty of them. The lot itself was ample and had been lovingly landscaped by the former owner, a Duke University professor with two green thumbs. It was not at all a pretentious house, but comfortable, and situated in a pleasant neighborhood built around the Country Club golf course. There was a good deal to be done on the house, however, so all that fall I was submerged in the myriad tasks necessary to put our new home in order, and of course, further occupied with making new friends and generally adjusting to a new community.

In Colonel Marshall's Christmas note in 1949, he reminded me that I hadn't written for a long time, but said he'd seen the mayor of Durham who reported that I was getting alone fine. The mayor was Dan Edwards, a new friend of John's and mine, who, Colonel Marshall remarked, was an able fellow and one whom he was going to boost at the proper time.

Dan Edwards was one of our local war heroes, although I didn't find that out until I had lived in Durham for some time. Back in the perilous days of 1942, Captain Daniel K. Edwards was senior aide to Lieutenant General Robert Eichelberger who had personally commanded American and Australian troops in the desperate fighting through the New Guinea jungles. General Eichelberger thought highly of Dan's ability and courage and was very fond of him as well—like father and son, the General once wrote. When a Japanese sniper shot down his young aide standing at his side, Eihelberger got him over a tortuous route to a field hospital where an operation had saved Dan's life. Neither Colonel Marshall nor Dan had mentioned Dan's war experiences, but knowing Colonel Marshall, I'm confident he was aware of our mayor's war record.

It wasn't long before Dan Edwards asked me to serve on the local Red Cross Board. He pulled a fast one on me, though, for when I arrived for my first meeting, he had the Board rigged to make me secretary. I'm sure he did it as a compliment to Colonel

Marshall, but I had to work like the devil for the next few years—interesting work, though.

One evening in late January of 1950, Colonel Marshall telephoned me from Pinehurst to tell me that as long as I had not gotten down there, he was coming up to see me, and how about inviting him for lunch on Saturday?

"Oh sure, come on!" I said happily, and told him Saturday would be great because John would be at home.

He said he wanted to see the boys too, and that I was not to send them off somewhere. I replied I didn't know where I could possibly send them, but anyhow I had a maid now, who helped me "as well as she was able" to ride herd on them. Page was now four years old and Thomas not quite three, and before Saturday I had several sessions with them on "how to behave when General Marshall comes." As they had heard about him all their short lives and were familiar with the pictures of him around the house, both boys were excited about meeting him.

Saturday turned out to be a bright, warmish day, so that when I saw Colonel Marshall's car drive up, I hurried out the door and down the walk to greet him. Before I could reach the car, however, Colonel Marshall was already coming toward me and the car was driving away. Although I was concentrating on Colonel Marshall, I caught a glimpse of passengers in the back seat of the automobile before it turned the corner.

After we'd embraced and told each other how well we looked, Colonel Marshall said, "That was Katherine and her Chinese amah in the car."

"Well, gosh," I lied, "I would have been glad to have Mrs. Marshall for lunch too, and we have plenty of food for the Chinese gal."

"Oh, I'm sure of that!" he said, laughing, "but Katherine wanted to do some shopping while she's here."

John came out to join us and once again, Colonel Marshall started to inspect the Wilson quarters. We all laughed when we

339

figured out that this was the sixth place John and I had lived that Colonel Marshall had had to tour. After we'd gone all over the outdoors and downstairs, Colonel Marshall asked where the kids were.

"Oh, Rose has 'em tied up until she gives the high sign for them to appear," John answered.

"Well, unloose them!" Colonel Marshall said, laughing.

I called upstairs where the maid was trying to keep the little boys clean and quiet, and told her to send them down. We repaired to the living room and after a few minutes Page came in. He did not do or say one single thing I had rehearsed with him all week. He marched stiffly across the room, halted abruptly in front of Colonel Marshall, and gave him a smart salute—with his left hand. As Colonel Marshall watched him approach, he wore an expression very familiar to me from my childhood: his eyes twinkled with amusement while a mere suspicion of a smile softened the corners of his lips. Immediately upon Page's saluting, Colonel Marshall rose from the sofa, drew himself up to full attention, and solemnly returned my four-year-old's salute.

Page broke into a pleased smile. "Wow!" he said. "You're a sure 'nuff soldier! I'm glad you're my godfather."

"Thank you," Colonel Marshall replied, "I am glad to be your godfather." While Colonel Marshall engaged Page's rapt attention in a conversation about soldiers, I sat fidgeting and wondering nervously what had happened to Thomas. I was about to go and check on him when I heard, "Here I comes!" Thomas whirled into the living room, toppling over and over in a series of somersaults which ended in a crash against the coffee table.

Colonel Marshall burst into laughter. "Well, anyhow," he said, "he looks like his father, though he does seem to have inherited certain of his mother's characteristics!"

We had a "lovely time" that day. Colonel Marshall played with the kids, and after they left for their naps, he and John carried on an animated conversation about John's job. We had a nice lunch and made a big to-do about eating ice cream out of the wedding present silver bowls. I told Colonel Marshall our maid was thrilled that such a famous man was at our house, so after lunch he went out to the kitchen, and to her speechless delight, shook hands and congratulated her on the wonderful lunch. Then, at John's suggestion, we three went outdoors so John could take snapshots of Colonel Marshall and me.

When my husband went back inside a moment to get fresh film, Colonel Marshall said how glad he was he'd come and seen how well things were with me. "You are very fortunate, Rosie," he told me; "you've got a solid man with a good head on his shoulders."

"Thanks, Colonel Marshall, I'm very proud of him."

"And he is a happy man," Colonel Marshall continued, "and your boys are bustin' with health and full of ginger." He put his arm around my shoulder and gave me an affectionate little squeeze. "You are doing a wonderful job, my dear," he said.

I felt as if I'd won the D.S.C.!

Mrs. Marshall returned to fetch Colonel Marshall shortly before dark, and he insisted that she take a modified tour of the house and yard. I remember his calling attention to the huge, old, cedar tree, and pointing out my drab rock garden. "Rose tells me she'll have all sorts of lovely blooms here in the spring," he said, smiling.

Mrs. Marshall made pleasant, courteous comments, and several times repeated that she wished Molly had a home "like this." After about fifteen minutes, she warned Colonel Marshall they had better leave because it would soon be dark.

I recall that sunny January day most wistfully; my godfather had looked so well and seemed so happy.

In April, Colonel Marshall sent me a note saying he was to precede President Truman in making a speech before an impressive audience of cultural and educational leaders. The occasion, he explained, was to acknowledge the gift of fifty volumes of

Thomas Jefferson's papers, writings, and other documents, being prepared at Princeton. "Who is this fellow?" Colonel Marshall asked. "What do you know about him?" "What should I say in my five minutes?" I sent him a facetious reply, saying that I had taught him all I knew about Mr. Jefferson and was surprised he had found it necessary to seek my help. On second thought, I added, as long as it was to be an intellectual audience, why not build his talk around Jefferson's dictum, "Error of opinion may be tolerated where reason is left free to combat it." That ought to lead into Truman's speech, which was bound to be about carrying the torch for freedom and liberty and all that stuff. "Or," I suggested, "You could define 'inalienable rights,' but then that would only use up 5 seconds."

I thanked him nicely, however, for his invitation at the close of his note asking the Wilsons to drive down and have lunch "some day" the end of the month. I told him we would be delighted to come whenever Mrs. Marshall found it convenient, but something went awry and we didn't drive down.

The press of daily events and other affections never dislodged Colonel Marshall from his special place in my mind and heart, even though he was not always in the forefront. During that period of 1949 and most of 1950 when I thought of him, it was always with a feeling of happy relief that at last he was out from under the tremendous pressures of the past decade. I knew he liked his work as president of the American Red Cross, because his interest in the Red Cross meshed with his regard for the well-being of mankind. His acceptance of the job was indicative of his basic nature.

In an interview with a reporter who asked him why he had taken on the presidency of the Red Cross after his strenuous years just past, Colonel Marshall replied, "I came to this work feeling that there is urgent need of regeneration of a real understanding among people in the interest of world peace. . . . We can't accomplish this regeneration by prayer alone, but by the individual giving of himself. The Red Cross, it seems to me affords that opportunity to literally give to your fellow man."

In another interview, Colonel Marshall said, "I consider it an honor to be the president of the American Red Cross." I can't remember his ever saying that in connection with any of his other public offices. It is very likely that had he been made head of the Civilian Conservation Corps, he would have termed that position an "honor," though I can't say for sure.

When a letter from Colonel Marshall arrived in July 1950, I opened it with pleasure. I guessed he would probably tell me of some delightful summer plans he'd made, and undoubtedly thank me dutifully for a framed photo of the boys I'd recently sent him. Sure enough, the letter started off, "I have just this moment opened the package containing the photograph . . ." After a few sweet remarks about the boys' appearances, he wrote that he had put the picture on his dresser to replace an earlier one; and I was surprised and pleased to learn he had put it "with the one of you and me in 1924 that Celeste sent me several years ago." His letter rambled on, saying that he had seen Dan Edwards in Detroit, and that he had been instrumental in getting Dan elected to the National Red Cross Board. He said he was going to the Huron Mountains in northern Michigan for August —and then the bubble burst. "Most confidentially," he wrote, "I have been trembling on the edge of being called again into public service in this crisis but I hope I get by unmolested, but when the President comes down and sits under our oaks and tells me of his difficulties, he has me at a disadvantage . . ."

Damn, damn, damn, I fumed, not again!

The "crisis" Colonel Marshall had mentioned was the Korean War. Less than a month before his letter reached me, the Communist North Koreans had launched their surprise invasion of South Korea on the twenty-fifth of June. President Truman had immediately ordered United States air and naval forces to rush to South Korea's aid, and had sent the Seventh Fleet to protect

Formosa where the Chinese Nationalist Government was now established. Later in the week, in support of the U.N. resolution calling on member nations for armed assistance, Truman ordered United States ground troops to South Korea. One by one, other U.N. members joined us until there were about fifteen nations altogether. On July 7, the U.N. authorized the United States to establish a unified command, and quickly approved the President's appointment of General Douglas MacArthur as Commander in Chief of the United Nations forces.

The situation following our entrance into the Korean War was tragically parallel, on a smaller scale, to that following Pearl Harbor. Ill-trained ROK (Republic of Korea) troops and our troops, green kids hurriedly yanked from their soft occupation berth in Japan, retreated, and retreated some more. The rout was finally halted by General Walton Walker's Eighth Army fighting a delaying action while U.N. reinforcements were rushed in. The next move called for a U.N. offensive.

The United Nations Security Council authorized General MacArthur either to force the North Koreans behind the thirty-eighth parallel (the boundary between North and South Korea) or to destroy their forces. If there was no evidence of Russian or Chinese forces, the Security Council recommended that U.N. forces attempt to occupy North Korea. A directive from the Joint Chiefs of Staff based on the U.N. recommendation was sent to General MacArthur on September 15.

That same day, MacArthur initiated his brilliantly successful gamble, the amphibious landings on Inchon commanded by Rear Admiral Struble, which led to the capture ten days later of the South Korean capital, Seoul.

On September 12, 1950, General George C. Marshall was sworn in as Secretary of Defense. He succeeded Louis Johnson whom the President had asked to resign because of Mr. Johnson's numerous squabbles with other members of the Cabinet and with Congress, and because of the drastic economies Johnson had instigated in our national defense.

In order for Colonel Marshall to be approved for Secretary of Defense, Congress had to pass an amendment to the National Security Act which prohibited the appointment of a military man before he had been out of active service for ten years.

Senator Taft and a few Republican isolationists raised moderate objections based on Colonel Marshall's hopeless mission to China, but Republican Senator William Jenner of Indiana screamed libelous, vulgar, and vituperative accusations against General Marshall. He called him "a front man for traitors," and said, "Marshall is a living lie." After Jenner's revolting tirade, Republican Senator Saltonstall of Massachusetts rose, quivering with rage, and announced that he was shocked almost speechless. ". . . If any man in public life," Saltonstall managed to say, "is more above censure than General Marshall, I do not know of him. I wish I had the vocabulary to answer the statement that General Marshall's life is a lie."

Democratic Senator Harry Byrd of Virginia stood up and said with cool dignity, "I challenge any man who opposes this appointment to propose a better one."

The stage was set, our defenses were cut to the bone, and we were at war—so, enter the selfless patriot, the voice of authority, "the organizer of victory," the organizer of peace, the *deus ex machina* of the troubled world drama—George C. Marshall.

The tributes paid Colonel Marshall on his assumption of office as Secretary of Defense were as extensive as those in 1944 and 1947. In summary, his appointment was hailed as bringing relief and reassurance to this country and to Europe. One editorial, however, depressed me. It emphasized his diversified talents, integrity, and broad outlook as being important assets for his job, but concluded, "The post he has agreed to assume is a killing one."

I wrote Colonel Marshall to tell him I was proud of him, but asked him how many more tough jobs he was going to accept, and said that he'd already broken all records for patriotism. I was only sorry about his latest honor, I wrote, because I wanted him to have some fun, but now I was afraid his conscience would never, ever permit him to retire and raise tomatoes.

As soon as Colonel Marshall came on stage, the action stepped up. In less than a month, he had put an end to interservice quarrels. That done, he set about straightening out the mobilization confusion. While Colonel Marshall was in China in 1946, it may be remembered, the whole Army had melted "like snow upon the desert's dusty face"; consequently, the desperate need for men in the Korean crisis was wrecking the Reserve and creating gross inequities in the draft. Colonel Marshall was an old pro when it came to mobilization, so while adjusting the interim mix-up, he ordered and directed the establishment of long-range plans to avoid future complications.

And what did Secretary Marshall do next? He set his sights on Universal Military Training! In November, he appointed the extraordinarily able and versatile Anna Rosenberg as Assistant Secretary of Defense in charge of manpower and personnel. ". . . The outstanding expert on the subject of manpower," Secretary Marshall called her. In January 1951, he went before Congress to plead for Universal Military Training. Mrs. Rosenberg attended with him, and snowed Congress with a blizzard of accurate manpower statistics and astute estimates.

One legislator, intending to insult Secretary Marshall, commented that it sounded to him like a shotgun wedding between the draft and Universal Military Training. Colonel Marshall replied that indeed it was, and that he was the papa insisting on the wedding. On June 19, 1951, Congress adopted the principle of Universal Military Training for the first time in our history.

On the fifteenth of October, 1950, one month after Colonel Marshall became Secretary of Defense, President Truman flew to Wake Island for a meeting with General MacArthur. The President wanted to learn MacArthur's assessment of the Korean War at first hand, and to review with him the necessity for integrating the Korean conflict with the complications existent in Europe, which were formidable at that time.

The Berlin blockade, broken in May 1949, had resulted in the formation of NATO for the mutual protection of the United States and free Europe, or the "containment" of communism. Though Stalin had been thwarted in his blockade, no one could prophesy what other perils his ambition might provoke, particularly since the USSR had successfully detonated an atom bomb the previous fall. Western Europe was menaced internally by communist subversion and externally by thousands of Soviet troops massed in Eastern Europe. Those were the fearful days when the line between the Cold War and World War III was stretched terrifyingly near the breaking point.

The consultation at Wake Island hinged on the President's direct question to MacArthur, asking his opinion concerning the possibility of communist intervention in Korea. General Mac-Arthur replied that the possibility of a Red Chinese attack was very slight, and uttered his oft-quoted observation, "If the Chinese try to get down to Pyongyang [the North Korean capital], there would be the greatest slaughter."

The President, greatly relieved and encouraged by Mac-Arthur's optimism, emphasized the precarious European situation and explained that it would inevitably affect the conduct of the Korean War. General MacArthur assured President Truman that he understood perfectly, and repeatedly told him that the Korean War was won, and that he would be able to send a division to Europe by January 1951. On the basis of the report he gave at Wake Island, General MacArthur was authorized to move U.N. forces north as far as the Yalu River boundary between North Korea and Manchuria, but was told under no circumstances to cross the boundary and risk the intervention of the Communist Chinese and probable Soviet retaliation in Europe.

From here on the story is tragic. General MacArthur, confident that he would not meet with a substantial Chinese attack, conceived what he supposed would be another brilliant strategic success. On November 24, he launched his "final" offensive; his forces split, one east and one west, and moved north to meet at

347

the Yalu and thus encircle and annihilate the North Korean army. What followed was a slaughter, as MacArthur had predicted, except that the slaughter was of U.N. troops. Hundreds of thousands of Chinese soldiers poured into North Korea and drove down the center of the divided U.N. forces. There ensued as bloody and devastating a retreat as any in history.

Unquestionably, General MacArthur had a brilliant mind and will be remembered in history for his military triumphs as well as for his able administration of American-occupied Japan. Unquestionably, too, his character was marred by an overweening conceit, and his intellect limited by stubborn parochialism. He was incapable of admitting an error and refused to attach importance to any world area outside his own sphere of interest. MacArthur was infallible to MacArthur.

After this terrible setback of the Korean War, General MacArthur, in open defiance of orders from his Commander in Chief, delivered public statements, amounting in cold fact to pronunciamentos, in direct and imperious opposition to the United Nations and Administration policies. On April 11, 1951, President Truman, the folksy little man from Missouri, rose to the full stature of his great office and relieved from all his commands, the glamorous god-hero, General Douglas MacArthur.

Many Americans have agreed with MacArthur's views on foreign policy and the conduct of the Korean War, and many others with Truman's, but neither partisan attitudes nor personal allegiance have the slightest bearing on MacArthur's dismissal. MacArthur was fired because he had challenged the Constitution of the United States which specifically provides for the dominance of civilian control over the military. That is why Secretary of State Acheson; Secretary of Defense Marshall; The Chairman of the Joint Chiefs of Staff, General Omar Bradley, speaking for himself and the unanimous Joint Chiefs; and Special Assistant to the President Ambassador Averell Harriman all agreed with President Truman's unavoidable decision.

When the news of MacArthur's dismissal broke, a huge emotional tidal wave surged across the nation. When the General returned home, he was accorded a frenzied welcome everywhere he appeared, which he acknowledged with dignified and aloof grandeur. The crowds worshipped him, like Caesar, though few of his idolizers understood or cared about the basic Constitutional reason for his dismissal.

Long and exhaustive hearings before joint sessions of the Senate Military and Foreign Policy Committees were begun before the General should "fade away," as he had suggested he might. One of MacArthur's statements at the hearing clearly explained the attitude which had prompted him to write a public letter to the House Republican Minority Leader, Joe Martin. In that letter, which had finally clinched the decision to cashier him, MacArthur, after criticizing the Government and the United Nations military and foreign policy, wrote: "Here we fight Europe's wars with arms, while the diplomats there fight it with words . . ." After close questioning at the hearing about important European issues of the day, however, MacArthur admitted he hadn't given much thought to such issues for fourteen years. From this startling admission, it was deduced that the global consequences of his views and public pronouncements were not apparent to MacArthur.

After General MacArthur's testimony was concluded, Secretary of Defense Marshall was called. Before he submitted to the questioning, Colonel Marshall said, ". . . I would like to observe that it is a very distressing necessity . . . that compels me to appear . . . in almost direct opposition to a great many views and actions of General MacArthur. He is a brother officer, a man for whom I have tremendous respect . . . as to his military performances."

This brings to mind the much touted so-called Marshall-MacArthur feud, which in my opinion, to quote one of Colonel Marshall's favorite colloquialisms, is "eyewash." It takes two to make a feud, and it takes jealousy and ill will on both sides to keep it going. I can vouch that jealousy and ill will were totally lacking in Colonel Marshall's make-up. There was no room for them in his heart and no time for them in his mind.

Colonel Marshall had been truthful when he told the Senators he respected MacArthur's military ability. There is plenty of public proof for his statement in the occasions he had boosted MacArthur during World War II. I also knew it to be so from my own experiences, a couple of which I have mentioned. Personally, I had not liked General MacArthur as a person since I was a little girl, and Colonel Marshall knew it; but one day when I was mimicking his "I have returned" speech, Colonel Marshall really shut me up, but good.

I was hamming around when my godfather used his cold, steely tone on me and ordered, "Stop that this instant!"

"O.K., yes sir!" I said; "but honestly, Colonel Marshall, you know as well as I do that General MacArthur is insufferably vain. It kind of irritates me for you always to be sticking up for him."

"Sometimes you can choose to be damnably difficult and stubborn," Colonel Marshall replied, but he was smiling. He went on to admit that of course General MacArthur was vain, but I knew as well as he did that MacArthur's conceit was nothing to him. He continued, dead seriously, "I have told you before, General MacArthur is unquestionably one of the ablest military men in our history. You are presumptuous to ridicule him."

I will not attempt to speculate on MacArthur's private feelings about Colonel Marshall, but I will present a few random examples of what he chose to publicize concerning those feelings after his dismissal from command.

After Colonel Marshall's widely acclaimed service as our wartime Chief of Staff, he stopped overnight with MacArthur in Japan en route to China in 1946. General MacArthur records this visit in his autobiography written in his retirement. He did not have one word of praise for the outstanding achievements of his

350

"brother officer," but wrote: "Mentally he had aged immeasurably since his visit to New Guinea. The former incisiveness and virility were gone." This was MacArthur's comment on the man who, after that visit, spent a hellish year in China; became Secretary of State and fathered the Marshall Plan; was a dynamic president of the American Red Cross; was Secretary of Defense and reorganized our defenses; was chairman of the American Battle Monuments Commission, and traveled all over Europe making speeches; and was chosen to be the recipient of a Nobel Peace Prize.

In the February 13, 1956 issue of *Life,* MacArthur wrote: "General Marshall's enmity [toward me] was an old one . . ." MacArthur flattered himself. Certainly, Colonel Marshall was always contemptuous of conceit, but regarding MacArthur, his contempt was subdued by patience and the recognition of MacArthur's military prowess. Colonel Marshall did not hesitate to censure MacArthur's insubordination and to uphold the Constitution when MacArthur defied it, but it was not enmity Colonel Marshall felt for him, it was pity.

Colonel Marshall told me himself he considered it a tragedy that vanity had "brought down" a man who was a real military genius. And "brought down" he was in Colonel Marshall's eyes. All the wild adulation accorded MacArthur on his return home would have been ashes to Colonel Marshall if he'd known he had failed in his duty as an officer of the Army. I don't know whether Colonel Marshall was mistaken in his pity for General MacArthur or not, because I don't know whether MacArthur ever believed in his innermost secret self that he was "brought down." He was a courageous man, but whether he was courageous enough to admit in his soul he was wrong, I cannot guess. Nor do I refer to the correctness or incorrectness of MacArthur's political utterances, but to his wrong action.

I think the above examples prove that the Marshall-MacArthur "feud," if any, was a one-sided affair. Come to think of it, if the term "feud" is to be used, why just a Marshall-MacArthur "feud"; why not Bradley-MacArthur or Eisenhower-MacArthur as well? Those two eminent Generals also met with MacArthur's displeasure. I suggest that a first-rate sensationalist could work up any old MacArthur-Peer or MacArthur-Superior feud, but the only one I know of that existed in fact was MacArthur-Navy.

Colonel Marshall had been yanked back into public life because the national defense required reorganization and rebuilding. General MacArthur's increasing recalcitrance and subsequent transgression had plunged the country into a temporary morale slump and had made Secretary Marshall's "killing" post more difficult in the light of the nation's well-being, and more painful, personally. MacArthur's behavior, however, probably drained the energies of his "brother officer" more than it did those of his country, for Lieutenant General Matthew Ridgway, MacArthur's competent successor to the U.N. Command, pulled the United Nations Army out of defeat and restored the confidence of the American people and their allies.

On the other hand, Colonel Marshall was seventy years old, and six days of continuing Congressional questioning on a most distasteful subject, added to his other pressing duties, must have unduly tired him whether he admitted it or not.

At the beginning of 1951, the period when Colonel Marshall was testifying for Universal Military Training, he sent me a nostalgic little note written from his office in the early morning before the ordeals of the day had begun. He had been prompted to write to me, he said, by his reminiscences as he was driving to work through our old "exploring grounds" of the 2400 days. The note was a clear indication that his exceptional self-discipline notwithstanding, Colonel Marshall was very human—he had looked back that morning with pleasure and yearning for the less strenuous days of a freer life. I replied that it was nice to be reminded of the time when he was merely a brilliant young Army officer and not the world figure he was today. It was a happy memory, I wrote, but he was the same Colonel Marshall. I meant it too. I had always been proud of Colonel Marshall, and I was no whit prouder of him at the height of his fame than I had been back then.

At the time of the MacArthur fiasco in the spring, I had intended to hold off writing my godfather until I had simmered down and could write a calm letter, but I heard from him first.

He sent me a brief longhand note in May, hurriedly written on a Secretary of Defense memo pad. "What has become of you?" he scribbled. "In my times of trial you usually come through with a morale boost." This poignant little paragraph was followed by a bum, far-fetched joke; he asked me if I was mad because he had taken on the mayor of Durham as his Assistant Secretary. Then, characteristically, never wanting to cause anyone else worry, he added that he was "feeling fine but pretty busy," and that his spring gardening chores had stimulated him tremendously. He ended, "With my love, Rosie, Affectionately."

He rarely referred to me in a letter as "Rosie," and indeed, even orally, had used this appellation of my childhood quite seldom in recent years.

I was deeply moved, and immediately after I'd read the note, I sat down and burned up my typewriter praising him and blasting MacArthur. When I'd gotten that off my chest, I asked how Dan was making out; I told Colonel Marshall I'd had dinner with him and his wife and that they were both thrilled with Dan's challenging new position.

It was probably better that I wrote Colonel Marshall a letter true to form than if I had labored over a more restrained one, for the letter amused him. He replied within a few days, observing that, as usual, I was generous with superlatives, and admitting, "I must say I am glad to have you 'on my side!'" Dan, he added, seemed to have "all four wheels on the track."

Around the middle or end of June, I was in Washington with my sister and Tom Morgan, and if my memory is correct, Colonel

Marshall and I went riding. We may have had lunch together, but the circumstances are unimportant; it is our conversation I remember so clearly. We talked about the undistinguished Senator Joe McCarthy, who at that time was transforming the national antipathy to communism into hysterical excesses. In a long, violent speech before the Senate, McCarthy had accused Secretary of Defense Marshall of "black infamy," "immense conspiracy," and of other preposterous, vile things. He dared accuse Colonel Marshall of "treason"!

The day I saw him in Washington, I commented bitterly to Colonel Marshall that McCarthy reminded me of the little boys who had thrown mud at our "tin Lizzie" many years ago. Like them, McCarthy was ignorant and irresponsible. The children had attacked from their hiding place behind the bushes and retreated into the woods when they were exposed. Similarly, McCarthy attacked from his hiding place behind his spurious "confidential reports," and retreated into a forest of lies when he was discovered.

"There's one important difference though," I said. "Those kids didn't realize the extent of the injury they might inflict, whereas McCarthy throws his mud clots at the innocent, trying his damndest to ruin them. All McCarthy wants is to use his unscrupulous political gimmick to further his demagogic ambitions."

"Colonel Marshall," I urged, "I wish you'd collar McCarthy like you did those boys and tell *him* what's what. I'll bet any stakes he would disintegrate if he ever faced up to you alone. Jeeze, but I'd like to see you freeze that guy!"

Colonel Marshall shrugged off my suggestion and remarked that aside from the fact that he always stayed clear of politics, clean or dirty, would I really want him to demean himself by exchanging words with McCarthy? I told him no, I was daydreaming, but it was frustrating that he wouldn't make a single public rebuttal.

"If I did that," Colonel Marshall explained, "I would acknowledge something that isn't true, that McCarthy's accusations are worthy of defense. There is no necessity for me to prove my loyalty to the United States; I have lived that loyalty every day of my life."

"That's for sure," I agreed. "Anyhow, Joseph 'Rabid' McCarthy's fake star is bound to fall in the trash heap before too long, but George 'Patriot' Marshall's real star will keep on shining forever and ever."

"Amen!" he smiled. "That's some fine speech!" Then he laughed and said he'd thought of an old joke that would be the most appropriate retort to all McCarthy's trumped-up accusations against decent citizens. Whereupon, he told this joke: "As the street cleaner said to the elephant, 'that's enough out of you.'"

I burst out laughing. I hadn't heard the joke before, and I thought it a singularly apt analogy for McCarthy's despicable slander. I still think so.

Colonel Marshall wrote me quite frequently during 1951. Sometimes he commented on various reports I had written for the Red Cross; sometimes he reminisced—for instance, he wrote me after a cold spell that he still slept under a Canadian blanket I'd given him when I was a little girl. Sometimes he gave personal news; for example, telling about the wonderful day he'd spent at his beloved V.M.I. when the Institute had celebrated "Marshall Day." Incidentally, Colonel Marshall had delivered two commencement addresses at V.M.I., one in 1940 and one in 1950. The interesting fact is that his opening words on both occasions were identical: "This is a day of high emotion for you men; it also might be one of the most fateful days in the history of the world." In 1940, the Germans were advancing on Paris. In 1950, the North Koreans were attacking South Korea. The letter about V.M.I. was written in June, the day he returned from Korea. The trip, he said, was "fast and furious," "interesting and tiring." I had not been surprised when I read in the newspapers that he was going to Korea. He had made a practice of getting on-the-spot

355

information at all the fronts during World War II, and I'd been wondering when he would do the same in Korea. In a press conference on his return, Colonel Marshall dismissed all insinuating questions about General MacArthur and said firmly his trip had been purely for "military purposes," which I'm sure it was.

I did not write Colonel Marshall very often, but when I did, I usually wrote what practically amounted in length to a novelette. He had always pressed me to write news of our children, and knowing of his interest in children generally, and in mine in particular, I realized I had an audience to whom I could brag and recount "cutisms" to my heart's content!

Colonel and Mrs. Marshall vacationed at Cape Cod for the summer of 1951, and he wrote to me from there because I'd written him that Page was sick. He said he was sorry about Page's illness, and commented, "in one of the pictures I noticed he had his hands up to his stomach and I was wondering if that is where his troubles lie—could it have been from too many green apples?" (Page had the measles!) Colonel Marshall also wrote Page from Cape Cod, a combination get-well note and sixth-birthday greeting.

On September 12, 1951, one year to the day since he had accepted the appointment, Colonel Marshall resigned as Secretary of Defense. He was succeeded by Robert A. Lovett, a man he counted his friend and in whose ability he had great faith; earlier, he had persuaded Lovett to become his Deputy Secretary of Defense, to assist him as he had done while Under Secretary of State. Colonel Marshall had made the fur fly that year! He had put the Defense Department in working order; more than doubled our armed forces (although he held out against total mobilization); convinced the country of the necessity for Universal Military Training; inspected the Korean front; led the planning for integrating the air, naval, and ground forces of the Atlantic Pact nations, and undoubtedly accomplished a good deal more that I never knew about.

I had been busy, too; I was pregnant again. I told Colonel Marshall the news when I congratulated him on his retirement. He wrote back, "that's grand, wonderful, . . . the larger the family the better you'll be." I only hoped he was right; I was not too enchanted with the prospect this time round.

Judging from Colonel Marshall's letters, he had a busy fall after the resignation, due partly to held-over engagements and partly to pleasure. He went on what he termed a "shooting spree" on Pinckney Island with our mutual friend, my cousin, former ambassador to Argentina, James Bruce; he got his turkey and pheasant limit, but flubbed on quail. His Christmas letter said he was going quail shooting at Baruch's place in South Carolina— where I trust he had better luck—and was thinking of spending two months in Cuernavaca, Mexico. He told me he'd been asked by the Carnegie Corporation to go on a good-will tour through New Zealand, Australia, and South Africa; and that he had just been invited to be the guest of the New Zealand Government, an invitation "*including* all the celebrated fishing I can manage." The italics are his. He and Mrs. Marshall, however, "thought not." He concluded that lapful of news by writing that he was "beginning to relax . . . though I have been far too busy. But I feel fine and they tell me I look all right?" The question mark is his, too.

I telephoned him soon after Christmas, and during the conversation asked if he wanted to go on the fabulous Carnegie trip. He told me no, he had done enough traveling to last him the rest of his life here on earth and afterwards too!

CHAPTER XXXIX

In JANUARY 1952, THE SUPREME COMMANDER OF NATO, GENERAL Dwight D. Eisenhower, announced his availability for the Republican nomination for President. On January 29, Greece and Turkey were admitted to NATO. These were undoubtedly momentous occasions for those concerned, but my prime interests lay elsewhere. On January 29, 1952, my daughter (another Celeste) was born. A daughter! Why had I complained for nine months about having a child in my "old age"?

I telephoned Colonel Marshall in high spirits the next day, intending to tell him that this time I had not contributed to the country's future military reserve. To my disappointment he was not at Pinehurst, although the itinerary he had sent me said he would be there until February first.

Colonel Marshall had "gone home" in a sense, but he was still extremely busy catching up with held-over engagements and attending various committee meetings, one of which was the Business Advisory Council. About a week before baby Celeste arrived, Colonel Marshall had written that he had seen my brother-in-law at a Business Advisory meeting; he said Tom had reported I was getting along well, and had told him my baby was due around the middle of February, which was true—she jumped the gun.

Colonel Marshall wrote that he and Katherine were leaving on February first to vacation in Cuernavaca, Mexico, for a month. He added. "I pray all goes well for you . . ." and he hoped the baby would be a girl.

After his return from Mexico, he said that he had a very crowded schedule, three dates in a row: one at Wellesley (". . . tell me what line to take with the young women") and one at Lawrenceville Preparatory School in New Jersey. The importance of informed youth was one of Colonel Marshall's pet projects, so he accepted speaking invitations at schools and colleges whenever he could manage to go. The third engagement was in New York, where he was scheduled to receive an award from the "Four Freedoms" which he said was three years overdue, but he wasn't exactly sure what it was!

After he'd filled me in on his whereabouts for the next couple of months, Colonel Marshall jumped right into another subject. He had received an out-of-print little book for his birthday which had been a great favorite of his and Lily's, and he was sending it on to me to read to the children. He treasured the book, and asked me to keep it for him until he could drive up and call on the baby and me. Most unfortunately, he was never able to make the trip. When I first offered to return his book, he said, "Keep it until Celeste is old enough for you to read it to her. Lily would want your little daughter to know that story."

I still have the book. The last time I suggested returning it was in the fall of 1958 when Celeste was seven years old and I had read it to her. Colonel Marshall declined. "No, not now," he said. "Put it with the other things you have of Lily's."

The book is *Timothy's Quest*, one of Kate Douglas Wiggin's first stories, published in 1890. It is a sunny, whimsical little tale, spiced with gentle humor, about the adventures of two small orphans. I can easily understand why *Timothy's Quest* had appealed to Lieutenant Marshall and his bride—Colonel Marshall being peculiarly sensitive to children, Lily being tender-hearted and sentimental, and both of them longing for children of their own.

Around the end of April, Colonel Marshall wrote inviting John, the boys, and me to come down to Pinehurst for the big North-South Golf Tournament. As he was to telephone me later in the week to find out if we could come, he gave me what he called "background information" so I'd be primed for his call— and sad information it was.

Clifton, Mrs. Marshall's elder son, was seriously ill in Walter Reed Hospital. Mrs. Marshall was also in Walter Reed undergoing a series of tests, but according to Colonel Marshall, she was comforted to be near Clifton. Colonel Marshall wrote he had returned to Pinehurst to oversee "a big reconstruction job ($2000 worth!) on the cottage due to termite destruction." Anyhow, he concluded, he would like to have the Wilsons come down to Pinehurst—if we could stand the bad smell of the termite poison —for the Tournament finals, unless Clifton took a turn for the worse and he should be called to Washington.

John and I were in Florida, so I missed his phone call, and didn't receive that letter or the next saying he must leave for Washington until after Colonel Marshall had gone.

The year 1952, which had started out so happily for me, turned out to be one of the most dolorous years of my life. My brother-in-law, Tom Morgan, of whom John and I are extremely fond, suffered a heart attack and lay at death's door for weeks. While he was still ill, Clifton Brown died. Clifton's death was not a great personal loss to me, for I had known him only casually; nevertheless, his untimely death disturbed me exceedingly for a long time. The fact that Mrs. Marshall had lost both her sons seemed so unbearable that I could not bring myself even to imagine the depth of her grief. I was not in a position to judge how Mrs. Marshall carried her loss in private, but I can state without reservation that in public or before me, she bore her grief with rare fortitude and grace.

In August, Colonel and Mrs. Marshall flew to Santa Barbara to spend some time with Mrs. Bowling Lee, whose daughter, Mary Lee, had been Clifton's fiancée at the time of his death. In September, taking Mary Lee with them, they sailed for Europe in connection with Colonel Marshall's chairmanship of the American Battle Monuments Commission. Colonel Marshall never told me whether his trip was unavoidable, or if he had agreed to go in the hope that the extensive traveling would distract Mrs. Marshall from her sorrow.

The Marshalls traveled far and fast on their European sojourn, although Colonel Marshall wrote that their traveling had been enormously simplified because General Ridgway had loaned them his Constellation. General Ridgway had succeeded General Eisenhower as Supreme Commander of NATO after Eisenhower was relieved to campaign for the Presidency. Another advantage which had made things pleasanter, Colonel Marshall wrote, was his temporary European aide-de-camp, Colonel Walters, who spoke seven languages. I don't know how well Mrs. Marshall spoke French, but I do know that Colonel Marshall's French was atrocious, and as probably neither of them spoke Italian or German, it must have been a great help to have the versatile interpreter along. The entire trip was work for Colonel Marshall, except for a week or so that the Marshalls spent at Capri where someone had placed a villa at their disposal, and where, as Colonel Marshall said, they had a "truly charming time." In spite of all the accommodations offered them, I personally didn't see how it could be a very entertaining trip for Colonel Marshall: inspecting the construction progress of about ten cemeteries in Western Europe and Africa, making speeches, and dedicating the first World War II military memorial in France.

The day after my birthday in September, my brother, Tom Page, died very suddenly after only one day's illness. It was the climactic misfortune of 1952. My letter telling Colonel Marshall of my brother's death reached him in Europe. He wrote by return mail:

> . . . We often use the word "shocked" at such a time but I am truly shocked terribly at your tragic news of Tom. . . . It is too hard to realize that the little boy I knew so well at 2400, 16th St., punted football with, and took sled rides with, has beaten me to the end. With a wife and fine family of children it's hard to explain such workings of Providence. Give Susie my affectionate sympathy. She had a fine man who I always admired, especially during the tough days of the depression.
>
> > I gotta brother and his name is Tom,
> > He ain't very wide and he ain't very long . . .

Poor Tom, whose superior intellect we had so admired, whose unique wit had been our delight, and whose affectionate nature had drawn us all to him; he who had cheated death so often in his childhood was cut down in the full blossoming of his maturity.

The Marshalls returned from Europe sometime in October. Colonel Marshall, as usual, was greeted by a battery of photographers and reporters who asked him for comments on General Eisenhower's campaign and particularly on what he thought of Eisenhower's relationship with Senator McCarthy. What a question to ask Colonel Marshall!

To give a little background information, soon after General Eisenhower's nomination, he had been urged by the press to express his attitude toward the Republican Senators McCarthy and Jenner who had insulted and maligned his old boss, General Marshall. Eisenhower had replied firmly, "I have no patience with anyone who can find in his [Marshall's] record of service to this country anything to criticize . . ." General Eisenhower, however, was a sub-novice at politics, and later during his summer campaign, he had fallen into the wily McCarthy's trap. McCarthy succeeded in persuading the General to delete a tribute to Colonel Marshall from one of his speeches. I suspect Eisenhower may have inserted the tribute to quell all suspicion that he distrusted the man whom he had publicly recognized as a great patriot, and who had given him the biggest boost of his career. Newsmen soon ferreted out Eisenhower's omission which was greeted by an uproar of nonpartisan indignation, except for McCarthy's extreme right followers. They, unfortunately, had been duped into identifying McCarthy as a Saint George slaying the Communist dragon. They were pitifully mixed up; McCarthy was a more evil, poison-spitting dragon than the bugaboo "commies" he pretended were lurking behind every bush.

When Colonel Marshall was pressed to comment on General Eisenhower's behavior, he parried the queries by replying that he had never involved himself in politics, that he had served under both Democratic and Republican Presidents, had never voted, and did not intend to vote in the coming elections.

The Marshalls came to Pinehurst around the middle of November, and their cottage, Liscombe Lodge, was Colonel Marshall's headquarters until early spring.

He wrote me that they would spend a very quiet Christmas, but there was one joyous aspect to it. Molly had bought a house in Pinehurst a year or so previously, and was there with her family at Christmas time, awaiting her husband's orders for foreign service—Jim Winn was now a Colonel. I was genuinely relieved to know that for her first Christmas after Clifton's death, Mrs. Marshall would have her daughter and grandchildren with her.

Aside from Mrs. Marshall's grief, Colonel Marshall's letter said she was having a hard time with her back. "She was well on her way to recovery," he wrote, "but persistently doing up some 60 packages about finished her." I have an idea Mrs. Marshall defied Colonel Marshall's entreaties to slow down, because I, myself, have found that keeping furiously busy is the best antidote to sorrow. Incidentally, Colonel Marshall's Christmas present to the boys that year was a huge, elaborate, Western village, complete with what I estimated to be about a hundred thousand pieces when I saw them scattered on the floor Christmas night. I must say I pitied poor Mrs. Marshall if she had wrapped that Christmas gift.

In February 1953, my fellow members on the Red Cross Board brought up for the third or fourth time a request that I ask General Marshall to come to Durham and make a speech. I had repeatedly declined to ask him because, in the first place, I didn't want to—I had only asked him one favor in my life—and in the second, I didn't think he would possibly be able to come. The nation-wide Red Cross Drive was beginning in the near future, however, and their request was so reasonable that I couldn't think up a plausible excuse; so I reluctantly agreed to invite him. I telephoned Colonel Marshall and issued the invitation. "You can't come to Durham and make a speech for the Red Cross, can you?"

He laughed and replied, "They must have really pressured you. No, I can't."

We talked a while of other things, but before we said good-bye, Colonel Marshall assured me that he would write a letter to get me off the hook, and that, in truth, he really was booked up for a long time ahead. "You are my favorite godchild and the Red Cross is my favorite philanthropic enterprise," he said. "I would come to Durham if I could."

His follow-up letter expressed his regret that he coldn't accept the Red Cross invitation; as I had already guessed, he had had to decline fifteen or twenty others because of prior commitments. I didn't know specifically what was keeping him on the go so much that season, but whatever it was, I thought it was too much. In his Red Cross letter, he wrote that he had just returned to Pinehurst from a trip to Washington, to Boston, and back to Washington, and in a few days he was due to fly to Savannah, then to Ohio. As I read his schedule, it made me uneasy that he was doing so much, as Colonel Marshall had passed his seventy-second birthday. The rest of his letter really worried me.

He said that when he returned from Ohio, he would try to find "the time and energy" to motor up to see me, but, "One sign of age is my reluctance to motor many miles. Also I find I grow very bored and restless sitting in a plane more than an hour or so." Colonel Marshall reluctant to motor? He used to love motor trips!

After his disturbing admission, he continued, *"Most* confidentially, I am to go to the Coronation [Elizabeth II] representing the President." He said he appreciated the compliment but was "bored stiff" with the prospect, and much preferred peaceful gardening at Leesburg. Colonel Marshall had the habit of saying "yes" when Presidents asked him to do something. He did add that he didn't mind the sea trip, because he thought it would be restful and pleasant. Colonel Marshall attended the Coronation as President Eisenhower's Special Representative, returned to Leesburg, came down with a virus, and stayed down a long, long time.

In November 1953, General Marshall was selected to receive the Nobel Peace Prize. Of all the Nobel prizes, the Peace Prize has been the one reserved most frequently, and had never before been awarded to a military man in the fifty-two years since the establishment of the Nobel institutes. I was overcome with pride and joy. To me, this coveted and distinguished award was a superb recognition of Colonel Marshall's long, selfless service to his country and to mankind.

I telephoned Leesburg as soon as I got the news, only to learn that Colonel Marshall was in Walter Reed Hospital. Mrs. Marshall assured me he was not seriously ill, but said that he had been plagued with a bothersome cough and had been unable to shake off the flu virus. When I inquired about her health, she reported that she was much better than she had been last year; I was glad for her sake, but I must confess, the thought occurred to me that her improved health would ease Colonel Marshall's mind.

Colonel Marshall's coughing bothered me especially, because I remembered his close brush with t.b. in his youth. In my letter of congratulations, I told him I was worried about his flu and cough, but I wasn't so dumb as to mention his old t.b. scare. He replied that the flu was one sickness that couldn't be cured overnight, even though Katherine had been a "modern Florence Nightingale," but that he was hopeful he'd be able to make the trip to Oslo. He said he wanted to go by the southern sea route on the new Italian liner *Andrea Doria,* and fly from Naples to Norway.

He did make the trip. I read the news accounts of the presentation ceremony with avid interest, and was outraged to learn, according to the newspapers, that just as Colonel Marshall was about to be presented with the Peace award, a bunch of Communists in the balcony rose up shouting, "We protest!" and simultaneously showered the hall with leaflets denigrating Colonel Marshall. (I never found out what the leaflets said, but I imagine the Communist attack on General Marshall was about as bad as McCarthy's and Jenner's—odd how demagogic fellows on opposite sides resemble each other.) The Communist demonstration produced a brief moment of stunned silence which was broken by King Haakon VII, who leapt to his feet applauding Colonel Marshall. Instantly, the audience recovered from its shock and let loose with a tremendous ovation while the Commies were hastily propelled from the hall.

Colonel Marshall's acceptance speech was as plain-spoken as his Marshall Plan speech had been. At Oslo, however, he expressed his deep personal concern for peace in terms of his Christian attitude toward humanity.

He mentioned various factors involved in establishing peace, such as economic problems and the necessity for a balance of powers, but he offered three specific recommendations which he considered essential guideposts for world peace. First, he called for education of the young in schools and colleges on the basic causes of war. In this category, he criticized the distortions of history, pointing out as an example the divergent treatment of our Civil War by Northern and Southern textbooks. His second recommendation strongly emphasized the urgent need to relieve the abject poverty suffered by millions of people all over the world. Lastly, he pleaded for an improvement in national attitudes, but not in political attitudes alone. Colonel Marshall stressed that a wide and genuine concern for other peoples' problems must preface any meaningful advance toward world peace. The main import of his speech was simply a restatement of his own formula for solving the problems of mankind, whether between proud, jealous nations, or between a recalcitrant child and her bitter, old-maid teacher: cooperation—teamwork; and charity, understanding, and compassion—*agape*.

> We must present democracy as a force holding within itself the seeds of unlimited progress by the human race . . . but make clear that such democracy is a means to a better way of life together with a better understanding between nations. . . . Material assistance alone is not sufficient. . . . The most important factor in the guarantee of future peace will be spiritual rejuvenation to produce good will and understanding between nations.

When he returned to Pinehurst, my godfather sent me a snapshot taken of him aboard ship en route to Naples. His longhand letter included the following interesting account:

> . . . My trip abroad was rather strenuous for a convalescent. I had thought the southern route would offer healing sunshine and tempered sea air but instead there was much of stormy weather and I left the boat at Naples less well off than when I started. Fortunately I had the use of the NATO Supreme Commander's plane so traveled comfortably and fast. Every day I was in Europe except at Oslo, I stayed in bed until dinner in the evening and did not go out at all. I flew back with Defense

Secretary Wilson and flew down here immediately from Washington. I've stayed in bed here to play safe with this damned virus bug that has been with me since September.

The Commy business was more press than fact, except for the time required for the leaflets to fall from the balcony. The one shouter only got off four words—"I thought this was" when the Agricultural Attache of the American Embassy slapped his mouth shut and jerked his head back, and my pilot sitting behind the fellow administered a one-two punch which terminated matters. They hustled him down stairs and the other two followed badly frightened and jumped in the police wagon to avoid punishment. Nothing was said of this to avoid embarrassing the Norwegian authorities who had allowed the demonstration to occur and then have it suppressed by two Americans.

It is my guess that Colonel Marshall never snapped back to his full physical vigor after his long siege with the flu. From 1954 on, he began to take his retirement more seriously, dividing his time mostly between Leesburg and Pinehurst.

When I saw him in the spring of 1954, he seemed to be quite well and rested, but not as physically energetic as he had been a year or so before. One day that spring, three of my cronies and I had planned an excursion to Pinehurst for a day of golf. As I always enjoyed seeing Colonel Marshall, and my friends were anxious to meet him, I telephoned to ask if I could bring the girls to call on him and Mrs. Marshall after our golf game. It was the first time I'd ever invited myself to his and Katherine's house, and I did so with considerable reservations. However, Colonel Marshall seemed genuinely pleased.

"What day are you coming?"

"Tomorrow," I told him, and right away he began pelting me with explicit instructions.

"I want you to bring your friends for tea—"

"Tea?"

"All right, for a drink. Wait a minute, I don't want you to be driving back to Durham at night. You and your friends have dinner with us. I'm sorry we can't put you up, but our cottage is too small, but they tell me there are some fine motels around here."

I demurred about descending on Mrs. Marshall for dinner, but he insisted, saying he would take us to the club and we wouldn't cause any commotion at all.

We had planned to stay in Pinehurst for dinner anyhow, but since I knew Colonel Marshall's spur of the moment invitation had been issued without consulting Mrs. Marshall, I thought it the better part of wisdom not to mention it to my friends.

We had a slow game on a crowded course, and afterwards, my friends took an eternity showering and primping.

"Hurry up!" I kept urging them. "We're going to be hopelessly late!"

We were due at the Marshalls at five, and I couldn't make them understand that five meant five *on the nose*. We arrived at about a quarter to six, and I was positively scared to go in.

Colonel Marshall answered the bell. "Gosh, Colonel Marshall, I'm sorry we're late," I blurted out. "We got behind a slow foursome."

He made a little private grimace at me but didn't raise a fuss, and greeted my friends with enthusiastic cordiality. Highballs appeared in a trice, and Colonel Marshall stood talking with my friends, giving them his whole attention, while I sat on the sofa with Mrs. Marshall. She was wearing a beautiful taffeta dress with matching shoes, and was so exquisitely coiffed she appeared to have just left her hairdresser.

"You look perfectly lovely, Mrs. Marshall," I said, and I meant it. Besides, I was flattered that she had dressed up for my friends. She thanked me for my compliment, and said she and Colonel Marshall were going out to dinner, so she had dressed for it before we arrived (dopey me!). Mrs. Marshall and I sat spinning our usual nothing-conversation when suddenly, in burst Molly;

her hair was blown askew, she was badly in need of fresh make-up, and her slip was showing. Her disarray was emphasized in my eyes because all of us were so gussied up and I was embarrassed for her. Damn, I thought, she does herself an injustice. But Molly couldn't have cared less; she had deserted her kids in the middle of some doings, and she only stayed a few minutes—probably Colonel Marshall had made her come—but while she was there, she filled the room with her contagious, bubbling laughter, and as she always had, charmed me with her easy, friendly, gracious manner.

After Molly left, Colonel Marshall suggested that Mrs. Marshall show my friends some of the more interesting things in the cottage. This was a happy suggestion because it gave Colonel Marshall and me a chance to catch up on each other. At the start of our conversation I overheard a few "ohs" and "ahs" from my friends, along with bits of Mrs. Marshall's talk.

"This exquisite painting was a gift from Madame Chiang Kai-shek."

"Ooo!"

"And here is an autographed picture of the General's dear friend, Queen Frederika of Greece."

"Oh, ah!"

As a matter of fact, Queen Frederika was right up Colonel Marshall's alley; she had the sort of pep and charm that I remembered had characterized the ladies he'd admired in days gone by. I'm sure she must have liked him, too, aside from her gratitude for all he had accomplished for Greece. I know that the two or three times she came to this country before his death, Queen Frederika made a point of calling on Colonel Marshall; the last time was in 1958 when he was sick in bed.

As Mrs. Marshall and my friends turned their attention toward inspecting the cottage, Colonal Marshall and I both started talking at once. I said, "I'm so happy to see you looking in the pink—"

He said, "I'm sorry, Rosie, about the dinner invitation but—"
We laughed. "You first," he offered.

I repeated my opening statement and asked how he was getting along. "As for your dinner date," I continued, "don't worry about it. I didn't even tell them we were invited; I knew you hadn't checked with Mrs. Marshall." He replied that he hadn't known they had an engagement, and Mrs. Marshall hadn't told him until that morning. More important, he said he felt pretty well on the whole but that he tired more easily than he used to.

He led me on to tell him news about my family, including Tom Morgan and Sis, while every now and then inserting a pertinent question which forced me to keep going.

"Colonel Marshall," I interrupted at last, "I'm tired of this monologue. Please let me ask you a question I'm dying to ask. How come you didn't stop Eisenhower from running for President?"

"I did once," he replied; "or at least, back in forty-eight, when he was sought after by the Democrats, he discussed it with me and I suggested he not run. Now listen," he laughed, "about that McCarthy thing which is what you're trying to lead up to—"

"Why, Colonel Marshall, I am not!" I denied indignantly.

"Why, Colonel Marshall!" he repeated. "Yes you are."

"Do you remember," he continued, "I told you I could never dabble in politics because of the compromises that have to be made? Eisenhower was forced into a compromise, that's all it was."

"Honestly, I wasn't going to bring it up," I interposed, "but as long as you have, I think it was disloyal of him, votes or not."

"Did you ever read Will Rogers' definition of politics?" Colonel Marshall asked.

"Which one?"

"The one I refer to is, 'There is no more independence in politics than there is in jail.'"

Suddenly we realized that Mrs. Marshall had shown my friends all there was to show in the cottage, and they were standing in a little group a small distance away, marking time.

"Well, would you girls like another drink?" Colonel Marshall asked.

Mrs. Marshall reminded him that they would be late for their dinner engagement.

"In a moment, in a moment," Colonel Marshall replied, and turned to me to say he hadn't told me yet what attractive friends I had.

"We had better go, George."

I began to get nervous; when Mrs. Marshall and I were together, Colonel Marshall had always stubbornly refused to pay the slightest attention to the uncomfortable relationship between her and me. At least he stood up, but unhurriedly launched into a long apology to my friends that he and Mrs. Marshall "had to run out on you," while they kept repeating, "Oh my goodness, we wouldn't keep you for anything in the world," and other such courtesies.

"Where are you going to have dinner?" he asked us.

We mentioned a couple of nice restaurants we knew of, but he disagreed with both of them.

By this time it was perfectly apparent to me that Mrs. Marshall was doing a slow burn. As for myself, I was about to have a heart attack; the last thing I wanted was to displease her at this stage of the game.

"Colonel Marshall," I said timidly, "I don't want to be the cause of your keeping your hostess waiting. You know she'll be all ready, you're always so prompt."

"Oh, she won't care, it's very informal," he replied testily; "I want to tell you where to have dinner."

He described the restaurant, praised the food, and gave us endless minute directions on how to get there before he finally said, "Well girls, I guess you'd better run along now."

I damn near knocked them down, hurrying us out of there. We drove all over Pinehurst and never found the restaurant, and we swore a pact together that I would never tell Colonel Marshall how dumb we were.

They thought Colonel Marshall was "an awfully nice man, so simple and friendly for a famous person," and they said Molly was "very pleasant"; but Mrs. Marshall had captivated them.

The Marshalls went to Eagles Mere, Pennsylvania, for their August vacation in 1955, and Colonel Marshall wrote me that they'd enjoyed that locale more than any they had visited in a long time. He told me both he and Mrs. Marshall were well, and looking forward to a quiet season at Pinehurst. A quiet season was Colonel Marshall's idea of Paradise—not that the Marshalls went into hibernation at Pinehurst. They had pleasant friends and enjoyed occasional informal entertaining; but Colonel Marshall was never partial to the cocktail circuit, and a round of pretentious social activities was the last thing he wanted. From time to time throughout the years of his retirement, one or another distinguished personage, usually one of Colonel Marshall's special friends, would make his way to Pinehurst to pay his respects, and undoubtedly those guests added a little fillip to the Marshalls' tranquil routine. There were many whom Colonel Marshall either mentioned to me or whom I read in the newspaper had been to the Marshalls': Mr. Baruch, Edna and Bill Pawley, industrialist and diplomat, Ellen and Jim Bruce, Queen Frederika and her son Constantine, now King of Greece, Mr. Dean Acheson, Mr. Lovett, Madame Chiang Kai-shek, Lady Astor, Mr. Hoffman, General Bradley, and Churchill, to name a few.

Colonel Marshall's letters to me tapered off considerably from 1955 on; he told me he didn't feel like writing letters any more, and he didn't want a secretary underfoot to "bust up our privacy." He'd telephone me once in a while when he was in Pinehurst, or I'd call him, not about anything important. We'd chat a few minutes about the kids or about something that had been going on with him. For example, one of our conversations was about Lady Astor who, I believe, had dined with the Marshalls at Pinehurst sometime in the spring of 1955. Lady Astor was from Virginia and had been well-known around the University in her youth. She was something of a character and had a keen sense of humor; and as I had a store of amusing anecdotes about her, I used up one of Colonel Marshall's telephone calls regaling him with Lady Astor chestnuts I'd heard from my father.

Sometime in November 1955, John had a business meeting in Pinehurst. When I told Colonel Marshall over the phone that John would probably drop in on him and Mrs. Marshall, he said that since John was coming down anyway, why didn't I drive the children down on Sunday and have lunch? Page and Thomas were now ten and eight, and Celeste was three; so I suggested to Colonel Marshall that in spite of his predilection for children, didn't he think perhaps three vitamin-stuffed, highly active kids would be "too much of a muchness?" He told me sharply not to be ridiculous, and I said, "Yes sir, thank you, we'll be there by noon."

He agreed to the time, and then instructed me to tell John to break away from his business lunch if possible, and join us at Liscombe Lodge for a cocktail, after which we'd all go to the club for lunch.

"John can return to his conference, you and the kids come back with us, and John can pick you up when he's through. We'll have 'a lovely time,'" he concluded.

I hoped we would, too, although I had certain misgivings. Both my sons could assume Chesterfieldian manners at will, but I knew well that such behavior was fragile armor, shattered all too soon by the turbulence and perpetual motion of their real natures.

The children and I arrived at Liscombe Lodge without undue commotion en route, and our visit started off very well. John was there already, and while we "grownups" had cocktails, Colonel Marshall gave the children Cokes, which delighted them, because

I'd cut out soft drinks when our dentist bills soared. I remembered later that we had all stood up during cocktails except for Celeste, who sat on the floor, and Colonel Marshall, who remained seated in his favorite easy chair. When we left for the club, Colonel Marshall instructed the children to go ahead and wait for us at the car (our car). We adults paired off as we always had, Mrs. Marshall and John leading off, with Colonel Marshall and me bringing up the rear. As Colonel Marshall and I walked to the door, he missed step and seemed to stagger a tiny bit. It was a barely perceptible irregularity, and I pretended not to have noticed, but it bothered me. Colonel Marshall remarked impatiently, and low enough not to be overheard, "I've been having a little trouble with my balance lately, but the doctors tell me it's nothing."

"Have you?" I asked, feigning surprise.

"Oh, just occasionally," he replied casually.

We reached the steps leading from the porch to the driveway, and again, he wavered ever so slightly. I took his arm. He resisted and said shortly that he was all right.

"I'm not," I answered. "I'm used to running around in flats and I've got on these wretched high heels."

He smiled, took my arm, squeezed it to let me know he understood my not-so-subtle gesture, and we descended the stairs. It was then I observed he was wearing loafers. His loafers, as I remembered his boots and shoes had always been, were polished to a high gloss, gleaming so brightly that when they caught a sunbeam, the reflection bounced off in a sharp, dazzling little ray. I laughed.

"Colonel Marshall," I said, "never would I think of you wearing loafers, and never in my life have I seen loafers with such a spit-'n'-polish military shine."

"I think they're very handsome," he replied proudly, "and they're extremely comfortable. I like them. Don't you agree my loafers are a nice symbol of my retirement?"

The club dining room was large and our table was at the far

end, near a window. I walked ahead of Colonel Marshall, but I asked John later if he'd noticed anything amiss in Colonel Marshall's walking. John told me no, the General had walked as he always had, except maybe a trifle slower. "He wouldn't race through the dining room anyhow," my husband reminded me.

We had a pleasant lunch. The conversation was geared to the children, who behaved very well, so I relaxed and enjoyed myself.

After lunch, Colonel Marshall asked John if he'd brought his camera along, which of course my foresighted husband had; so Colonel Marshall suggested that John take snapshots of him and the boys. While the picture-taking was in progress, Mrs. Marshall sat on the veranda in the warm Indian summer sunshine, and I chased after little Celeste who chased after the gentle breeze.

As soon as he finished the pictures, John drove us all back to the Marshalls' cottage and left for his meeting. Before Mrs. Marshall excused herself for her afternoon rest, she thoughtfully produced a box of dominoes for Celeste to play with, explaining that her little granddaughter didn't know how to play dominoes but had often entertained herself by laying them out in patterns on the rug. Celeste thanked her, dumped out the dominoes, and began her project. The boys went outdoors to blow off steam, and Colonel Marshall, declining my earnest suggestion that he take his rest too, insisted that he could rest any time, and that he and I would pass the time of day.

We touched on many subjects. He told me a little of his life at Pinehurst, saying it varied only slightly from the way he lived "these days" at Leesburg. One thing that fascinated him in Pinehurst, he remarked, was going to the supermarket and pushing a cart around "all those corridors lined with every conceivable thing to eat." It seemed a dreary pastime to me, to whom marketing had long since become a boring routine, and I told him so.

"If you were as conscious as I am of the starvation in the world; if you had seen the pitiful hungry children I have seen," he said, "you would regard those A & P shelves with a different eye."

Colonel Marshall talked with delight about a little boy who lived next door whom he found amusing good company. I was glad there was a child near enough for Colonel Marshall to enjoy, and suspected that the little boy came over to see him as often as he could.

Colonel Marshall had given up riding, he told me, but he took walks nearly every day the weather was fine. I'd noticed that his step had not faltered again since we'd come from lunch, and I asked him if he was much troubled by his occasional lapse of balance. He replied, "Very little," and added that he hoped it was a temporary affliction that would go away.

We spoke briefly of his bad year in China, mostly of Chiang Kai-shek's and Madame Chiang's respective personalities.

"You liked them, didn't you?" I asked.

"Yes," he agreed. "Madame Chiang is intelligent in addition to her good looks and highly publicized charm. Furthermore, I appreciated her warm hospitality to Katherine. I liked Chiang too. Personally, we got along very well—he was always most agreeable and friendly to me; but he was a poor leader, as I told you before. If Chiang had been able to weed out his corrupt officials . . ." Colonel Marshall paused and added reflectively, "or if he had wanted to . . ." Then, speeding up to his rapid speaking pace, he said, "If Chiang had cared about or even had directed his attention to the woeful plight of the Chinese people—the masses—he could have knocked the props out from under Mao." My godfather checked himself, shrugged his shoulders, and sighed a deep, tired sigh. "Ah well, Chiang is a War Lord; if not, perhaps history would have written a different, happier story."

"He liked you too, didn't he?" I asked, "I read in *Time* that in a public statement about you, Chiang said, 'Our confidence in him is unbounded.'"

Colonel Marshall replied drily, "Chiang's confidence in me may have been unbounded but it did not restrain him from disregarding my advice."

I brought up the subject again to Colonel Marshall of writing his autobiography. He had told me before, and stated publicly, that he would never write it, but I thought perhaps I could change his mind. It was a futile supposition, even though I argued that he owed his personal account to history. He said he had turned down a fortune that had been offered him for his memoirs, and there was nothing I could say to make him decide otherwise. He said he could not write an accurate account of his public life without revealing unpleasant things about people still living, and a revelation of this sort would contribute nothing but harm.

"Like who?" I asked.

"Roosevelt, for instance."

"He's not living."

"That's why I chose him. I can tell you I had some very difficult sessions with Roosevelt!"

"Like what?"

"Like none of your business!"

We talked a little about Eisenhower too. His name came up after a light-hearted discourse on the relative merits of horseback riding and golf. I made some casual comment about the President's love of golf and about his easy geniality, and Colonel Marshall told me not to underestimate the importance of Eisenhower's personality. He explained that one of the major reasons he had recommended him for the Supreme Allied Command was directly associated with his outgoing personality. Colonel Marshall maintained that Eisenhower's open-hearted affability was an invaluable asset in running a show, the success of which depended in large measure on the likeableness of the man who ran it.

"We had other unusually able Generals over there," Colonel Marshall said, "so it was not General Eisenhower's military ability alone that contributed to the Allied victory. His faculty for getting along well with top brass—Americans and Allies alike—and his immense popularity with the troops were extremely important."

We talked a long time, all afternoon. Celeste fell asleep on the floor; and I had been so absorbed that I hadn't noticed the after-noon had waned into early evening, and I'd completely forgotten about the boys playing in the yard. Colonel Marshall was talking about the breadth and depth of Dean Acheson's intellect when we were interrupted by howls from outside. I rushed out to find Page and Thomas rolling around on the ground socking each other, in an effort to settle an argument by the usual means resorted to by little boys and big nations. Colonel Marshall broke up the fight by suggesting that the boys and Celeste, who had been awakened by the hullabaloo, repair to the kitchen and have some ice cream.

From then on the visit deteriorated for me into an agonizing embarrassment that we were fast wearing out our welcome. Where the hell is John, I wondered? During that last miserable three-quarters of an hour, I relished the thought of Reno.

"When is Mizz Marshall coming out of that room?" little Celeste asked.

"When you and the rest of your family are well on the road to Durham," Colonel Marshall answered, looking at me and laughing.

John showed up at long last, and for the second time, I pushed everybody out of the Marshalls' cottage in desperate haste.

To the best of my knowledge, the Marshalls' "quiet season" was not interrupted again until Colonel Marshall's seventy-fifth birthday, December 31, 1955. Many reporters came to interview him and he appeared briefly on TV in an informal pose with Mrs. Marshall. Along with its Marshall story, *The New York Times* carried an enchanting front-page picture of Colonel Marshall sitting in a chair outdoors smiling up at his little neighbor, John Bertrand, standing beside him.

Most of the birthday stories carried reviews of the highlights of Colonel Marshall's career, interspersed with numerous quota-tions about him gathered from his great or well-known con-temporaries: "the overall architect of victory," "first in war, first in peace," "the greatest living American," "selfless patriot," and so

379

on. For some strange reason now forgotten, I wrote down only one, a commendation by former Secretary of State James Byrnes. As I read it now, I think I may have recorded it because Secretary Byrnes summed up most of the published tributes with a simplicity similar to Colonel Marshall's own style. Byrnes said, "In war and peace, General George Catlett Marshall rendered countless service to his country."

"Catlett"—how Colonel Marshall and I hated his ugly middle name! In fact, it was a long time before I even knew what the "C" in his name stood for. Lily and I used to call him Catlett sometimes just to get his goat.

Back to the birthday—telegrams and letters poured into Pinehurst from all over the world. They came from President Eisenhower and former President Truman; from Trygvie Lie; from Churchill; from the Secretary General of the North Atlantic Council; from the chairman of the Nobel Prize Committee of the Norwegian Parliament; from various other dignitaries, including the heads of state of every free nation in the world; and from hundreds of friends, including me.

CHAPTER XL

MY GODFATHER DIED ON OCTOBER 16, 1959. WHAT TRANSPIRED BE-
tween us during the two years before that date has been all but
blotted out by the poignant memories I keep of the times we spent
together near the end.

In July 1956, Colonel Marshall dictated a note to my sister in
reply to a letter from her urging him to write his autobiography.
"My autobiography," he wrote, "is an old story. I'm afraid I'm no
good now. The [George C. Marshall] Foundation at the Virginia
Military Institute is starting on a write-up based on the records—
official and personal. I agree to fill in the blind spots . . ."*

Sis sent the note on to me, calling attention to the phrase, "I'm
no good now," and asking if anything serious was wrong with
Colonel Marshall.

I wrote him immediately, one of my novelettes in which I

---

* The first two volumes of a three-volume biography of General Marshall have
been published: Pogue, Forrest C., Vol. I, *General George C. Marshall, Education
of a General 1880–1939;* Vol. II, *General George C. Marshall, Ordeal and Hope,
1939–1942.* New York, Viking Press, 1963; 1966.

buried an inquiry about his health. I had no answer until September—it was the last longhand letter I was ever to receive from Colonel Marshall. He wrote, ". . . I have not done well this summer but am improving. Katherine is in better shape, thank goodness . . ." He said he'd gone to Washington for the first time in three months to attend a Business Advisory Council meeting, but that Tom Morgan had not been there. He asked if my brother-in-law was ill, which unfortunately, he had been at that time.

Sometime during 1956, Colonel Marshall received another award, this one in connection with the centennial celebration of Woodrow Wilson's birthday. The award was presented to him as the American whose services to the country most typified Wilson's ideal, "Freedom for man—a world safe for mankind."

The Marshalls came to Pinehurst in the fall, as usual, and Colonel Marshall and I talked on the phone from time to time, as usual, but that's all I remember.

If he had not looked well or had appeared feeble or different in any way when I saw him in 1956 or 1957, I would certainly have noticed; but I have no remembrance of any startling change in his appearance or behavior. Looking back, I see that although I realized at the time Colonel Marshall was in his seventies, my reaction to his advancing years was purely theoretical. I thought he should "slow down" and "take things easier," because that was the accepted routine elderly people should follow. In reality, when I was with him, I never thought about his age at all. He was just "Colonel Marshall," my godfather, my "pretend parent" who had always been older than I, my lifetime friend, confidant, adviser, interesting companion. His hair turned gray and I scarcely noticed; his lithe, slender figure thickened slightly with age, but as he was never overweight, I paid no attention to the gradual alterations in his build. Colonel Marshall had remained ageless to me because I loved him, and because his keen mind disallowed any thought of an "old man."

Colonel Marshall's 1956 Christmas letter came from Washington, where he had gone for a hospital checkup. His sense of balance had worsened considerably, "vanished with I don't know what, my hearing or something of that sort." He said he would return to Pinehurst, and maybe in the spring I would "feel inclined" to make a visit. Regarding that little dig, of course I had many commitments of my own, but there was never a time I did not "feel inclined" to visit Colonel Marshall. I had repeatedly told him, however, that I did not think I should come without an invitation from Mrs. Marshall, or at least without her foreknowledge. For one thing, it was a matter of courtesy, especially after my two long intrusions at Liscombe Lodge. Another reason was that I had convinced myself I would never presume to force my way in on them. Since Colonel Marshall was such a famous figure, I did not want Mrs. Marshall to think I was trying to hover around the edge of his limelight. Now, I think perhaps I was suffering from false pride, and I regret it.

I had a brief, dictated note from Colonel Marshall in May 1957, informing me that he and Katherine were both entering the hospital for their semi-annual checkups. He said the place at Leesburg looked pretty well, although it lacked flowers. That's all he wrote just a note to keep me posted.

The year 1957 marked the tenth anniversary of the Marshall Plan speech, and I read in the news that in June, Colonel and Mrs. Marshall had attended a ceremony honoring him in Washington at the Blair-Lee House. The British Ambassador presented Colonel Marshall with a medal struck by the Organization for European Economic Cooperation. The French ambassador gave him a tapestry, and gave Mrs. Marshall a clock in the name of the grateful French people.

President Eisenhower was there and said a few commendatory words about Colonel Marshall. There were other speeches, and a notation that the European press was observing the anniversary by printing tributes from the various European heads of State.

John and I attended John's class reunion at Harvard that June. The brilliant British economist Barbara Ward received an honorary degree and delivered a splendid commencement address enumerating the remarkable results accomplished by the Marshall Plan. I thought her speech so impressive that I asked John to get a copy for Colonel Marshall. John found out that Miss Ward had spoken from notes with a good deal of ad-libbing, so that no printed copy was available, but my husband is a resourceful fellow. He arranged through a classmate, the Chief Justice of Massachusetts, Paul Reardon, to have another tape cut from the recording of Miss Ward's address. I sent the tape to Colonel Marshall and told him to be sure to write Justice Reardon, because he had gone to a lot of trouble in having the tape made.

Of course he did, and of course he wrote to thank John and me too. I was distressed to read in his thank-you note, "I have not been feeling very well." He admitted he was having considerable trouble with his balance and told me he suffered from an almost "total lack of energy. I stay close to home," he wrote, "and participate in very few activities." But Katherine, he said, was "in better shape."

For the past couple of years or so, Colonel Marshall had been writing me that Katherine was in "better shape," and it reminded me of a funny story he used to tell on Lily. When Colonel Marshall was a young Lieutenant in the Philippines, Lily wrote him almost daily, and in every few letters she would gleefully tell him how many pounds she had lost. One boring day, he and another young officer decided to amuse themselves by calculating what Lily's weight might be. They added up all the pounds she reported she had lost, and subtracted the sum from the weight she had been been before Colonel Marshall left home. The answer came out that Lily weighed minus ten! I dashed off a little note to Colonel Marshall, and reminding him of that tale, I told him I supposed Mrs. Marshall was now in such good shape that she was ready to compete in the Olympics.

The last letter I ever received from my godfather was dictated on January 11, 1958. It was a sweet, friendly, lovely letter. It was a reply to one of my novelettes in which I had written the family news, and apparently lamented Page's and Thomas's interest in things other than study.

He wrote that my family news gave him "a great deal of pleasure." He told me about his condition: "I am pretty much the same. I get in about a half-mile walk or more a day. Other than that, I don't get around much." He teased me, saying, "Apropos of your note, I would ask you to define extra curricular activities at the Cathedral School. As I recall, for a time you were something of a 'bust.' " He said he hoped my brother-in-law, Tom Morgan, was improving "materially." He sent his love to my sister, Celeste, and then he said, "As for you, my dear, everything you do and are is of interest to me."

I treasure that last letter of his.

I heard nothing further from or about Colonel Marshall until August, when Page received a birthday note from Colonel C. J. George, Colonel Marshall's aide.

Every year, beginning with Page's sixth birthday, he had received a note from our godfather. Sometimes Colonel Marshall sent a present—for example, a silver spoon from Mexico engraved with his and Page's birth dates and initials. Another year he sent his autographed photograph in a silver frame engraved with the words, "Page Wilson, from his Godfather, G. C. Marshall." But most birthdays he sent ten dollars, an astronomical sum to Page. In August 1958, however, Colonel George wrote to Page telling him that General Marshall was in the hospital undergoing tests, and had asked him to convey the birthday wishes. Colonel George enclosed the usual ten dollars with instructions from General Marshall that Page was to spend the money for anything he wished.

I was not unduly concerned, for I knew Colonel Marshall was having "balance trouble," and reminded myself that when a man reached seventy-eight years of age, it was time he took precautions with his health.

The Marshalls ordinarily came to Pinehurst in November, but in 1958 they arrived a little earlier than usual. I only knew they were there because I read about Queen Frederika's flying visit to Colonel Marshall in October. As the paper said he was sick in bed, I didn't telephone him for two weeks or more, because I didn't want to disturb him. I assumed if he were seriously ill, Mrs. Marshall would let me know; but as the days went by with no word from Pinehurst, I grew more and more uneasy. At length, I gave up, and telephoned to inquire about him. I talked to Mrs. Marshall, who sounded very glum and told me Colonel Marshall was not at all well, and no, it was not the flu. "Just about everything is wrong with him," she said unhappily. I was frightened, and hesitated before I spoke so that my voice would not shake. Mrs. Marshall, however, must have sensed my anxiety. "I think he would enjoy seeing you," she said.

"When may I come?" I asked.

"Any time you like, we'll be here." Her voice was heavy with discouragement.

"Tomorrow?"

"Yes," she replied. "Tomorrow will be fine."

She said she would only be able to provide a light lunch, for she was burdened with the nurse-Sergeant and something or other else. I assured her I would arrive after lunch time; I could tell that Mrs. Marshall was tired.

I picked up lunch en route and arrived at Liscombe Lodge a little after one. The Sergeant let me in and asked me to wait a moment, saying he would call me. Everything was very quiet; I could hear my own heart beating. I don't suppose I paced up and down the living room more than five or ten minutes, but it seemed an eternity before the Sergeant returned and said, "The General is waiting for you, Mrs. Wilson."

I stood at Colonel Marshall's door and looked across the small, austere room. He was sitting up in bed, dressed in a handsome, heavy silk dark-blue dressing gown. It was oriental, and it flashed through my mind that he must have gotten it in China. My godfather's face was gaunt and lean; his skin stretched tightly across his jutting cheekbones, and the sharp outline of his skull was clearly visible under his neatly combed hair. His hair had become dead white. I stood in the doorway a moment, smiling at him, but shocked and unable to move. My God, I thought, he's an old man! Instantly, I knew. He's not going to get well; dear God, he's not going to get well!

Colonel Marshall smiled back. He opened his arms and held them out to me. "Rosie!" he called. I ran to him and leaned over and put my arms around him and kissed him, and said how wonderful he looked, and how handsome he was in his snazzy Chinese robe. He pulled me down to sit on the side of his bed, and I sat there for hours while he held on to my hand.

He looked at me steadily for a moment and said, "I have so much time now to remember." He began to reminisce, though he did not mention a single incident of his public life. He talked of the old days, sometimes of the days even before I knew him. I had often listened to elderly people recall their far past, some wandering about vaguely in a maze of disconnected episodes, and others falling into a garrulous, boring monologue. Colonel Marshall was not like any of them. It was as if I were a child again, listening to him tell his fascinating stories. He was entertaining, articulate, and clear-headed.

There was just one thing he said that first afternoon which I do not believe he would have said under different circumstances. It was too revealing.

"You know," he said, "this morning as I lay here I was thinking of my father, and about the brisk, snowy winters in Uniontown. When I was very small, my father would sometimes take

387

me tobogganing down a steep hill right in the center of the town." Colonel Marshall broke into a bright smile. "What great sport that was!"

He had seldom mentioned his father to me, and not at all for many years. Lily used to tell me indignantly, "George's father never understood him. He never appreciated George and it hurt his feelings."

"Colonel Marshall," I said, "I'm sorry your father didn't live long enough to know what a great son he had. He would have been very proud of you."

"Do you really think so?" he asked quite seriously. I laughed and told him it was a silly question, of course he would.

"Well," he replied, "maybe that's why I was thinking about him. I'd like to believe he would have approved of me."

We talked a lot about Lily and about our excursions when I was a little girl. Once he remarked, not bitterly, but with quiet resignation, "Lily always did more than she should have. I made a great mistake permitting her to take Mrs. Coles to China."

The hours ticked away, and I began to worry that he was getting overtired. I suggested I'd better go, but he said, "No, not yet." It never occurred to me to disobey him, so I stayed a while longer. Before I left, I promised to come back in a week or so, and kissed him good-bye. As I walked out of the room, he called, "Thanks for coming, I'll look forward to your next visit." I did not see Mrs. Marshall that day, but I told the Sergeant to tell her I would return a week from Friday. There was no question anymore that I could be hankering after reflected glory.

I went to Pinehurst every ten days or so. After my first visit, Mrs. Marshall would appear when I arrived and again when I left. She began to take advantage of my visits to rest or do little errands with a free mind; she needed those breaks, and I'm glad she was able to take them. Also after my first visit, Colonel Marshall became used to my coming, and my presence did not revive old memories as it had at first. He continued to reminisce occasionally, but we talked of many other things. It amused him to hear about my children, particularly about their latest scrapes and escapades. It was on one of my trips to Pinehurst that he told me to keep *Timothy's Quest*. He asked about my current reading and what the kids read; and once he made me try to recite "The Ancient Mariner," and laughed because I had forgotten most of it. We ranged over many subjects, and I tried to keep our conversations gay. Colonel Marshall spoke of Katherine with affection, and often repeated how wonderfully attentive she was. Frequently, I would forget he was slipping away, but the knowledge that he was, always returned to chill me.

One day as I was just sitting by Colonel Marshall's bed—a silence had fallen and neither one of us felt constrained to fill it. I lit a cigarette and went to get an ashtray, and when I sat down again, Colonel Marshall asked if I were comfortable now. I assumed he was about to scold me for the millionth time about smoking; but no, he said he wanted me to do something for him.

"Sure," I said, "anything."

I turned my head to look directly at him and recognized the familiar expression of absolute concentration spread over his face; as always, he kept his keen eyes riveted on me as I listened to what he wanted me to do.

"This is not an easy thing I'm asking you," he began, "but you must trust me that I am right. I know that you know I am not going to get well. How long I will last, neither of us can say. I am troubled because I do not believe Katherine understands the situation and I want her to be prepared and to be making sound plans for her future."

"Always taking the long view," I said, with tears streaming down my face.

"Stop crying now," he ordered in his I'm-accustomed-to-being-obeyed tone. "You can do that later if you must. Right now, I want you to pay close attention. The doctors may have told

Katherine I will not recover, but I doubt it. I want you to tell her I am definitely going to die before long and she'd better damn well start planning accordingly."

I pulled myself together and replied steadily that of course I would tell her because he had asked me to, but I was a poor choice. "She would think me presumptuous," I said, "she would even think me hateful. I'm sure she would resent it very much. But most important, she wouldn't believe me."

He replied that all those possibilities had occurred to him, but there was no one else he would be willing to ask.

"How about Molly?" I suggested.

Molly was too close to her mother, he said, and anyway, he doubted if Molly, herself, was facing up to the truth about him. I reminded him that Molly was a sensible girl and that if I ever had a chance to see her, I could talk to her and she could make plans for her mother. Molly had rented her Pinehurst house and was with her husband at his post, somewhere in New England, I think.

I thought a minute and added, "If you give me Molly's address, I'll hop in the car and go to see her and take care of the whole business."

"I will think about it and let you know," he replied.

Colonel Marshall dismissed the subject abruptly and started talking of other things as naturally as if we had been discussing the weather. I, however, was struggling so hard to cover up my distress that I have no idea to this day what he was talking about.

I hadn't seen Molly since the afternoon four years previously when she came to Liscombe Lodge for those few minutes to speak to my friends. Nevertheless, I was not surprised when she and Colonel Winn stopped by my house not long after that afternoon. They had been to see "Colonel" (her appellation for him), she told me, and thought it would be nice to come to see me on their way back home. We had a pleasant conversation for about a half an hour. Molly said she thought Colonel was a little better, and that her mother seemed quite well. We exchanged anecdotes about our children, as mothers are apt to do, each of us bragging a tiny bit. Her husband contributed pleasant and amusing remarks to our conversation, helping to make their visit a really friendly one. Jim Winn is an affable man, very easy to like. All the while, I kept angling for an opening so I could complete my mission, but I had not yet succeeded when Molly and Jim said they must be on their way. I protested; they insisted. I walked out to the car with them—I had to speak before they got in. "Molly," I asked, "have you thought at all about what you should do, I mean about your mother, in case Colonel Marshall doesn't make it?"

Molly burst into tears and replied, "I haven't given up hope"— and I don't know what else she said. Colonel Winn put a protective arm around his weeping wife, and they stared at me in shocked surprise. I felt like a damned dog, but I kept plugging. I told Molly that I, too, hoped to God Colonel Marshall would get well, but I did not honestly think he would. "I know it's awfully hard to be practical now," I said, fighting against tears myself, "but you must, Molly, you have to for your mother's sake, for Colonel Marshall's sake. It would ease his mind to know Mrs. Marshall was all set and prepared for a future without him." I was too upset to remember what Molly answered. I only remember that they got into the car and drove hurriedly away, and that I felt terribly sorry for Molly, and sorrier for myself.

On my next visit to Pinehurst, I told Colonel Marshall that Molly had come and I had done my best, but I was not at all sure my best had been good enough. He nodded and smiled, and we never discussed the subject again.

As Christmas drew near, Colonel Marshall told me he wanted me to get a Christmas present from him for Page. When I asked if there was anything special he had in mind, he said no, just to be sure it was a very nice present, not a football or anything like that, but something good. When the time came for me to leave, Mrs.

Marshall joined us for the last five minutes, as she usually did, and Colonel Marshall repeated his instructions.

"Go ahead and buy the present," he added, "and bring it down here for me to see. Katherine will reimburse you with a check."

I had no idea how much he wanted me to spend, so when Mrs. Marshall came out to the living room with me, I asked for her advice.

"Has he ever given Page a present before?" she inquired.

"Why, yes," I replied surprised, "every birthday and sometimes at Christmas."

She asked what he sent for birthday presents, and I told her he usually sent ten bucks.

"Well," she said practically, "then get something for ten dollars."

It isn't easy to find a "good" present for a thirteen-year-old boy, and Colonel Marshall had intimated I should get something that Page could keep, and yet enjoy right away. I bought four black-and-white drawings, two baseball and two football pictures. They were no examples of great art, but were well drawn and full of motion. I had them framed and took them down to Pinehurst.

"What did you get?" Colonel Marshall asked me eagerly as soon as I walked into his room.

When I told him I'd bought pictures for Page's room, he was furious, and said disgustedly, "What would an active boy like Page want with pictures?" I wasn't the least disturbed—I knew both he and Page would like them, so I told Colonel Marshall to hold his horses and I'd get them out of the car.

He was absolutely delighted with them. I set the pictures up where he could see them, and every once in a while during the afternoon he'd look at them and say, "They're splendid, they really are very fine pictures!" He told me to be sure and get a check from Katherine, but I never asked her for it, because the pictures had come to considerably more than ten dollars. Just the same, Colonel Marshall gave those pictures to Page; my son is twenty-two now, and he still enjoys Colonel Marshall's Christmas present.

Mrs. Marshall telephoned me around the end of January to tell me not to come to see Colonel Marshall the day I was due because he'd had a "little attack," and they had moved him to the hospital at Fort Bragg. She said she would let me know if, and when, I could see him at Bragg. She sounded quite calm, and assured me there was no reason to be overly concerned. Mrs. Marshall called me back in February to say I could come down to Bragg on Sunday.

Sunday was February 14, 1959. It was about one thirty when I knocked on the door of the hospital's VIP suite. The sergeant ushered me straight through the sitting room into Colonel Marshall's bedroom, saying that the General was waiting for me. Colonel Marshall lay uncovered on the bed, which had been slightly elevated at the head; it was a vibrating hospital bed. He looked very thin in his perfectly pressed blue pajamas, but otherwise he seemed unchanged since I had last seen him. His expression was alert, his eyes keen, and his voice steady when he asked if I'd had much trouble finding him.

We chatted a while. He joked that his "jiggly bed" made him feel like a hula dancer, but they'd told him the vibration was good for his circulation. He was in a gay mood. He told me to be sure to observe the tall flagpole before I left Fort Bragg, and suggested that if I'd like to come early some morning, he could arrange for me to raise the flag. He made me go into his sitting room and see what I thought of the color TV. (It was lousy.)

"They pretend it's for me," he laughed, "but it's really there for Katherine and the Sergeant."

Every now and then he would interrupt himself, or me, to say, "You look so young!" Once I reminded him I was nearly fifty years old, and he told me he didn't believe it, "You are my little girl and you will always be young."

During the afternoon, one of our companionable silences came

393

over us, but I noticed Colonel Marshall was watching me closely. Suddenly he said, "I would like to ask you something very confidentially."

"Yes?" I said.

He made me swear I would not repeat to anyone what he was going to ask; he was embarrassed, so that twice I reassured him he could trust me.

"Rose," he said gravely, his forehead wrinkling and his eyes narrowing with perplexity, "I'm not sure where I am. I don't want to alarm Katherine and I most assuredly will not ask the Sergeant. Will you please tell me? Where am I?"

"You are in Womack Hospital at Fort Bragg," I replied calmly. "The reason you don't know where you are is because you were taken ill at Pinehurst and you were unconscious when they brought you here."

Damn! Why hadn't he been told? Or had he? I thought in alarm.

"I am?" he answered surprised. "That's most reassuring. I had a notion I was in Walter Reed, but these surroundings are unfamiliar and I was puzzled."

Colonel Marshall had had a stroke. That question was the single indication during all the recent times I had seen him that perhaps his brain had been slightly affected. His question hurt me so! I couldn't bear to think that Colonel Marshall's prodigious mind might deteriorate. I said a silent prayer begging that death would take him before serious damage could occur. "Spare Colonel Marshall that indignity," I prayed; I was churning inside, and furiously reminded God, "You owe him that much!"

Out loud I said, "Well, that's settled," and to divert him, I asked the first question that popped into my head. "Why is this hospital named 'Womack'; was that an Indian battle or something?"

Colonel Marshall burst out laughing and said, "Good Lord no, *Womack* is a commonly known North Carolina name." He told me that when he was Chief of Staff, he had directed that all Army hospitals, old and new, were to be named for an outstanding war hero from the general locality of the hospital. His orders left the selection of the name up to the local people, but stipulated that it must be chosen from the rolls of enlisted men. Since that day, I've noticed the name *Womack* all over North Carolina.

Shortly before I was to return to Durham, Mrs. Marshall arrived carrying a gaily wrapped box in her hand. Colonel Marshall exclaimed, "Oh good, you didn't forget! Give it to her now."

Katherine handed me the box with a smile, and while I was opening it, Colonel Marshall said happily, "That is my Valentine present to you." I was deeply touched, and made a big to-do over the unwrapping. The box contained a lovely pale-blue Lenox-china powder box, but it was not the present itself which was important to me. Mrs. Marshall told me later in the adjoining sitting room that George had only asked her to get a present that morning, and as it was Sunday, she'd had to bring something she already had at home. I understood her predicament and appreciated the trouble she'd taken.

The time came for me to go; I put my Valentine present down beside my pocketbook and went to kiss Colonel Marshall good-bye.

"Good-bye, my wonderful Colonel Marshall," I said; "I'll be back soon. Thank you again; I love my Valentine present and I love you!"

"Good-bye, Rosie," he said, "and I love you too!"

We laughed and I left him. It was the last time he ever spoke to me.

Some Army officer telephoned me in March to tell me that Colonel Marshall had had another serious heart attack and had been flown immediately to Walter Reed. Mrs. Marshall had followed the next day. Mrs. Marshall, I learned later, was distraught and half sick all summer, so I had no news from her, but

Page received a letter on his birthday from Colonel Marshall's aide.

Dear Page:

In the years gone by, you have always received a personal note of birthday greetings from General Marshall. However, his health is so poor that his greetings this year must come through me.

I regret to say that he has been doing poorly in recent weeks, and it is very difficult to say what tomorrow might bring.

With my personal greetings and the hope that you will have a very fine day,

Sincerely,

C. J. George
Lt. Colonel, U.S.A.
Aide to General Marshall

I was most unhappy. I guessed, however, that a letter to Mrs. Marshall would only burden her, and I was sure she would let me know if Colonel Marshall's condition became critical. In September I drove Page to Alexandria, Virginia, to enter him in the Episcopal High School, and while I was there I telephoned Mrs. Marshall. I asked if I could see Colonel Marshall and invited her to dinner. She agreed to both, and we arranged to meet in front of the Hostess House on the Walter Reed grounds.

Mrs. Marshall led me through a labyrinth of basement corridors to a back elevator, explaining that she preferred the back way for privacy.

"I want you to know that you are specially honored to be allowed to see George," she told me. "I permit very few people to see him." She continued that Presidents Truman and Eisenhower had been in, and only a few days ago, Churchill had come to see him.

"Mr. Churchill didn't say a word," she went on. "He just stood in the doorway with tears in his eyes."

"He didn't speak?" I asked.

I listened in horror while Mrs. Marshall warned me that I must not expect George to know me; he had not known anyone for many weeks, she told me, including herself. I wished I hadn't come. I wished I could have kept only the lovely memory of him at Fort Bragg. I wished I could get out of there and run as fast and as far away as I could.

"I understand," I said to Mrs. Marshall.

We went into his room; my heart was pounding and I was wet with sweat. I forced myself to look at Colonel Marshall, and when I saw him, I smiled.

Colonel Marshall lay on his side in a coma. His eyes were shut and he was breathing deeply, but evenly. I'd seen him sleep that way a hundred times when I was little. He was not slack-mouthed; his face was not disfigured by the vapid stupidity that characterizes most stroke victims. Was he really in a coma or was he sleeping peacefully? He looked comfortable, as if at long last he was enjoying a good, sound rest.

"Colonel Marshall, Colonel Marshall," I called softly, "it's Rose."

He slept on.

I leaned forward and kissed his forehead lightly.

"Oh Min!" I whispered, turned, and walked out of his room.

I was not sad. I was glad I had come. I kept repeating to myself that Colonel Marshall had earned the right to peace.

Colonel Marshall's funeral was small and simple, as he had instructed it to be. John and I received an envelope with a tag for our car to let us through to the small chapel at Fort Myer. We picked up Page from nearby Episcopal High School and took him with us. John reasoned that inasmuch as Page had seldom seen Colonel Marshall, he would not suffer from grief, and would profit by the opportunity to see the celebrities attending the funeral.

There were plenty of them there, but I hardly noticed. I

remember that John nudged our son when President Eisenhower entered; and I watched impassively as Eisenhower walked down the aisle to the pew in front of President Truman. Truman arose and the two shook hands. I thought idly that the gesture would be recorded in the newspapers as Truman and Eisenhower were not on the best of terms.

I heard the muffled drums sounding the approach of Colonel Marshall's flag-draped casket, and I stood up as if I were a robot. I could feel nothing—my mind was absolutely blank. The brief Episcopal service was soon over and I hadn't heard a word.

Mrs. Marshall came down the aisle on Colonel Winn's arm. She was heavily veiled. I was aroused sufficiently from my comatose state to remember that this was her fourth great loss, two sons and two husbands. Does one get used to the death of people one loves? I wondered. No, I answered myself, no.

Molly and her son followed Mrs. Marshall, and her little girls followed Molly. Molly and her daughters were weeping. The girls wore polo coats and had long pigtails with black ribbons on the ends. Why do I notice trivialities at such a time, I mused? Suddenly I thought of Lily's funeral and how I had noticed Colonel Marshall's fresh haircut.

We followed the other mourners out into the bright sunlight, and John spotted Edna and Bill Pawley, whom we had known for years. We walked over to speak to them and John introduced Page. We stood with the Pawleys while everyone waited for the cars to depart carrying Mrs. Marshall and the Winns to the burial service. The cars started to move away.

"Aren't you going to the grave?" Bill asked me.

"No," I replied, "I was not invited."

"No?" Bill asked, and added quickly, "neither were we."

"Only the family is going," I said.

I watched the cars disappear slowly around the curve. When they were out of sight, an almost uncontrollable panic seized me. Colonel Marshall was gone! He was really gone!

My head was ringing, Colonel Marshall! Colonel Marshall! My heart cried out, Colonel Marshall! I looked at John; he moved closer, took my arm, and we left the churchyard.